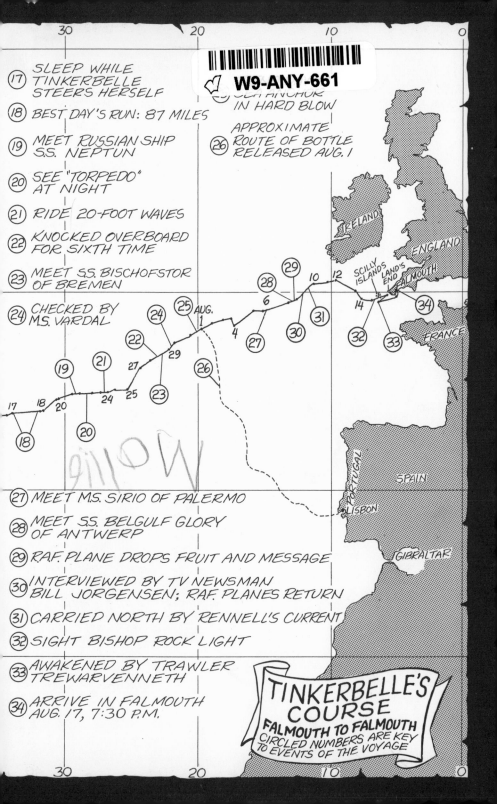

TINKERBELLE

Drawings by Roy C. Hearn ⇥

Robert Manry

TINKERBELLE

HARPER & ROW, PUBLISHERS   *   NEW YORK

FIRST EDITION

LIBRARY OF CONGRESS CATALOG CARD NUMBER: 66-15735

For Virginia, Robin and Douglas

*

Contents

Photographs follow pages 54 and 182

TINKERBELLE

—Herblock, Washington *Post*

"Say, that guy made it across the Atlantic in the sailboat okay."

*

1

Even with shortened canvas *Tinkerbelle* rushed headlong through the darkness at about seven knots, her top speed. Her spray-soaked sails strained against their fastenings as the relentless wind probed for some point of weakness that could be forced to give way. Every now and then a foaming wave cap slammed into her starboard side, sending up a geyser of spume and sloshing rivers of salt water back along her deck, half filling her self-bailing cockpit. Under each blow of the waves she lurched like a wounded doe, dipping to leeward with a tense, stomach-churning heave. She told me through her tiller, by the way she wanted to point closer to the wind, that she was unhappy. But I forced her to go on, full tilt.

What time was it? How many more grueling hours to dawn?

I wrapped the mainsheet once around the tiller and held both in my left hand. Then, struggling to keep *Tinkerbelle* on course with this hand, I shined a flashlight into the cabin with my right hand and peered through the tiny porthole in the drop panel of the battened-down hatch. I'd hung a wristwatch inside where it was relatively dry. From the Greenwich mean time indicated by the watch, I calculated it was roughly 2 A.M. at our meridian of longitude; 2 A.M. *Tinkerbelle* time. Oh, God. Another two and a half hours to sunrise! I'd be frozen stiff by then. Not to mention blown silly or drowned.

My teeth chattered even though I had on four layers of clothing. I wore padded thermal long johns next to my skin, regular cotton underwear over these, then a woolen shirt and woolen trousers and, on top of everything, a yellow rubberized anti-exposure suit. And still I shivered.

⚓ 1

My socks, canvas shoes, feet and the lower halves of my trousers and legs were soaked despite the waterproof outer suit. Rivulets from my sodden hair trickled across my face and down my neck, stabbing icily at my back, making me wince. My hands were puckered and swollen from prolonged saturation. They hurt, especially the tips of the fingers and thumbs, which made untying knots and adjusting the sheets painful tasks. Salt-water sores on my buttocks turned the necessity of sitting into pure misery.

The cabin barometer was an enigma. I wasn't sure what its strange behavior presaged. During the day it had fallen gradually. Then, between sunset and about 11 P.M., it had held steady. But since eleven it had zipped upward again at an alarming rate. I suspected it meant we'd soon encounter even stronger winds than those we were already battling.

The wind, whistling out of the south at twenty-five knots, the most that *Tinkerbelle* could stand up to under reefed main, built up menacing seas that threatened to bowl her over on her beam ends. She had to be swerved around periodically to meet the biggest of the cross-waves almost head-on or she'd have got into serious trouble.

Yet we kept moving, despite our vulnerability, because I wanted to make up for the seven or eight hours we'd spent hove to in a hard blow during the day. It would take forever to reach England if we had to spend that many hours out of every twenty-four lying to a sea anchor. We were already several days behind schedule. So on we raced, taxing our endurance to the limit, reeling off a fraction less than two nautical miles every fifteen minutes.

Except for glimpses at ocean, sails and sky, I kept my eyes fastened on the orange glow of the compass, shifting the tiller to right and left as required to keep the index line opposite the mark for 105°, our eastward course, printed on the swaying card. We bucketed along, our position at that hour being approximately 40° 43′ N and 60° 50′ W, which meant we were some two hundred and ninety nautical miles south of Canada's Cape Breton Island and four hundred and eighty miles east of Long Island.

It was Monday, June 14th, and we were fourteen days out from Falmouth, Massachusetts, on the first leg of a transatlantic voyage I had dreamed of most of my life and carefully planned for more than a year.

"England, here we come!" I yelled at the stars.

2   That was one of the moments I remember best during a voyage that had had its practical beginning about seven years before. As a rim man on the copy desk of a morning newspaper, the *Plain Dealer* of Cleveland, Ohio, I had a chance at about ten-forty every working night to peek at the ads the regular subscribers didn't see until they got out of bed the next morning. It was a benefit I hadn't even considered when I applied for the job, but during the summer of 1958 I availed myself of it with considerable appreciation because Virginia, my wife, and I had decided that at long last our heads were far enough above water, financially, to permit us to buy a small sailboat.

Every night when first-edition copies of the paper were brought up from the presses to the second-floor city room, I took advantage of the first lull in the night's work to turn to the want ads listed under "Boats—Marine Supplies" to see what I could find. Most of the ads concerned motorboats; only a few sailboats were offered for sale and none of these seemed suited to us. We needed a boat large enough to accommodate both of us, our daughter, Robin, and our son, Douglas, and yet small enough to keep at our home in suburban Willowick, in the garage we hoped to have before long. This would enable us to avoid dockage fees that, at that stage of our fortunes, would have bankrupted us. But it also meant that the boat had to be a centerboard craft that could be rolled on and off a conventional boat trailer with ease. A sailboat with a keel sticking down was out of the question as it would be much too difficult to haul on a trailer.

Finally, after weeks of looking, I found a promising ad in the paper of August 2nd. It said:

> SAILBOAT, 13½-ft. Old Town, needs
> some repair, cheap. EN 1-7298.

Getting the drop on the *P.D.*'s three hundred thousand-plus paying readers, I dialed that telephone number at once and made arrangements to see the boat early the next day. It turned out to be a most memorable occasion.

The owner was a fine old gentleman of Greek descent who met me with a twinkle in his eyes. From the way he spoke, I could tell the boat had played the same unifying role in his family that Virginia and I hoped it would play in ours. He and his wife had raised their daughter on sailboating very much as we hoped to raise our youngsters, for, in addition to all the other reasons we had for wanting a sailboat, we listed the character-building part it could have in shaping our children's personalities.

But my first glimpse of the boat gave me quite a shock. It looked so lonely and forlorn turned bottom up in the owner's back yard, its bow and stern resting on rough crates. What struck me like a blow, however, was the sight of two enormous splits in the hull, one on each side at about waterline level. They were about five feet long and up to a quarter of an inch wide. I couldn't imagine what had caused them and I didn't ask for fear of embarrassing the owner; he was such a nice old man. The cause didn't matter, anyway; all I needed to know was whether they could be repaired.

Sensing that I wanted to examine the boat thoroughly, the elderly gentleman left us alone. He had said the boat was thirty years old, and she showed her age in her multilayered and multicolored coatings of paint, which, in spots, was peeling. But the planking, except for the two splits, appeared healthy and strong.

I lay on my back, pushed my head and shoulders under the

boat and, as soon as my eyes grew accustomed to the gloom, studied every nook and cranny of her interior. I discovered the "needs some repair" of the ad was an understatement. Nearly two dozen of the boat's steam-bent ribs were broken and half a dozen others were infected with dry rot, which also had decayed chunks of the mast step and a portion of the centerboard trunk. The canvas deck was badly worn and needed replacement, and the sails, as I discovered later, were too mildewed and threadbare to use. Everything else, though, was basically sound.

For about forty-five minutes I lay there under the boat. After I'd examined her insides completely and had decided her split planks were mendable, I drifted off into woolgathering about our plans for her, fixing her up, the place she'd occupy in our family and how she'd fare with us and we with her. Finally I got down to the business of listing all the pros and cons, weighing her cost, a hundred and sixty dollars, and the expense of repairing her and buying new sails, which I estimated would come to around three hundred dollars, against the cost and the possibility of buying a boat in better condition. I decided that, dilapidated as she was, she was the boat for us. So I paid a deposit and told the owner I'd be back soon to pick her up.

On August 4th (Virginia has the date underlined in her diary) the whole family bundled into our car and, with a rented trailer hitched on behind, we drove off to take possession of our little craft. The owner and his friendly wife and daughter came out to greet us on our arrival. We chatted for a few minutes, completed our transaction, and then everyone pitched in to turn the boat right side up and winch it onto the trailer. Virginia told me later that, as we drove slowly down the driveway, she noticed tears glistening in the old man's eyes as he and his wife kissed their hands and patted the boat with affectionate gestures of farewell. We were sorry to be taking away an object that had meant so much to them, but at the same time we were happy to know that, despite its run-down state,

the boat had been deeply loved. Unquestionably, it had provided this pleasant family with many happy experiences, and we
felt certain it would do the same for us.

Earlier in the day Robin and Douglas had broadcast the
news to their friends that we were going to get a boat, so nearly
all the children of the neighborhood were waiting for us on
our return home. They paraded along shouting to one another
as we proudly towed our new acquisition up our driveway, and,
from that moment on, the boat seemed to be surrounded by
children. It apparently was a magnet, although I suspect the
neighborhood mothers often told their offspring to "go up and
watch what Mr. Manry's doing" just to get them out from
underfoot for a while. Anyway, they seemed to congregate
around the boat whenever I was working on it, which was
practically every day between 9:30 A.M. and 4 P.M., when I had
to stop to have dinner and then leave for my job on the *P.D.*
copy desk.

Sometimes I was able to pull off a stunt like Tom Sawyer's
the day he had to whitewash his Aunt Polly's fence, except
that I was taking paint off, not putting it on. I'd scrape away
as though the task were sheer ecstasy and pretty soon one of
the young observers would ask if he could share my fun; and
I'd say yes and give him a scraper or some sandpaper. And then
another would ask, and then another. Once I had four junior
boat renovators working at the same time. Usually they didn't
get a great deal accomplished; the paint-removal project was
too arduous. But we all had a good time.

I used every minute I could take from the demands of my
job, family and home to work on the boat, for steady progress
had to be made if it was to be ready in time for the 1959
boating season, which opened in May. In fact, I spent so much
time working on the boat I'm sure Virginia and the children
often wondered whether we had taken possession of it or it had
taken possession of us. I must say, though, that they bore up
remarkably well under the intra-family strains created by occa-

sional conflicts between its needs and ours. Like the time I had to soak the new ash ribs I'd ordered in the bathtub for five days to make them pliable enough to bend into place. That was a time of tribulation for everyone.

The grim days of having to take sponge baths or none came to an end as the new ribs were installed and bolted down to the planking. A new mast step was put in next, and the decayed portion of the centerboard trunk was cut out and replaced with fresh wood. Then those cruel, ugly splits in the sides were repaired with plywood strips, waterproof glue and fiberglass.

During all this time we had to be careful to keep the boat dry. Whenever I wasn't working on it, we kept it covered with tarpaulins and old plastic tablecloths. And, of course, the necessity of keeping it dry made that fall seem like the rainiest one we'd ever had.

One night Virginia was ready for bed when I telephoned from the *Plain Dealer,* as I always did at about 10:00 P.M., during my supper hour.

"Is it raining?" I asked. (It was impossible to tell from the *P.D.* city room, which had no windows.)

"Yes."

"Better make sure the boat isn't getting wet."

"O.K."

So my wonderful wife put a raincoat on over her pajamas and rubber boots on over her bedroom slippers and went out into the cold, blustery, wet night to make sure the boat—this nautical thing that was being treated with the deference we might have shown a third child—was not suffering from the dampness.

One of the tarps was flapping wildly, threatening to come adrift; so Virginia took hold of an automobile tire we used to weigh the tarps down and heaved it into position. It was an easy operation. She'd done it scores of times before. The only trouble was that this time the tire was full of ice-cold rain water.

Virginia gasped and sputtered beneath the resulting shower, drenched to the skin in spite of the rain gear she wore, and nearly frozen. It was a moment of dreadful crisis for me and for the boat, although, at the time, I remained tranquilly oblivious at my *P.D.* post miles away, with nothing more serious on my mind than the split infinitives and faulty syntax in a reporter's news copy. I didn't hear of it until the next day, at breakfast.

We passed through such troubled waters as these on several

occasions. However, a rising tide of good humor always saw us through, as the boat gradually changed in appearance from an abandoned hulk to a craft that might conceivably return some-day to the element for which it was designed.

Our developing plans for the boat were rather unconventional. In fact, our intentions went far beyond simply restoring it to a seaworthy condition. We wanted it to become our little yacht, to take us on cruises, which meant that it had to have sleeping accommodations for all four of us within the meager space provided by its 13½-foot length and 5¼-foot beam. Seldom has so much been expected of so small a boat. And yet these expectations were, in a manner of speaking, realized.

The mid-section of the hull was converted into a tiny "cabin" separated from the cockpit by a watertight bulkhead and covered with a roof that could be partly opened, to permit entry and use of the folding-down seats at its rear, or removed entirely. Virginia and I could sleep on air mattresses, in sleeping bags, in this area; one on each side of the centerboard trunk, with our feet extending into the bow.

Next, I built a removable panel that could be fitted over the foot well to convert the cockpit into a flat space where Robin and Douglas could put their air mattresses and sleeping bags. Since this cockpit sleeping area was elevated eight or ten inches above the floor where Virginia and I would sleep, it gave our accommodation plan a split-level effect that was certainly in tune with the times, from the viewpoint of home architecture if not naval architecture.

Naturally we had to consider the weather, for it wouldn't have been very pleasant on our yacht in a rainstorm; the joint between the two sections of the cabin roof wasn't absolutely rainproof, despite the use of weather stripping, and would have let water drip below, maddeningly. Besides which, the cockpit double-bunk layout was entirely open to the elements. These difficulties were overcome through the fabrication of a tent we could sling over the boom and snap to fasteners installed on either side of the boat just below the rubbing strake. The tent enclosed both cabin and cockpit, giving us all the headroom we needed, as well as privacy and shelter for cruising.

At last, in early May, after more than nine months of toil, our tiny yacht was ready. Then came the unforgettable day we brought home our own trailer, pulled the boat onto it for the first time and, just for practice, pitched the tent to see how it would look. It looked great; at least, it did to us. I think it would be accurate to say the boat was unique; and the entire rig, assembled with the tent up, had the extraordinary appearance of an amphibious Conestoga wagon. Robin and Douglas and their friends had a wonderful time playing in it. And Virginia and I began to feel like pioneers on the threshold of exciting explorations that would add an entirely new dimension to our lives. We could hardly wait to get started.

Mother's Day, Sunday, May 10th, was only a day or two away and I thought what a treat it would be for Virginia if we launched our boat and went for our first sail on this special day. So that's what we did; only it didn't work out quite the way I'd hoped it would.

We trailed the boat to Cleveland's Gordon Park and utilized the public launching ramps there to get it into the water. That much was easy. But then the complications set in. First it began to rain and, for half an hour or so, Virginia and the children huddled uncomfortably in semi-reclining positions in the minute cabin to keep relatively dry. There wasn't room for me in there, too, so I stayed outside tending the mooring lines and getting soaked.

When the rain finally stopped, the wind began to blow with alarming force. Frankly, it scared me. Even as a novice sailor I realized it would be dangerous to be out on Lake Erie in such a stiff and gusty breeze. But we'd come to sail and sail we would. At least, one of us would—me.

I felt like Captain Bligh when I told my family I'd decided to go it alone; under the circumstances, I simply couldn't be responsible for the safety of anyone but myself. However, they must have realized I spoke words of wisdom for there were no significant protests. All three got out of the boat and into our car and sat there, protected from the wind, eating the picnic lunch Virginia had prepared, as the boat and I left the shore.

As we headed into the maelstrom of winds and waves the words of Tennyson's "Crossing the Bar" came to me:

> Sunset and evening star,
>   And one clear call for me!
> And may there be no moaning of the bar,
>   When I put out to sea.

It wasn't the time of sunset, either actually or figuratively, and there was no evening star in sight, but I could hear that "clear call for me" and a frightful moaning that filled me with dread. Fortunately, the moaning was of the wind in the rigging, not of the bar. That was a relief.

I didn't dare to venture far into the lake; in fact, I stayed within the protecting arm of a nearby breakwall. Even so, it was one of the most breath-taking sails of my life. The boat whizzed along so fast that I had to come about every twenty seconds or so to stay within the breakwall's shelter, which I was determined to do. Violent puffs of wind made the craft heel over so far and so fast that I repeatedly let go of the main-sheet in alarm, whereupon it would run through the boom block as far as it could go. Only the knot in its end kept it from going all the way, which would have created a very sticky situation indeed.

In less than fifteen minutes I'd had my fill of sailing under those conditions and returned to the dock. We soon had the boat back on the trailer and were on our way home.

"It was kinda gusty," I told Virginia.

"Kind of gusty!" she exclaimed. "I was sure you were going to upset. And the waves were so big we couldn't even see you when you were down between them! All we could see was the tip of the sail!"

"Yeah. I guess it must have looked pretty exciting from the shore. And it sure wasn't much of an outing for you. All you got to do was sit in the car and watch your husband sail."

"You mean watch him nearly drown!"

When we got home, the neighbors hurried out to greet us as though we had all returned from the grave. They said that, to tell the truth, they hadn't expected to see us again—alive. However, I couldn't afford to hang around wallowing in the delightful role of a latter-day Lazarus; I had to eat a quick lunch and rush off to work at the *P.D.* Virginia, left with the duty of hanging up the sails to dry, spent most of the evening in deep reflection, pondering the meaning of Mother's Day.

Undaunted, we set forth again a few days later for another

attempt at sailing. It was a bright, sunny afternoon and for me a day off from work, which meant we wouldn't have to hurry home as we had before. We had an opportunity to sail and sail; until dark, if we wanted to, or even later than that. I'd never been sailing in the moonlight and wondered how it would be. Marvelous, I guessed.

This time we decided to launch the boat at Wildwood Park, nearer our home. We got it off the trailer and into the water again without any trouble, stepped the mast, then, with what seemed to us an exceedingly seaman-like flourish, hoisted the sails and headed for the narrow channel leading from the harbor into the lake. We were propelled by a wind that had had its teeth pulled, a gentle breeze that couldn't have hurt a fly. It was comforting to know that, whatever else might happen, we had nothing to fear from Aeolus, god of the winds.

But, alas, that "else" began happening almost at once. The boat seemed to have a will of its own. Refusing to respond to my excited pushes and pulls on the tiller, it moved with unwavering aim on a course destined to pile us up on the huge blocks of stone that formed one of the harbor's walls. I had a nightmare vision of losing my dear wife and children in a grotesque in-harbor shipwreck and of spending the rest of my days racked by remorse, imprisoned for improper operation of a sailing vessel. I believe I was as close to skidding into utter panic as I have ever been, and the children didn't help to calm my nerves. Both of them hollered in terror, "We're going to hit the rocks! We're going to turn over!"

Fortunately, I retained enough of a grip on myself to get out the oars. I gave one to Virginia, and together we fended the boat off the rocks. Then it came to me—I hadn't lowered the centerboard! That's why I hadn't been able to steer; why the boat had seemed bent on dashing itself to pieces.

In a matter of seconds we had the board down and immediately almost everything subsided into normality. I say almost everything because, even though the wind caught our sails and wafted us peacefully out into the lake, even though the boat was now fully under control, Douglas, then not quite five, was far from gleeful.

"Take me back to the shore!" he yelled at the top of his lungs. "Take me back! Take me back!"

Virginia and I held a hurried conference. We agreed that he was truly frightened and, if we wanted him to grow up enjoying boats and sailing, it would be prudent to respect his

wishes and return to shore, to await a more auspicious time to start him off as a sailor. So, without any sailing in the moonlight, or even much sailing in the daylight, we returned to the dock and set off for home.

For a while Virginia and I saw our hopes of family unity built on a foundation of happy sailing experiences slipping into oblivion. But we persevered. Recalling the horseback riders' dictum to remount at once after a bad fall in order to maintain confidence, we soon cast off from home again, this time on an overnight voyage of discovery to Pymatuning Lake, a fetching reservoir sixty miles east of Willowick. This was to be our shakedown camping cruise.

When we got to the campgrounds, our fellow campers found us, or rather our boat, a trifle startling. In fact, it was plain they had never seen anything like it in their lives. A woman at a neighboring campsite watched spellbound as I prepared our yacht for the night. When I hoisted the tent over the boom and started to fasten it down, Virginia overheard her exclaim to her husband, "George, look! He's building a house on that boat!"

I must confess that, secretly, we were both amused and pleased by the apparent consternation our little craft caused among the more conservatively equipped campers who saw it. We loved the dropped jaws and surprised looks it produced. And we were pleased with ourselves, in a way, for our refusal, in this one respect at least, to follow in the crowd's footsteps like sheep. We enjoyed daring to be different.

Also, on later trips, we found our boat-tent paid unexpected dividends, for we were allowed to sleep in it offshore at crowded camps where all the onshore sites were occupied.

As we settled down for the night at Pymatuning Lake, Virginia, unknown to the rest of us, began what was undoubtedly the supreme test of her life, an excruciating ordeal of physical endurance. This terrible night of torture was imposed by a regulation government-issue sleeping bag, otherwise known as a mummy sack. The children and I fell asleep in our sacks almost at once. It wasn't until morning that we learned Virginia had spent most of the night tugging, turning, twisting and thumping—struggling to find a comfortable position in the too-tight shroud that encased her. To top it off, she nearly froze; and in silence. She allowed the rest of us to go on sleeping, undisturbed, as she played martyr, suffering without a word of complaint. Even at dawn, when we awoke, she continued to be brave. The nearest she came to releasing the inner pressures that threatened to explode was to say, "I take my hat off to the American soldier. Any man who can go out and fight after spending a night in one of these woolen booby traps has my undying admiration."

A surge of admiration flowed through me, too, at that moment, but it wasn't for the American soldier.

After breakfast we provided our fellow campers and boaters with a spectacle that no doubt, to them, was hugely entertaining. It happened as we were launching our boat. I was busily engaged in sliding the boat off the trailer into the water when Virginia, at the wheel of the car, mistook something I said for the signal that the boat was launched and the trailer could be hauled away. She took off prematurely with a forward jerk that sent the boat careening into the water with a mighty splash and me following after, legs and arms whirling like windmills. By the time she heeded my shouts of distress and looked around, I was on my hands and knees in the lake and the boat—with Robin, our beloved first-born, on board—was skimming off beyond reach.

I swam out and towed the boat back to shore; getting soaked, but saving our daughter. Meanwhile, Virginia remarked to a camper standing near her that perhaps, in view of the havoc she'd wrought, she had better start driving and never come back. And he said he reckoned that might be a good idea.

Robin and Douglas thought the whole episode was the most fun they'd ever had. In fact, it was then they decided that sailing was a great sport, after all, and began to enjoy it thoroughly. Virginia and I were a little slower about savoring the humor of the situation, but as soon as we got under way, spanking along in our windboat before a fresh breeze, we regained the capacity to laugh at ourselves. We could imagine how energetically tongues were wagging back at the camp about the performance of that nutty family with the boat that converted into a tent, or the tent that converted into a boat, or whatever it was.

During the months that the driveway of our home had had the appearance of a boatyard, and the weeks since then, our craft had been nameless. It had been known simply as "the boat" or as "our boat" or (when its seemingly excessive consumption of time and/or money piqued other members of the family) as "Daddy's boat." Now, however, the time had come to give it a name and we put our heads together in a brainstorming session to choose one we all liked.

Douglas at that time was tapering off from an amazing adulation of bullfighters—where he acquired it, I don't know—and entering a phase of his life in which he regarded pirates as the most wonderful of men, the only real heroes worthy of acclaim. He knew more about Blackbeard, Captain Kidd, Long John Silver, Henry Morgan, Captain Hook and the other factual and fictional freebooters of the Spanish Main than other boys his age knew about baseball greats. He and his friends were constantly playing pirate on the boat, making imaginary foes walk the plank and sailing off to hidden islands to bury chests full of treasure. And whenever we went sailing on Lake Erie or Lake Pymatuning, we always had to fly the Jolly Roger from the masthead, as befitted a buccaneer's sloop.

It was Doug's love of pirates that led, indirectly, to the name we chose for our boat. It got us to thinking about Captain Hook, and that led to Peter Pan and Tinker Bell, who, at one point in J. M. Barrie's story, was poisoned by Hook and brought to the brink of death. The only thing that could save her was for the children of the world to affirm their belief in fairies, which they did. So, believing in our boat fully as much as these children believed in fairies, we decided to name her after Tinker Bell. We thought this name was particularly appropriate because, in addition to the connotations of the fairy tale, it reflected the fact that I was forever tinkering with her. However, we changed the spelling to Tinkerbelle, since the boat certainly was an enchanting belle, although, like its namesake and all things feminine, it could on occasion be exasperating.

Tinkerbelle, now definitely a "she" rather than an "it," exhibited her exasperating side on our next cruise, a gunkholing expedition to Erie, Pennsylvania, a lakeshore city about ninety miles east of our home. We launched her in the bay formed by the curving arm of Presque Isle Peninsula and planned to sail through the channel into Lake Erie and on to a beach where we could go swimming. It was a sunny day and the lapping waves and glistening sails made us feel vigorously alive. We looked forward to an exceptionally enjoyable afternoon.

All went well until we got to the channel and then the breeze dropped to less than a whisper. We stopped moving. *Tinkerbelle* just sat there motionless as motorboat after motorboat passed by. When an excursion boat out for a tour of the peninsula came along, we were admired, photographed and waved to. And then, an hour later, when the excursion boat returned, we were admired, photographed and waved to again; but this time, since we hadn't moved ahead more than a few feet, we also became the butt of some snide remarks, such as: "Get a horse." "Why don't you use a motor?" and "Maybe you better swim for it." Even the fishermen on the banks of the channel chimed in with caustic comments.

"Sailing is like watching grass grow," one of them remarked, plainly for our benefit.

We had prided ourselves that, in the great tradition of the sea, ours was both a happy ship and a taut one. But it didn't require 20/20 vision to see that the first mate was going into a maneuver that even in nonnautical circles was known as "coming to the end of one's rope." So, finally, when one of those beastly motorboats offered us a tow, I accepted.

The return trip, after our swim, was just as slow, maybe slower. It took us more than twice as long to sail the four miles from the beach back to the dock as it had taken to drive the ninety miles from Willowick to Erie. Without a doubt, Virginia and the children earned their Ph.D.s in patience that day. I guess I'd already picked one up somewhere but nevertheless I resolved that, as soon as possible, we'd get a little outboard motor to use when the wind faltered. That would make our seafaring ever so much pleasanter.

In June and July we did a lot of day sailing on Lake Erie from launching ramps in Cleveland and went on several more overnight trips to other, smaller bodies of water. Then, in August, we climaxed the summer with a seven-day amphibi-cruise through Michigan.

Virginia and the kids look back on this as our nonstop vacation race through Michigan because we didn't spend more than one night at each place we visited. Nevertheless, the trip became a high spot of our lives. Our most vivid memories are of lovely Higgins Lake, where, for the first time, we slept aboard *Tinkerbelle* while she was water-borne; of the gigantic Mackinac Bridge connecting the state's upper and lower peninsulas; of Manistique, a former logging town which still has a friendly frontier atmosphere; of Indian Lake in the heart of the Hiawatha country, where we imagined ourselves camping "by the shore of Gitche Gumee"; of Traverse City, where we nestled in a grove of sweet-scented pines, and of Ludington State Park, where we again spent a night afloat, snug and dry in our boat-tent despite the driving rain of a thunderstorm.

During the summers of 1960 and 1961 we continued our day sailing on Lake Erie and occasional overnight gunkholing trips elsewhere, but our three-week vacation each summer was devoted to camping and sailing in the delightfully remote wilds of Algonquin Provincial Park in Canada's Ontario Province. The fun we had living on an island in the park's Lake Opeongo has left indelible impressions of bliss on our minds, and the sailing experiences we had there were equally joyful.

It was on an enchanting blue-sky day on Lake Opeongo, as we ghosted along in our boat listening to the charming songs of tiny white-throated sparrows, that we came to the realization, suddenly, that *Tinkerbelle* had crept deeply into our lives and hearts. She wasn't a boat any more; she was a friend. She was helping us to grow, individually and as a family, by bringing us, together, into confrontation with basic forces of nature and fundamental situations in living. She was giving us a foundation on which to make wise decisions about what was important in life and what wasn't. She was providing experiences through which we were acquiring self-reliance, appreciation for the outdoors, respect for others, instincts of mutual aid and co-operation and all the other qualities, skills and attitudes that contribute toward the development of mature personalities. She was teaching us how to endure what couldn't be cured. And she was helping us to avoid some of the pitfalls that abound in today's urbanized environment, where the impact of Madison Avenue's bullyboy exponents of the hard sell has tended to transfer human values from their normal climate to a hothouse atmosphere almost totally unrelated to reality.

Don't assume for a second that the children were the only beneficiaries, or even the principal ones. Virginia and I gained enormously, too, in our understanding of our children, of sibling rivalry and how to deal with it, in our comprehension of ourselves and of each other and in innumerable other ways. We didn't always act with flawless wisdom and love, we were far too imperfect for that; but we seemed to be moving in the right direction. Anyway, I hoped we were.

And we owed a debt of gratitude to our boat. She was accomplishing for us what we had originally hoped she would accomplish, and more. This does not imply that these things might not have been achieved equally well, or even better, in some other way, by some other family. It simply means that for us the key to fulfillment was our beloved *Tinkerbelle*.

*

3 Our proficiency as sailors gradually increased. As we gained in experience, we also gained in skill and we became better and better acquainted with our boat, her good points and her shortcomings.

We found that her beaminess and flattish bottom gave her considerable initial stability, making her stiff, up to a point, so that she preferred to sail fairly upright rather than heeled far over to one side. If she did heel over farther than was comfortable for her, she developed a strong weather helm that called for a firm hand on the tiller to make her behave herself and stay on course. This, over a long haul, could be exhausting. However, adjustment of the mains'l, by taking a reef in it or by easing off on the sheet to allow more of the wind to spill out of it, usually restored the helm to normal balance.

The bright side of this pattern of conduct was that if an unexpected puff of wind struck *Tinkerbelle* it forced her bow to windward as she heeled over, thus lessening the danger of capsizing. Instead of going "bottoms up," she tended to swerve around into the wind and stop, "in irons." I liked this for I saw it as a valuable safety factor.

Another thing we discovered was that she was far from being a racing machine. She was lamentably slow in light breezes; so slow, in fact, that we joked about the way it took a hurricane to make her get up and go. Actually, we did some of our most enjoyable sailing when small-craft warnings were hoisted aloft and the wind was blowing so hard few other sailboats ventured out on the lake. In light airs, though, *Tinkerbelle* simply wallowed in the water like a decoy duck while racing boats of comparable size moved along as effortlessly as swans. It was embarrassing to be left behind, but this facet of *Tinkerbelle's* personality also had its advantageous side. The squat sail plan that made her slow in light airs gave her extra stability in hard blows. She could stand up to strong winds better than the racing machines.

As we became more and more familiar with *Tinkerbelle* and her idiosyncrasies, I couldn't help thinking of ways to make her more seaworthy. Most sailors, I'm sure, study their boats with an eye to improving them, in one way or another, and I was no different, except that the changes I proposed to make in our boat were a trifle drastic and, some of them, perhaps, of questionable value. Nevertheless, in the late spring of 1962, I began to rebuild *Tinkerbelle* nearer to my heart's desire; to make her as able a vessel as I possibly could, without spoiling her portability by trailer.

About eighteen months before this we had acquired a garage, so I took over the whole place as my boat-rebuilding shop and, for the time being, relegated our car to the driveway. Virginia, who invariably anthropomorphizes the family car, thought this was scandalous. To her it was disrespectful, if not downright cruel, not to mention immoral, to leave the poor thing outside, exposed to the ravages of wind and rain. I had somewhat the same feelings, only they were directed toward the boat, not the car. An automobile, to me, was simply a mass-produced contraption of metal, glass and rubber, stinking of gasoline and oil, that couldn't possibly have feelings, much less a soul. But a sailboat . . . That was different. A sailboat could feel joy and pain, hope and despair; it could be cooperative or cantankerous, well-mannered or insulting, a lady or a floozie. And every sailboat had an individuality, a specialness that set it apart from all others, even those of the same class. It also, most assuredly, had a soul.

If anyone deserved to inhabit the garage, I told Virginia, it was our sailboat. I reminded her that before we got the garage our car had endured the rigors of more than one winter outdoors; and I recalled the troubles we'd had keeping the boat covered with tarpaulins. I think the memory of the tarps was what turned the tables in *Tinkerbelle*'s favor, for it was right after I'd mentioned them that Virginia agreed to let her have the garage to herself.

So, for the second time since she had become ours, the boat underwent something like a nautical metamorphosis. I was adequately skillful with woodworking tools, having taken a manual-training course in high school, and had acquired from my reading a sufficient understanding of boat-designing principles to plan and execute the metamorphosis with confidence. It required a full year of spare-time labor to complete the transformation, but when it was done *Tinkerbelle* was a proper little yacht, with a cabin, cockpit, running lights, compass and other gear usually found only on much larger vessels.

Instead of her original centerboard, she now had a daggerboard-keel that could be moved up and down by winch in the slot of a watertight housing that passed through the keel timber and extended upward through the cabin roof. When the daggerboard-keel was retracted, *Tinkerbelle* could be moved onto a trailer without difficulty, and when it was lowered it provided the same lateral resistance the centerboard had supplied, plus a dividend of increased stability, for it was made of iron plate and weighed a little more than a hundred pounds.

The cabin roof's height above the deck was proportionately much greater in *Tinkerbelle* than it was in larger sailboats and this detracted somewhat from her appearance, but there were three good reasons for making this dimension as ample as practicable: to give plenty of headroom in the cabin; to house (in the through-cabin slot) as deep a daggerboard-keel as possible, and thus (when the daggerboard-keel was down) lower the hull's center of gravity to the maximum, and to provide, in effect, additional freeboard, thus raising the hull's center of buoyancy.

The second and third factors, taken together, reduced the chance of a capsize and also mightily improved the prospect of righting the boat if she should happen to be overturned.

Abaft the self-bailing cockpit was a lazarette, accessible through a small hatch at the stern and separated from the rest of the boat by a watertight bulkhead. By bolting down the lazarette and cabin hatches, the hull now could be sealed shut, giving it many of the storm-weathering properties of, say, a corked bottle. This, it seemed to me, was approaching the ultimate in seaworthiness.

I also made a new mast, eight inches taller than the original, so that the boom would be high enough to clear the cabin top, and hinged in a tabernacle to permit easy raising and lowering. The hull's lapstrake planking was coated with white fiberglass, and the cabin top, cockpit foot well and deck were coated with red fiberglass, the deck also being treated with an anti-skid preparation.

When all the work was done, *Tinkerbelle* looked like a brand-new boat. Her white hull, red deck and cabin top and varnished mast, cockpit seats and cabin sides gleamed in the sunshine. She was a thing of beauty, at least to me, and there was no disputing the fact that no other boat like her existed anywhere in the world. She had a place all her own.

We decided she should be christened, to give her a decent start in her reincarnation, but we didn't particularly favor the customary boat christening with a bottle of champagne smashed against the bow. We were afraid the blow might mar her lustrous finish and, anyway, the symbolism of champagne was entirely out of keeping with both our financial circumstances and our drinking habits. So we settled on a ritual that diverged slightly from standard boat-christening protocol, and, of course, Virginia did the honors.

"I christen thee *Tinkerbelle*," she intoned gravely as, watched intently by the rest of us, she ceremoniously sprinkled the stem of our lovely craft with soda pop. It was a scene of breathtaking pageantry.

Naturally, now that the boat was ready to take to the water again, I wanted to try her out to see if she measured up to my expectations. There were skeptics in the neighborhood who silently pitied Virginia for being tied to a husband gone berserk and who needed to be shown that the remodeled boat was not the feckless creation of a deranged mind. These doubters were mostly men, of course. The women, none of them sailors or even the wives of sailors, had no doubts whatever that I was balmy; anyone interested in boats was bound to be. They were beyond

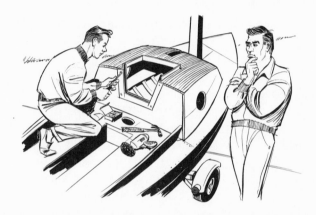

being shown the error of their belief. With the men, however, I had hopes. They were willing to grant that a fellow male who fooled around with boats could be sane. It was only what I'd done to the boat that made them doubt my sanity.

During the rebuilding several men had dropped by periodically to see how the work was progressing and to chat. They were always polite, but when they got home they loosened up and, quite often, word got back through their wives to Virginia and through her to me that they thought I had lost my marbles, as the saying goes.

"That old tub will never take him anywhere," one man told his wife. Another said, "It'll never go to windward; cabin makes too much resistance. Makes it top-heavy, too."

A third fellow came over one afternoon while I was away on

some family errand and, with Virginia's permission, studied the boat for about fifteen minutes to see exactly what I was up to. Later, his wife revealed his private opinion: "He's making a mess of that boat. The tabernacle will never stand up; too much strain on it. And that daggerboard thing he's got! That's pure Rube Goldberg!"

So there was a lot riding on the outcome of the new *Tinker-belle*'s trial runs: my reputation for soundness of mind. Fortunately, nothing untoward happened. The boat and I, and all who sailed with us, came back safely every time. I'm not sure that this immediately scotched the rumor that I was a nut, but at least it tended to show that, if I was a nut, I was a passably competent one, or else exceedingly lucky. In any case, no more unflattering comments came my way via the housewives' grapevine.

I think what did more than anything else to restore my reputation was my first singlehanded cruise, a seventy-mile sail from Fairport, a city east of Willowick, to Erie. By surviving that voyage on Lake Erie I did more than I could have done in any other way to bring myself back from beyond the pale, to convince my friends and neighbors that I actually did know enough about boats and sailing to indulge my passion safely.

It pleased me to find that *Tinkerbelle*'s behavior had been changed scarcely at all, except for the better, by the alterations she had undergone. The cabin's windage did keep her from sailing quite as close to the wind as she had before, but the difference was so slight, only a degree or two, that it didn't distress me. Anyway, she had never been a good pointer. The best she had been able to do was sail within fifty or fifty-five degrees of the wind, whereas most modern boats could sail within forty-five degrees of it.

The loss in windward ability was more than compensated for by the added stability imparted by the below-hull weight of the daggerboard-keel, the all-weather comfort of the cabin and,

when the two hatches were closed, the watertight integrity of
the hull. This last point, especially, made me confident of the
boat's ability to weather rather severe sailing conditions. In
fact, on the voyage to Erie, she took a beating off Presque Isle
Peninsula as winds of thirty to thirty-five miles an hour built
up steep, six-foot waves; but she bore up under the pummeling
in fine style. I began to feel she was fit to embark on much
longer voyages.

The next winter, in January or February, 1964, a friend who
owned a 25-foot cruising sloop proposed that we sail it across
the Atlantic Ocean together to England. I guess he said it half
in jest, not knowing that such a voyage had been a dream of
mine for nearly three decades and that I would latch onto the
idea with enormous enthusiasm and tenacity. We had long
discussions about the problems of ocean cruising, both of us
having read widely on the subject, and began making plans and
assembling the necessary equipment. Virginia, and Robin and
Douglas, knew of the proposed voyage, of course, and approved.
So I was jubilant. I have seldom been happier than I was during
those days when the prospect of achieving my long-time ambition seemed within easy reach. I went about my work at the
Plain Dealer in a sort of ecstatic trance, the course my life was
following (most unexpectedly) was so unbelievably wonderful.

After more than a month of planning I wrote, on March 18th,
to Philip W. Porter, the newspaper's executive editor, request-
ing a leave of absence in the summer of 1965 to make the
voyage. When he wrote back granting the request, my joy knew
no bounds. I felt the major obstacle in our path had been surmounted. In an all but uncontrollable surge of elation I told
my friends of our plan to cross the great Atlantic under sail;
and, despite my fears, I was pleased to find they received the
news fairly calmly. Most of them made it clear they thought the
voyage would be hazardous, but very few of them thought we
had lost our minds, and two or three even admitted they wished
they could accompany us.

I was on Cloud 9 for about six weeks. Then came a crushing blow. The prospective skipper backed out of the venture, persuaded by his wife, father and business associates that it was ill advised; not that it was too risky, but that it would require too much time. I was heartbroken; inconsolably wretched. It was like dropping from paradise to purgatory at the flip of a switch. The instant descent left me stunned. But, of course, groggy as I was, life had to go on. Somehow I continued to perform my duties as husband, father and newsman, but it was a desperately trying period of my life.

As I regained my psychological balance, however, the thought struck me: Why not make the voyage in *Tinkerbelle?* And the more I mulled over the idea, the less fantastic it appeared. After all, voyages had been made in small boats before. There was the 19-foot-long *Pacific* that Bernard Gilboy sailed from California almost to Australia in 1882-83. There was the 18-foot *Elaine* in which Fred Rebell, using a homemade sextant, sailed from Australia to California in 1931-33. There was the 19-foot *Mermaid* sailed by Kenichi Horie from Japan to California in 1962. There was the 16-foot *Little Western* that Frederick Norman and George P. Thomas sailed from Massachusetts to England in 1880 and, the following year, sailed back to Nova Scotia. There was the 15-foot *Sea Serpent* that Si Lawlor sailed nonstop from Massachusetts to England in 1891. And there was the 14½-foot *Sapolio* that William Andrews sailed, in 1892 (the four-hundredth anniversary of Columbus's famous voyage), from New Jersey to Palos, Spain (Columbus's port of embarkation), with a stop at the Azores.

Other unusual Atlantic crossings had been made by the 18-foot rowboat *Richard K. Fox* (1897), the 15-foot pneumatic raft *L'Hérétique* (1952) and the 17-foot folding kayak *Liberia III* (1956).

All these voyages were remarkable. But there was another, even more remarkable, voyage that made me feel *Tinkerbelle* should be able to sail across the Atlantic. This was the voyage of *Half Safe*, an 18-foot amphibious Jeep that Ben Carlin and his wife took from Halifax to West Africa, via the Azores, in 1950-51. If a getup such as Carlin's aquatic auto could traverse the broad ocean, *Tinkerbelle* could do it, too; I was convinced of that.

So, without telling anyone except my wife and children of this change in plans, I began making preparations.

*

4 Sailors have seldom been envied by confirmed land-
lubbers and, until recent times, with good reason.
Their lives were hard and usually short.

Boswell reported in 1759 that Samuel Johnson said: "No man
will be a sailor who has contrivance enough to get himself into
a jail; for being in a ship is being in jail with the chance of
being drowned. . . . A man in a jail has more room, better food,
and commonly better company." This was a widely held view
in those days, I imagine, because the conditions under which
seamen existed were so atrocious that press gangs often had to be
employed to fill out the crews of naval ships; and once a man
was pressed into service he usually did not escape, except
through death.

About a hundred years later Ralph Waldo Emerson echoed
Johnson's opinion. Writing of a voyage he took to England in
1847, he said, "The wonder is always new that any sane man
can be a sailor." He was referring to the sailor's "life of risks,
incessant abuse and the worst pay," for conditions at sea hadn't
improved greatly in a century.

Nowadays, of course, few persons talk this way about life
at sea, either in the merchant marine or in the navy. The lot
of today's seafarers is so much better that it bears scarcely any
resemblance to the lot of seamen of Emerson's or Johnson's
time. The impressment, harsh discipline, bad food, outbreaks
of scurvy and brutalizing environment of the old, old days are
gone. Yet, while life aboard a commercial freighter or naval
battleship is no longer regarded with horror, a rather large
segment of the landbound population (at least in the United

States) now looks askance at a new breed of sailors—those who go down to the sea in small pleasure boats. With Emerson, this group wonders how any sane man can do such a thing.

The reason for the attitude today is, I suppose, compounded of a fear of deep water and the widespread thumb-rule judgment that a vessel's safeness depends on its size—the bigger the safer.

Although I hadn't conducted any private opinion polls, I had learned enough in the course of everyday living to have a fairly good idea of the reaction I would get if I let it be known that I planned to sail across the Atlantic in little *Tinkerbelle*. I could plainly see the raised eyebrows and hear the expressions of alarm such a confession would produce among my *Plain Dealer* associates and Willowick neighbors. I wouldn't have minded if that had been all, for these things couldn't have hurt me or my family. What did worry me, though, was the possibility that some well-intentioned person who knew nothing about boats or the ocean, but who had an unreasoning fear of both, would go to work on Virginia and try to convince her that, for my own good, she should refuse to give the voyage her blessing. I'm sure Virginia would have withstood such pressures admirably, but at the same time they would have made her life a great deal more difficult, psychologically, than it needed to be, and I didn't want that.

So I engaged in a deception for which I hope the good Lord and my friends will forgive me. I let everyone continue thinking I expected to cross the ocean with another man, in his 25-foot boat, and whenever anyone inquired about our plans I answered as if a voyage in the larger boat were still in prospect. Actually, almost all the planning I did for the voyage in *Tinkerbelle* was the same as it would have been for a voyage in the bigger craft (except that the provisions were reduced by half), so the amount of fabricating I had to do was minimal. It consisted mainly of simply allowing a false impression to remain uncorrected.

I started my studying and planning with the determination

that if at any time prior to embarkation I encountered a difficulty of such magnitude as to be what I considered a serious
threat to success, I would decide against attempting the voyage.
I was resolved not to let foolish pride sweep me into a bad
situation or, being in one, make me continue in it to the bitter
end. For my family's sake as well as my own I refused to be concerned about loss of face, for I considered it far better to be a
live coward than a dead hero.

What I had to do first of all, it seemed to me, was to determine
as precisely as I could the nature and full extent of the hazards
to be expected on a transatlantic voyage, and then, once this
was done, come to a levelheaded decision as to whether or not
these hazards were surmountable. If they weren't, I'd simply
have to go back to being a copy-desk Walter Mitty, at least
until another, more propitious opportunity for oceanic adventure came along.

The weather was the first major hazard to be reckoned with.
I knew from reading about other voyages and from studying
the marvelously informative pilot charts of the North Atlantic
issued by the U.S. Naval Oceanographic Office that the summer
months were best, but I lacked more precise information. I
wrote to the U.S. Weather Bureau in Washington and the
summaries it sent me, while still not so detailed as I had hoped
for, were most encouraging. They contained sentences such as
these: "The weather of June is usually very pleasant over the
North Atlantic. . . . The wind speeds average force 3 to 4 over
most of the ocean. . . . Gales are infrequent. . . . Weather conditions are relatively settled during July with the buildup of the
Azores high. . . . Wind speeds average 10 knots or less 40 to 60
per cent of the time. . . ."

Then I ordered, from the Naval Oceanographic Office, an
Oceanographic Atlas of the North Atlantic Ocean and a book
entitled *Wind Waves at Sea* and these gave me all the information I was looking for, as precisely as was feasible. I learned that
the highest wave ever reliably reported was a monster a hun-

dred and twelve feet high observed from the U.S.S. *Ramapo* in the North Pacific in February, 1933, and that the highest waves seen in the North Atlantic were sixty-footers, also observed in the winter. The *Atlas* yielded the prediction that on a transatlantic voyage lasting through June, July and August I would have approximately two days of waves twelve feet high or higher, about four days of eight- to twelve-foot waves, about nine days of five- to eight-foot waves, and smaller waves the rest of the time. It also forecast roughly four days with winds of twenty-eight knots or stronger, eighteen days of seventeen- to twenty-seven-knot winds, nineteen days of eleven- to sixteen-knot winds and weaker winds on the remaining days, with nine or ten days of calm.

Tinkerbelle already had taken six-foot waves and about thirty-knot winds on Lake Erie without having to heave to and I was confident that, hove to, she could survive conditions that were far more severe. I realized, of course, that the Oceanographic Office statistics were averages that wouldn't necessarily hold true for a given summer; there was always a chance one of those infrequent storms would strike. Red tracks on the pilot charts showed that storms had crossed my proposed transatlantic course in the summers of 1952, '54, '55, '56, '59 and '60, so the probability seemed to be much greater than fifty-fifty that I would take either a head-on or a glancing blow from a storm. Still, I was confident my little boat would acquit herself well, especially since I planned to make her unsinkable. I won't say I believed she could live through a hurricane, but I did believe she could take a terrific amount of punishment.

Many small-boat voyagers have stated in their books that size has little or no bearing on a boat's seaworthiness and, visualizing conditions at sea in a storm, I was inclined to believe they were right. A small boat, first of all, is a great deal stronger, pound for pound, than a big ship. Secondly, a small boat, being light and buoyant, will recoil before the waves and tend to ride over them, whereas a big ship will offer immense resistance.

The predicament of a big ship in a storm is that of an almost irresistible force meeting an almost immovable object; something is likely to give, and fairly often it is the rivets or plates in the big ship's hull. That is why big ships are sometimes battered and broken, even sunk, by storms that do no more than cause a few hours' inconvenience to properly handled small boats.

So far so good. But what about the differences between my boat and other sailboats less than, say, twenty-five feet in length? Would *Tinkerbelle* equal them in ability to weather a storm?

It seemed to me that the Achilles' heel of the usual ocean-going yacht was its keel, a thick slab of iron or lead that, in some boats, weighed more than a ton. The purpose of this weight was to keep the boat sailing right side up, a most worthy objective. But what if the boat sprang a bad leak or through some other misfortune filled with water? It would sink to the bottom like a lead casket.

As I saw it, the prime function of a boat was to float, and, preferably, to go on floating no matter what calamities befell it. For even if its sails were torn, its rudder lost, its mast broken, even if it capsized or had its planking ruptured, those aboard it would have a fighting chance to stay alive as long as it continued to float. So, to insure that *Tinkerbelle* would remain afloat (with me and all my supplies and equipment on board), I filled the spaces between her deck beams with polyethylene-foam flotation material and, in addition, made five or six thick planks of the material to be packed inside the hull with my supplies. Of course, the boat and all my gear had to be weighed to make certain the total weight didn't exceed the buoyancy factor of the flotation material, but when all this was accomplished, I had a vessel that was virtually unsinkable. And that contributed greatly to my peace of mind.

I came to the conclusion that the dangers posed by the winds and the waves had been successfully neutralized; that there was nothing about them to make me give up my plan. This meant, to me, that the biggest single obstacle to the voyage had been hurdled.

Then it occurred to me that next in importance to the assurance of staying afloat was the assurance of being able to call for help in case of need, so I bought a surplus Air Force "Victory Girl" distress-signal transmitter, a neat little waterproof gadget that, on being cranked, automatically sent out SOS signals on two frequencies. One of these, 500 kilocycles, the marine distress call frequency, had a range of a little more than a hundred miles; the other, 8364 kilocycles, the aircraft distress channel, had a range of about fifteen hundred miles, which was far enough to reach shore from the middle of the ocean.

Taken together, the guarantee of staying afloat and the guarantee of being able to summon aid, if necessary, seemed to me to eliminate or reduce most of the risks of the voyage. A lot of things could still go wrong, certainly, but the likelihood of their being fatal was now slight. Consequently, from this point on, my preparations went full steam ahead.

The next biggest problem, the danger of being run down by a big ship while I was asleep, was disposed of much more easily. I would prevent this from happening by, insofar as possible, staying away from the regular shipping lanes, all of which were clearly marked on the pilot charts. Where it was impossible to stay clear of these lanes, while crossing them near New York and at the entrance to the English Channel, I would stay awake, with the aid of pills if necessary, until I was safely into the untraveled sea beyond.

O.K. Next problem.

What about navigation? It was obvious that simply by sailing east I was bound to fetch up, sooner or later, somewhere on the western coast of Europe; but I hoped I could be a little more accurate about my landfall than that. I wanted to sail to England. It would be mortifying if, instead of landing there, I landed in France or Spain or Portugal or Ireland. It was essential that I learn the rudiments of celestial navigation, a subject

whose very name filled me with dread, for as a mathematician
I was a great tennis player. Calculus, spherical geometry and
related areas of mental torture were distinctly not my forte.
I was the sort of guy who, in college, had had to take high-school
algebra.

But as it turned out navigation wasn't the bugaboo I had
thought it was. Some wonderful, anonymous men had taken
all the pain out of it by producing a book of logarithmic tables

called *H.O. 214,* which reduced all the required calculations
to simple addition and subtraction. And add and subtract I
could, just.

So, armed with George W. Mixter's *Primer of Navigation,*
Carl D. Lane and John Montgomery's *Navigation the Easy Way,*
H.O. 214, the *Nautical Almanac,* charts on which I could pinpoint the position of our home and a surplus Air Force sextant,
I set out to teach myself how to guide a boat from one port to
another across the trackless, roadless, signpostless sea. And I did
it on our home's front porch.

My sextant could be used either with the natural horizon or

with an artificial bubble horizon. In my practice sessions I used the bubble, and the check I had on the accuracy of my calculations was the known latitude and longitude of our house. If my sun lines came close to this position, I knew my sextant sights and figuring were reasonably accurate. They didn't come close at the beginning, though. If I remember correctly, my first sight put me somewhere in the middle of Hudson Bay, Canada, hundreds of miles to the north. That was a mite alarming. If I couldn't do better than that, I might as well throw away the sextant and rely on a Ouija board. But I improved in time, happily. In the end my position lines usually came within nine or ten miles of being right on the nose and, from my reading, I gathered that that was pretty good going with a bubble sextant.

Of course, it remained to be seen whether I could do as well from the cockpit of a little boat on the bounding main, but I had the feeling I could. So I decided another difficulty had been overcome.

Next I bought a short-wave radio with which to get the time signals that were essential for navigation and to maintain some sort of contact, through news programs, with what was happening in the world ashore while I was alone at sea. I also hoped musical and entertainment programs would help me while away some of the hours I'd have to spend at the tiller.

I had an idea sharks wouldn't bother *Tinkerbelle* or me, as long as I stayed out of the water (and I planned, in any case, to take along chemical shark repellant), but I was a little concerned about what whales might do. I knew of several lone voyagers whose boats had been damaged by whales and also two instances of real-life Moby Dicks having sent large whaling vessels to the bottom. In November, 1820, the Nantucket whaler *Essex* was attacked by a whale in the Pacific and sunk, thus providing a model for the climax of Melville's novel. And in August, 1851, while the novel was at the printer's, the *Ann Alexander* of New Bedford was done in by a whale, also in the

Pacific. I didn't enjoy contemplating what might happen if an enraged whale were to assault my miniature sloop and yet I couldn't decide what I might do to guard against such a catastrophe. The best plan I could devise was to blast away on the compressed-gas foghorn I expected to carry with me and to put my faith in the theory that an animal won't bother you if you don't bother it.

One danger at a time, I tried to think of every conceivable misfortune that could beset' us and to contrive a way of taking the sting out of it. What if lightning struck? I put a lightning rod at *Tinkerbelle*'s masthead and grounded it through the shrouds to a hefty copper plate on her bottom. What if a wave washed me overboard? I rigged a lifeline to prevent my being separated from the boat. What if the rudder broke or was somehow lost? I built a spare rudder and, in addition, bought spare gudgeons and pintles. What if the hull was damaged or the mast broken? I assembled a complete tool kit and a supply of lumber of various types and sizes with which to make repairs. What if the boat capsized? I bought an inflatable life raft and figured out a way of using it, with a line running from it to the sunken masthead, to right the boat. What about my health? I had a complete medical checkup (in fact, I had two) and passed without any ifs or buts. What if my water supply was spoiled or lost? I bought a solar still for converting sea water into fresh water. What if my food supply didn't last? I acquired an extensive fishing outfit. What if my SOS transmitter failed? I collected flares, signaling mirrors and dye markers. What if something forced me to abandon *Tinkerbelle* and take to the life raft, how would I stay alive? I studied survival techniques perfected by the Navy and put together a complete survival kit, including emergency food and water. What if I was becalmed in the path of a ship? I took along a radar reflector to make my presence known to ships equipped with radar and also took along oars with which to row out of the way. (I decided against taking our little 1.7-horsepower outboard motor, or any other outboard. I couldn't have carried enough fuel to make it worth while.) What if the sails were badly torn? I got together a sail repair kit and spare sails; in fact, I bought a red nylon mains'l to make the boat as highly visible as I could. What if a shroud parted, the stem plate gave way or something else broke? I bought replacements for every piece of equipment that was under strain. What if I became ill or suffered a serious injury? I put together a complete kit of medical supplies, including antibiotics, disinfectants and pain killers, with the help of a Cleveland physician and pharmacist.

What about appendicitis? I knew that this malady had almost brought William A. Robinson to grief while he was cruising among the Galapagos Islands off the coast of Ecuador and I certainly didn't want to go through the same ordeal. However, I felt the chance that my appendix would act up was so remote that I didn't need to have it taken out in advance. If it did act up, I hoped to be able to keep the infection under control with antibiotics until I reached help.

And so it went.

In the summer of 1964, before the planning had gone very far, Douglas, then ten, and I took a cruise on Lake Erie that was the longest voyage yet for *Tinkerbelle*. We sailed in easy stages from Cleveland's Wildwood Park to Thunder Bay, Ontario, Canada (seven miles west of Buffalo, New York). covering more than two hundred miles. This was a trial voyage for me, in preparation for the assault on the Atlantic, and it made me more confident than ever of *Tinkerbelle*'s capability. In a thunderstorm one day she ran up against stiff, squally winds and the biggest waves she had yet encountered, white-crested rollers six to eight feet high. The spirited way in which she rode the waves made me more optimistic than ever about the Atlantic venture, especially when I remembered having read somewhere that Howard Blackburn of Gloucester, Massachusetts, a former Grand Banks fisherman who had lost the fingers of both hands through frostbite and yet had twice taken small

boats across the Atlantic, believed the sailing he had once experienced on Lake Erie was more dangerous than anything he
had met on the ocean.

I began in January, 1965, to gather food supplies from widely
separated sources: dehydrated meat bars from Chicago; com-
ponents of Army C rations from Council Bluffs, Iowa, St. James,
Minnesota, and Dawson, Georgia; canned white bread and
fruitcakes from Nashville, Tennessee, and cereal bars, dehydrated eggs and a number of other items from Newton, Massachusetts. Most of the food was purchased at neighborhood
grocery stores, however, and all of it was acquired with an eye
to easy preparation of meals. I didn't want to spend much time
cooking, so practically all the food was precooked. It needed
only to be warmed, or, if I was hard pressed, it could be eaten
cold. I had a little canned-heat stove in gimbals, a frying pan,
a saucepan and a knife, fork and spoon with which to prepare
and eat my victuals. And, naturally, I had a can opener; in fact,
several of them.

A few weeks later, when I broke the news of my proposed
voyage to my mother, one of her great fears was that I would
forget to take a can opener and would find myself out on the
ocean with plenty of food, but with no way of breaking into
the cans to get at it. She was relieved to hear I was taking pre-
cautions to avoid this catastrophe.

Acting on the principle that it is unwise to put all one's eggs
in one basket, I decided to carry twenty-eight gallons of water
divided among forty half-gallon plastic bottles, three one-gallon
plastic bottles and one five-gallon plastic container. By doing
this I hoped to prevent any mass loss or spoilage and to facilitate keeping track of my water consumption. And, by refilling
emptied bottles with sea water, I hoped to maintain most of the
boat's inside ballast. According to the usual allowance of half a
gallon a day I had enough water to last fifty-six days. However,
this was supplemented by numerous cans of fruit juice and
carbonated drinks, plus a supply of canned water in my survival

kit, so I felt it was adequate. Besides, I knew from experience that my consumption of water would be far less than half a gallon a day. And if I did run short, I could use the solar still to make more, or catch rain water in a sail.

I expected the voyage to take about sixty days, but guessed that it might possibly take as long as seventy-five days so, to be on the safe side, collected enough provisions to last a minimum of ninety days. Other west-to-east crossings of the Atlantic had taken between twenty-two and a hundred and twenty-three days, which indicated to me that my estimate of the trip's duration was reasonably realistic.

One point about my food supply worried me. How would I protect all those cans from the corrosive action of sea water? The contents of any cans that rusted through would spoil very quickly so that, if worst came to worst, I might be reduced to living on fish and plankton, a prospect that didn't appeal to me in the least. Some earlier voyagers had protected their cans of food by noting the contents on each one with paint or indelible ink, removing the labels and then varnishing the cans thoroughly. This method, I felt, had now been made obsolete by the introduction of plastic materials; so I packed my food supplies into heavy plastic bags sealed shut with a hot iron, two bags containing the food required for one day. Each week's supply of food was then packaged in a larger plastic bag, which, in turn, was put into a protective canvas bag. I had eight of these large bags of food, enough for two months at sea, with enough additional food in the form of emergency rations to last more than another month. As all these preparations neared completion, I began to feel confident that, no matter what my other misfortunes might be, I would at least have plenty to eat.

My provisions included two canned plum puddings Virginia had got me, with hard sauce to go with them, and my plan was to eat one of these when I reached the halfway point of the voyage and the other when I reached England. These little celebrations, I thought, would give me something special to look forward to.

As spring arrived, my preparations moved ahead more quickly. I wanted extra insurance coverage during the voyage so that if by some unlucky stroke of fate I lost my life Virginia and the children would be protected. I wanted to be sure of funds for the children's education and Virginia's future.

In applying for this insurance I, naturally, revealed my real intention of sailing in *Tinkerbelle,* and I was distressed to find that Lloyd's, which reputedly stood ready to insure anything, wouldn't insure me. That gave me a bad jolt, for it made me feel I wouldn't secure coverage anywhere. But then two other companies, apparently impressed by my knowledge of previous voyages, extensive preparations and the emphasis I put on safety factors, decided to risk rather large sums of money on me. Each of them insured me for twenty-five thousand dollars at a premium of two hundred and fifty dollars; so, in effect, they were betting a hundred to one that I'd make it. That encouraged me greatly, for it meant that if I was lost at sea Virginia would receive fifty thousand dollars over and above the insurance we already had, and it also meant that a couple of hardheaded business organizations had enough faith in me to regard my voyage as something more than a harebrained stunt.

By this time my close relatives had been told of my planned expedition in *Tinkerbelle* (all of them being sworn to secrecy) and, on the whole, they took the news calmly. My father and father-in-law were no longer living, but, had they been, I believe they would have given me their blessing. Virginia's mother accepted the project with good grace, and my own mother wrote, "Of course, your letter made me catch my breath; I am sure you can understand. But I can understand the urge within you to do this thing, and this will be your adventure of a lifetime!" Later I learned that her greatest fear was that the loneliness of the ocean would drive me insane, a possibility that, I confess, hadn't even occurred to me.

One of my sisters, Dorothy Dole, also was concerned about the loneliness, but believed I would be able to endure it without ill effects. In a letter to my mother, my other sister, Louise, said: ". . . at first I couldn't take it [the planned voyage] in, it seemed incredible, and then I became very excited about it. I can't say that I really understand it; it's something I think we'd all like to do in the abstract, but when it gets to actuality, most of us draw back. The main thing I feel is that it is wonderful to see someone carry out his dream—so few of us get or take the chance. And Robert is a dreamer. . . ." I'm not sure the characterization of dreamer was meant entirely as a compliment, but I was pleased to hear that Louise believed in the pursuit of dreams.

My brother, John, and Virginia's brother, John, also gave their full support, each of them having yearned at one point in their lives to take a voyage such as I was planning. They offered many good ideas for making the trip safer and more comfortable and even assisted in more tangible ways. One bought me some excellent waterproof bags in which to store books and film, and the other presented me with a wondrous little contrivance—a hand warmer.

My colleagues on the *Plain Dealer,* still believing I was going with someone else in a boat nearly twice the length and several times the weight of *Tinkerbelle,* offered all their good wishes as well as innumerable helpful or humorous suggestions. During our supper hour from nine-fifteen to ten-fifteen every night we frequently gathered in the paper's cafeteria and discussed the voyage. I remember one night someone brought up the possibility of our meeting icebergs. And then someone else, recalling the *Titanic* disaster, suggested that we'd better take along a phonograph and a recording of "Nearer My God to Thee" to play if the occasion arose.

"You at least ought to write down the words of the hymn," said Ted Mellow, the *P.D.*'s news editor, "so you'll be able to sing it as you go down."

Ted also secretly solicited contributions from my companions on the copy desk and used the money to buy a bottle of brandy to be taken on the voyage "strictly for medicinal purposes." The bottle was presented to me in a ceremony that left me all choked up. I was deeply moved, partly because I thought Robert Havel, chief of the copy desk, had called us together to chastise us for lousy headlines we'd been writing or for some other dereliction. It was indeed a pleasant surprise to receive liquor instead of a licking.

"You'll need that stuff in case of snake bite," said Robert Murphy, one of my fellow rim men.

"Yeah," chimed in John Metcalfe, my neighbor on the rim. "But don't do like the doctors and drink all the 'medicine' yourself."

The bottle had been prepared to render valuable service in a moment of crisis, as an auxiliary communications device. Directions affixed to it said, "In case of emergency: 1. Remove contents. 2. Insert message. 3. Launch." It was thoughtful of my friends to be so concerned about communications.

On another occasion Walter Berkov, an assistant news editor, and I were talking about the voyage and I happened to mention that I'd cross the Rubicon (that is, make a firm decision about going) in April.

"You mean you'll cross the Styx, don't you?" said Walt.

"No," I replied, with what I imagined was exactly the right inflection for a debonair adventurer to use, "I won't do that until June or July at sea."

Not long after this, at about 12:45 A.M. when our night's work was done, I happened to walk out to the *P.D.* parking lot with Chet Downing and Charlie Mulcahy, two more of my copy-desk friends, as we set off for our respective homes.

"All ready for your voyage this summer?" Charlie asked.

"Just about."

"I've got to admire your fortitude," Chet said.

"Yes, I do, too," Charlie agreed, adding, "I wouldn't do what you're doing for a million dollars. I'm afraid of water. Why, I'm even scared to look down in the shower!"

I enjoyed that remark hugely and later, on the ocean, I occasionally conjured up a picture of Charlie standing in the shower, terrified, and it always made me chuckle.

In April, as I'd said I would, I crossed the Rubicon with a firm "On we go," and then, in what seemed to be scarcely enough time to turn around, it was May 1st and I was up to my neck in last-minute preparations. I had already gathered all the necessary charts, pilot books, light lists and so on, but I still had to get a passport and a smallpox vaccination, fill out a voyage plan and check-off list and have a signed disclaimer statement notarized for the Coast Guard, fit a bilge pump to *Tinkerbelle* and do a number of other chores. Every minute away from my job was spent attending to these details.

The plan was for my mother to come from her home in Warner, New Hampshire, on Saturday, May 15th, to be with us for a week before my departure. She would remain to care for Robin and Douglas, whose vacations from school were still two weeks away, while Virginia and I and Virginia's brother set out on Sunday, May 23rd (the day my leave of absence from the *Plain Dealer* began), to drive with *Tinkerbelle* to Falmouth, Massachusetts. After two or three days of exploring about Cape Cod and launching and loading the boat, John and Virginia were to return with the boat's trailer to Willowick. (Before setting sail I wanted to be sure Virginia reached home safely through the heavy pre-Memorial Day highway traffic.) Then, on June 1st, *Tinkerbelle* and I would begin our transatlantic adventure.

My mother arrived on schedule on May 15th, at the beginning of what I'm sure was one of the most hectic weeks of her life; but she endured it with good cheer and before we knew what had happened we began what was to be my last day of newspapering for some time to come.

That morning, in anticipation of the coming weeks at sea, I

had the local barber give me a close-cropped butch haircut. I hadn't worn my hair in that style since my Army days and the reaction to it was mixed. Virginia didn't like it because, she said, it reminded her of the haircut a condemned man receives before he is strapped into the electric chair. And John Hilton, an Englishman who had joined the *Plain Dealer* copy desk six or eight months before, didn't like it either (Englishmen being partial to longish hair).

"They'll never let you into England with that haircut," he said.

Gerry Lee, sitting across the copy desk from me, didn't particularly mind the haircut, but, molding his features into an expression of grave concern, he made the sign of the cross as he said, "Old man, you look as if you've already got a touch of scurvy."

During the supper-hour break, when the copy-desk crew adjourned to the cafeteria, there was a lot of kidding about my having my last supper; and, with a knowing nod in my direction, William Evans, a police-beat reporter, remarked, "Some people will do anything to get out of writing headlines."

Copy editors, of course, are irrepressible punsters and many puns were exchanged that night. I've forgotten most of them, but I do recall that someone asked why they have knots on the ocean and, before I could reply, someone else broke in with "Because, if there were no knots, they couldn't have the ocean 'tide.' "

Later on, when we returned from supper and were hard at work again, Russell Bacon, the desk's acknowledged master punster, quietly slipped me a note that injected a pun into a friendly bon-voyage message. It said, "May the Atlantic surfeit your greatest hopes." Bacon, now retired, was one of the kindest men I've known. In addition to doing many other favors, he introduced me to a lotion that, during the voyage, saved my hands from the worst effects of prolonged contact with salt water.

La Rue Daniels, the *P.D.*'s expert on dogs and horses, presented me with a lucky twenty-five-cent piece to take with me, and my good friend Metcalfe, whom I have already mentioned, gave me the snappiest yachting cap I have ever seen, as well as what he described in a typewritten note as "a guaranteed instant panic stopper," an item I might need desperately in the days ahead. On being unwrapped, this extraordinary contrivance, dangling from a string, turned out to be a battered, worn, decidedly secondhand bathtub plug. It served its purpose well; and so did the twenty-five-cent piece.

When quitting time rolled around, I was deeply touched by the sincerity with which my colleagues shook my hand and wished me a pleasant voyage. It made a lump rise in my throat to have these men with whom I had worked for so long, through torrents of written words, express genuine concern for my welfare. Some were so overcome with emotion they couldn't speak, and a few, I think, were convinced they would never see me again. I felt uncomfortable about being the cause of such intense concern and yet how much more concern there would have been if they had known I was about to set sail in a 13½-foot boat rather than a 25-footer.

When I went to bed that night, on the eve of departure for Falmouth, I felt that I'd probably done the right thing after all to keep the true nature of my voyage a secret.

*

5 We arose early the next morning, Sunday, May 23rd, and, after a hurried breakfast, started loading my supplies into our little station wagon. This job took much longer than expected, so we weren't ready to leave until after 3 P.M.

The goodbyes were relatively painless, for no tears were shed. We kissed and hugged with assurance that we weren't doing it for the last time. My mother and the two children understood what I aimed to do and were confident I would survive, although they may have had some doubts about whether I would get all the way across the ocean. It may seem odd, but the goodbye I was most concerned about at this time was my goodbye to Chrissy, our five-year-old German shepherd. After all, I was able to explain to my mother and the children why I was leaving and how long I'd be away, but to Chrissy it would almost certainly seem as though she had been deserted. I couldn't possibly explain to her that I'd be back in three months. Nevertheless, I tried to be reassuring by speaking affectionately and rubbing noses with her and scratching her neck the way she loved me to. And anyway, maybe she wouldn't miss me so much at that, for now, instead of having to sleep at the foot of my bed, she'd get the whole bed to herself. Come to think of it, after three months of such indulgence she might be sorry to see me return. No matter; she was my special girl and I loved her.

Then I bade a fond farewell to Fred, our cat, and to Puff, Douglas's iguana, and climbed into the driver's seat beside Virginia and her brother. The car's springs sagged with the weight of the provisions and of *Tinkerbelle* hitched on behind, but all we could do was hope the strain wouldn't be too much for them. We had to get moving. So, with waves to mother, the children and the gathering neighbors, we struggled off, the engine laboring mightily.

We were blessed with good fortune, for the next day at about 7:30 P.M. we arrived in Falmouth, after an overnight stay at a motel near Batavia, New York, without the car's having suffered any sort of breakdown. We put up at a very comfortable

motel about a quarter-mile from Vineyard Sound, and before we went to bed that night, we drove down to the shore and looked out over the water which, in a few more days, *Tinkerbelle* and I would traverse. I'm not sure what the others felt, but I tingled with an intense sensation of awe.

The next day we devoted to sightseeing, as if we were a group of tourists. We had breakfast at a charming little place in Woods Hole and, afterward, looked over the buildings of the Woods Hole Oceanographic Institution where my brother had once been employed. Then we drove to Chatham, at the southeast corner of the Cape, and browsed through some souvenir shops, in one of which I bought Virginia a little silver dolphin for her charm bracelet. "A lucky dolphin," I called it.

What made Chatham especially interesting to me was the

fact that in 1877 Thomas Crapo and his wife had sailed from there in the 19½-foot *New Bedford,* bound for England. They arrived at Newlyn, near Penzance, Cornwall, fifty-one days later, after a truly remarkable voyage.

We went on, next, to a lovely sandy beach where we ate a fine picnic lunch as we looked out over the blue Atlantic, which, that day, was in a warm, contented mood. And then we visited Provincetown and saw some of the fascinating characters of that famous art colony. We also fed a huge flock of sea gulls from the end of a long pier where the fishing boats docked.

The following day, Wednesday, May 26th, we trailed *Tinkerbelle* over to Falmouth's Inner Harbor and, at a marina operated by F. W. (Bill) Litzkow, a big, friendly man, *Tinkerbelle* was hoisted from her trailer and lowered into the salt water. It was her first taste of the sea and she took to it as though she'd been tasting it all her life.

But I couldn't stand around just admiring her; there was a lot to be done. We had to load her. I paddled her over to a nearby dock and went to work raising her mast and bending on her sails while Virginia and John filled all the plastic containers with water and brought them over to be stowed away under her cockpit. Then I packed in the eight big bags of food and the Victory Girl, sextant, radio, blankets, charts, spare batteries, flotation planks and all the rest of my equipment. There were an awful lot of things to get into that little boat, but somehow I found a spot for everything. When the loading was completed, *Tinkerbelle* was sitting lower in the water than she'd ever done before. I guess she had only eight or nine inches of freeboard although, empty, she had had more than twelve inches.

The lack of freeboard didn't worry me. I believed the weight would give her increased stability. And I kept thinking of something Ben Carlin had written in *Half Safe.* He had said freeboard was like a chin stuck out to be hit. To me, that made a lot of sense.

While the loading was under way, Bill Litzkow's eyes must have bulged at the sight of all the material we were putting aboard.

"Where's he going?" he asked Virginia and John in a confidential tone. "England?"

My two fellow conspirators were taken aback, for no one else had suspected our secret.

"How'd you guess?" said John, with a mysterious grin.

Then he and Virginia swore Bill to silence, and Bill promised he wouldn't breathe a word to anyone. He kept his word, too. He didn't even mention it to me in the five days I remained at his dock preparing for departure. I found out later that after I'd gone he telephoned Virginia and finally got her permission to break his silence. Bill was a man you could trust.

Another man you could trust was Virginia's brother, John Place, a rewrite expert on the Pittsburgh *Press*. He was using a week of his vacation to help Virginia and me, and, although he considered my voyage extremely newsworthy, he didn't even tip off his own newspaper until I was safely out of reach at sea. That was rare trustworthiness.

Late that afternoon we did some more shopping. Virginia bought me a fine sweater and a book about sea birds to help me identify the birds I saw on the Atlantic (I already had two other books I hoped to read along the way: Margaret Mitchell's *Gone With the Wind* and John Le Carré's *The Spy Who Came In from the Cold*), and John got me a harmonica and some books of music to help pass the time if and when I was becalmed. And in the evening we had a delicious farewell dinner at a restaurant overlooking the harbor. I think we all felt a little self-conscious, not knowing quite what to say, but we enjoyed ourselves, anyway.

The next morning John and Virginia began their journey back to Willowick with *Tinkerbelle*'s trailer.

There is an old superstition of the sea that if you wave a ship out of sight you'll never see it again. John and Virginia wouldn't be there to wave me out of sight when I set sail, but I was there to wave them out of sight as they set off for Willowick; and I brought them a heap of misfortune. Not even the lucky dolphin I'd given Virginia could forestall it. On the New York Thruway, near Oneida, right at a tollgate, the car gave up the ghost and refused to budge. Virginia told me about it later over the telephone.

They'd had the car towed to a garage, where it was learned that the engine was beyond repair; they'd need a new one. So Virginia wired our bank for some money and they got the new engine and finally, after dark on May 29th, a day late, they arrived back in Willowick.

For the next two days I occupied myself aboard *Tinkerbelle* with moving my stores into what I hoped would be the most convenient arrangement and in lashing them down so firmly that they wouldn't shift even if the boat was turned over. I also did some last-minute varnishing and worked out a way to carry the oars on either side of the cockpit with their blades extending out beyond the stern of the boat. I wanted them where I could get at them easily, for I might have to put them to use at a moment's notice.

Once all my gear was packed away as I wanted it, I swung the boat to check the compass. It's a good thing I did, for I found a substantial error on the east-west heading. However, once it was discovered, it was easily corrected and I gained the satisfaction of knowing that I could then rely on the instrument.

The night of Monday, May 31st, my last night ashore for some time, I had supper at a little restaurant on the city's main street and, while I was eating, reviewed the circumstances that had led me to select Falmouth as my port of departure. Actually, the first thing I'd done was to choose the port I wanted to arrive at in England and, in the beginning, I'd thought the best one would be Penzance, for it was near a tip of England that stretched out toward the United States like a hand offered to a friend. But the *Sailing Directions* mentioned various difficulties and dangers connected with entering Penzance, or Newlyn, the adjacent harbor where the Crapos had landed, so I decided to go on to Falmouth, which seemed to have an excellent harbor that could be entered without danger, although there was one sentence in the *Sailing Directions* that made me a bit nervous: "Falmouth experiences a remarkably high number of strong winds and gales."

I'd just have to hope no gale was blowing when I arrived on the scene. Anyway, I decided to end my voyage at Falmouth, in Cornwall, and it remained only to decide where to start it.

I thought I'd best embark at a port from which I could sail southeastward handily to get across the shipping lanes out of New York City as soon as possible. Next to the approach to England, I expected this first part of the voyage to be the most dangerous because of the heavy ship traffic. On studying the map I decided that some harbor on the southern shore of Cape Cod would do very nicely as a starting point and then I discovered a Falmouth there, too. So that settled it. I'd sail from Falmouth, U.S.A., a former shipbuilding center and whaling port, to Falmouth, England, a famous maritime town and resort.

About 9 P.M. I telephoned Willowick and said goodbye to mother, Robin, Douglas and Virginia, all of whom were still confident of my success. As I left the telephone booth and walked slowly back to *Tinkerbelle,* I was seized by an intense realization of my great good fortune in having a mother and family like mine. How many mothers, sons, daughters and wives were there in the United States or the world who would let their son, father or husband do what I was doing? It struck me that probably there were very few. I'd seen too many men whose lives were hemmed in by strict adherence to the conventional demands of a business or profession or marriage; too many whose lives were made pallid by the fear of being different, of being criticized, of failing to meet all their responsibilities (as *others* saw them). I knew these fears well indeed because I had cringed before them myself. The pressure to conform that pervades our society has a basically useful function, I suppose, but I wonder if it isn't too intense, too rigid, or perhaps misdirected, so that it stifles the freedom of living that leads to happiness and, incidentally, to an intellectually richer environment for everyone.

I was positive no one in the world had as wonderful a wife as mine. Virginia's quiet faith was an extraordinary compliment and a priceless gift such as few men received in their lives from anyone. She could have insisted that I behave as other "rational" men did and give up any notion of taking this "crazy" voyage. But she didn't. She knew I was stepping to the music of a different drummer and she granted me the invaluable boon of self-realization by allowing me to keep pace with the music I heard. I was poor in dollars and cents, but rich in love. I hoped I would prove worthy.

On the way back to the boat I mailed some letters. One was to the *Plain Dealer*'s executive editor and others were to friends on the copy desk, and they all revealed the truth about my voyage: that instead of going with someone else in his 25-foot boat, as I had originally expected to, I was going alone in my own *Tinkerbelle*. I hoped that no one at the *P.D.* would think too harshly of me for my deception.

There were also letters for Virginia and close relatives who already knew the facts.

When I got to the dock, *Tinkerbelle* somehow seemed to be in an expectant mood, as though she knew what was ahead. She was certainly as ready, as prepared, as any boat her size could be. There was just one thing missing. I hadn't been able to find the chemical shark repellant anywhere and, earlier, on the phone, when I'd mentioned it to Virginia, she had informed me the repellant had accidentally been left at home. It was there now.

"You'll just have to make friends with a dolphin and have him keep the sharks away," Virginia had said.

I said, yes, I guessed that was what I'd have to do. It didn't

Scraping paint—an early stage in the repair of original boat, August, 1958.

First repair job on boat nearly completed.

Sailing on
Lake Pymatuning,
Ohio.

Ready to set forth at
Ludington State Park in
Michigan.

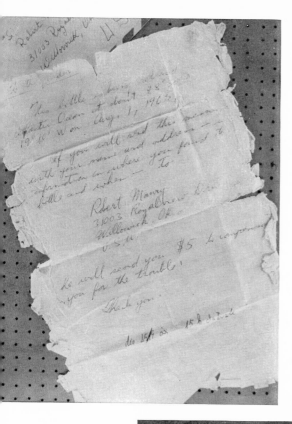

The message that drifted to Portugal in a bottle and the reply.

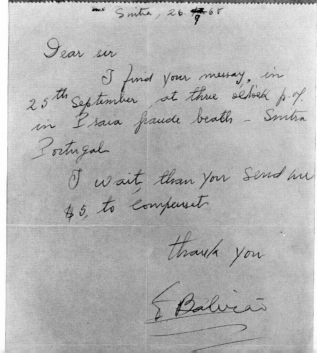

S.S. *Belgulf Glory* churns up from astern.

Banquet provided by Capt. Emile J. A. Sart of *Belgulf Glory*.

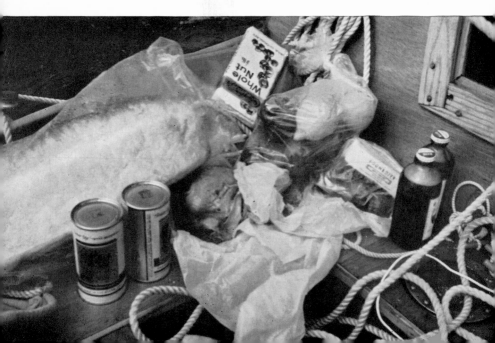

worry me because I understood the repellant wasn't especially effective. I'd read a report by a "shark research panel" of Navy and civilian scientists that said the trouble with most shark repellants was that those that worked at all were as likely to attract sharks as to shoo them off. So maybe I was better off without the chemical shark chasers.

Soon I was in *Tinkerbelle*'s cabin, curled up under a blanket. Tomorrow would be a long, hard day of sailing; in fact, I might have to continue sailing for two or three days and nights without sleep to get safely across the shipping lanes. I told myself I'd better get all the rest I could that night, for it was the last one I'd spend in the safety of a harbor for many days to come.

6 A tremor ran through *Tinkerbelle* as she bumped gently against the dock. Lying doubled up in her tiny darkened cabin, I felt the tremor and it sent a sympathetic tingle of anticipation coursing down my spine.

I shifted to the most comfortable position I could find in that cramped space and tried to sleep. It was difficult. I was keyed up. I couldn't help listening to the mingled sounds of the sea and the land that came through the night air.

Across the small harbor a burst of "quack-quacks" marked the spot where I knew a family of semi-tame ducks was bedded down. I knew, too, that an elderly duck couple spent each night under a cruiser stored on a wooden cradle scarcely a dozen paces from where *Tinkerbelle* lay, and I waited for their reply. Finally it came, a single no-nonsense "quack." And then I heard the singing of distant truck tires rolling fast over concrete, and then the splash of a fish jumping and the slap, slap of the ripples it stirred up striking *Tinkerbelle*'s hull, and then the wail of a police siren (or was it an ambulance?), and then the muffled hum of an outboard motor, the bang of a door slamming shut, the cat-like meow of a sea gull, a woman's voice far away calling in the darkness, the beep of an auto horn, the crunch, crunch of footsteps on gravel, and then the throbbing rumble of the returning Martha's Vineyard ferry, which, for several minutes, drowned out every other sound.

It was a clear night. Through the open hatch I could see a patch of bright stars. It was a bit on the cool side, too, and I pulled the blanket around me more tightly, trying to seal in my body's warmth.

When the wake of the ferry reached *Tinkerbelle,* it jostled her against the dock. I could feel another tremor each time her rub rail bumped the pilings. It seemed as though she were quivering with excitement.

It won't be long now, old girl, I thought.

Both of us were tugging at our moorings, anxious to be off. *Tinkerbelle*'s mooring lines were strong, of three-eighths-inch dacron; mine were made of invisible stuff, the social conventions, habits, thought patterns and bonds of affection that held me to the life on shore. But in their own way mine were as strong as hers, maybe stronger.

Nevertheless, in the morning we would cast off the lines, sever our links to the familiar land and begin a new life, an ocean voyage under sail. Soon after daybreak the voyage would begin, an ages-old *élan vital,* the wind, expelling us from the comfort of the harbor and the sound beyond, pushing us forth into the vast outer world of the North Atlantic Ocean, bound for England, 3,200 miles away.

I watched a pattern of light reflected from the water as it shimmered and danced on the cabin ceiling, little more than a foot above my face. It cast a hypnotic spell, and soon I was drifting back mentally to the eternal questions of time and space, cause and effect, questions that had fascinated me since my teens. Only now, as I lay sprawled in *Tinkerbelle*'s diminutive cabin, on the brink of a long, lonely voyage, they seemed more poignant than ever.

A great many thoughts sailed through my mind that night. I can't remember them all exactly, but I do recall the general outlines of some of them.

I remember I nearly had to pinch myself, literally, to make myself realize it was really *me* in that cabin, ready to begin a voyage that had been a dream of mine since high-school days in India, where I had been born and raised by American missionary parents, the eldest of four children. It seemed incredible that a dream so old was on the point of actually becoming a deed.

Most of the thoughts that flowed from this wonderment

sprang from questions that began with "How" or "Why." The most basic one of all was: Why was I there? That is, why was a middle-aged, married, sober, sedentary and presumably sane copy editor of the *Plain Dealer* now, on the night of May 31, 1965, lying in the cabin of a 13½-foot sailboat in the harbor at Falmouth, Massachusetts, intent on departing the next day on a voyage to Falmouth, England? What interplay of events, thoughts, feelings, desires and other causes had brought it about?

The causes began, I suppose, at Woodstock School in Landour, a town situated 7,000 feet above sea level on the first range of the Himalayan Mountains, about as far as one could be from the ocean and still be in India. To an assembly program one Thursday in the early summer of 1935 came a handsome German man of about twenty-six to tell of a voyage he and some friends had made from Sweden to the island of Tierra del Fuego at the southern tip of South America. They had rented a fair-sized sailing vessel for the weekend and then had kept it for the six months or so it took to complete their voyage. The young German showed movies that included some spectacular shots of mid-ocean storms and skiing on the snow-covered slopes of a Fuego mountain.

I was enthralled by the adventures of the voyage. Vicariously, I had never enjoyed anything so much in my life, and inevitably, although from afar, I fell in love with sailboats and the ocean. I became a sort of landlocked Dante pining for a seaborne Beatrice.

It was a love seldom gratified for I wasn't able to acquire a sailboat of my own until August, 1958, when I bought the craft that became *Tinkerbelle*, but from that day on I read every book I could find about voyages in small sailboats. The first one was William A. Robinson's tale of sailing around the world in his lovely *Svaap*. Then came Harry Pidgeon's story of circling the earth in *Islander*, which he had built himself, Dwight Long's book about his circumnavigation in *Idle Hour* and Captain John C. Voss's report of his venturesome voyage in the converted Canadian Indian dugout *Tilikum*.

By the time I got to Captain Joshua Slocum's classic account of his pioneering singlehanded voyage around the world in the *Spray*, I had made up my mind that if I ever got the chance I, too, would sail around the globe or, at least, make a long voyage in a boat under thirty feet in length. And so a dream was born.

The dream never died although there was seldom any noticeable evidence that it was still alive. Whole years went by without my so much as mentioning boats to anyone, as I graduated from Woodstock; attended Lingnan University in Canton, China, for a semester; visited Japan (where one afternoon I did my only pre-*Tinkerbelle* ocean sailing); earned a degree at Antioch College; served with the 66th Infantry Division in France, Germany and Austria during and after World War II; worked as a reporter on newspapers in Washington Court House, Ohio, and Pittsburgh and Erie, Pennsylvania; married the former Virginia Place of Pittsburgh; acquired a daughter and a son and, in 1953, joined the *Plain Dealer* copy desk.

During all these events the dream of ocean voyaging remained in the back of my mind like an incubating microbe waiting for the right moment to flare up as a full-blown disease. Every so often, after reading some particularly gripping tale, I became afflicted with virulent sailboat fever. Books about adventurous voyages periodically raised my temperature alarmingly, making it an enormous struggle to continue on course through college and into a journalistic career. But somehow I always manged to get a grip on myself and wrestle the fever back down to normal before it was too late; that is, I managed it every time but the last time, which was why I finally found myself in *Tinkerbelle* in the harbor at Falmouth, Massachusetts.

The first actual sailing I did was on the Jumna River at Allahabad, India, where my father, Dr. James C. Manry, taught philosophy at Ewing College and where my brother, two sisters and I spent our winter vacations from school. That first sailing experience became a landmark in my life. I'll never forget it.

A couple of the young American instructors at Ewing College had bought an Indian rowboat, a craft about sixteen feet long made of galvanized sheet metal stretched over a heavy wooden frame, and had converted it into a sailboat. They had equipped it with a sheet-iron centerboard, a mast and boom of bamboo, galvanized solid-wire shrouds, and a mains'l and jib of light canvas. I'm sure it was the only boat of its kind anywhere on the Jumna or, for that matter, on the Ganges, either, except possibly at Calcutta on the seacoast.

My brother and I obtained permission to use this little sloop soon after its completion. As we bent on the sails, a crowd of Indians gathered on the shore and on a nearby bridge, and every Indian boatman in the area turned our way to see the fun. I feel certain that very few of these spectators had ever seen a fore-and-aft rigged sailboat, since all the Indian vessels that plied the Jumna and Ganges had square sails that could be used only when the wind blew from astern. The Indian boats also lacked centerboards, which undoubtedly made our craft seem that much stranger to the massing crowd.

I don't know what went through John's head as we prepared to sail, but I do know that I had feelings that must have paralleled those of the Wright brothers as they took to the air at Kitty Hawk, North Carolina, and of Edison as he gave the electric light bulb to the world. We were pioneering a great step forward in sailing technique and, by demonstrating it for all the Indians ashore and afloat to see, passing it on to them as a priceless boon. Now, after centuries of abysmal ignorance, they would at last learn how to sail with the wind abeam; even how to sail upwind by tacking from side to side. My pleasure and pride at being able to bestow this great blessing on the Indians was only made more intense by the skeptical expressions of some of the watchers who seemed to be saying to themselves, "It'll never work."

We'll show 'em, I thought. We'll show 'em it works and that we know how to make it work. It didn't matter to me that neither John nor I had sailed a boat of any sort before, fore-and-aft rigged or not. Our only asset was some reading I'd done. But that was enough for me. The reputation of all Americans, if not all westerners, was at stake.

Despite my cockiness we started out rather timidly, John stationed near the mast to handle the jib sheets while I sat in the stern controlling the mainsheet and tiller. It was pure beginners' luck that we weren't immediately caught in irons, bow to windward, and blown ashore stern first. Surprisingly, we got under way with reasonable dispatch and as we picked up speed I could sense a wave of amazement sweeping through the crowd. You see, I said to myself, we aren't being pushed sidewise as you expected; we're moving ahead just fine, and at a pretty good clip. And look! We can even go a little bit into the wind! You never saw one of your flat-bottomed barges doing that!

Everything went well, considering it was our very first attempt at sailing, and as we glided back and forth under the bridge and from one side of the river to the other, we rapidly gained self-assurance. We discovered that sailing was a delightful, exhilarating sport, and that we were pretty good at it; no, very good at it. Our confidence soared.

"Let's put on a real show for 'em," I said.

We adjusted the sails for maximum draw on a beam reach until the boat, heeling excitingly, knifed through the water at top speed. Wow! What a frolic! We knew our audience had never before seen wind power move a boat so fast and the thought made us, or at least me, delirious with the heady pleasure that accompanies unrestrained showing off.

And then *it* happened.

The centerboard and rudder caught on a sand bar and spun the boat into a jibe. The boom lashed around like a giant club.

I ducked just in time. John didn't.

My brother took the full force of that flailing boom on the side of his head and it nearly knocked him out double, meaning both unconscious and overboard. He could easily have been killed. I was lucky; only my pride was hurt, although that grievously. My face turned as red as John's turned white.

We limped back to the boat landing, disembarked and slunk away. To the everlasting credit of the dozens of Indians who

witnessed our comeuppance, not one made a gloating remark or in any way called attention to our embarrassment. Every single one was a gentleman. And I'm still grateful.

As the wounds to skull and pride healed, we discerned a lesson in our mishap. It was that the Indians' boats were perfectly adapted to navigation conditions on the Jumna and Ganges. Centerboards and fore-and-aft rigs were out of place there. Tradition and centuries of experience, we had to admit, should not be scorned or tossed overboard lightly.

After that whack on the head my brother's main recreational interest turned from boating to mountain climbing. I guess he decided in the quietness of his own mind that it was much better to risk being clobbered by falling rocks at high altitude than by whiplashing booms at water level. It was a good decision, for he has developed into an accomplished mountaineer.

My own enthusiasm for sailboats and sailing not only survived the catastrophe on the Jumna, but increased in the months and years that followed. However, it is conceivable that if that swishing spar had struck me instead of John I might never have followed the trail that eventually led to *Tinkerbelle* and to the Atlantic. John might then have taken to the ocean while I scaled lofty peaks in India and western Canada. Psychologists agree, I think, that bumps on the head (or the lack of them) can have a profound influence on one's life. They call it the pleasure-pain principle.

I don't want to give the impression that my thoughts on that last night of May, 1965, percolated exactly as I have described them. They didn't. But I did meditate about why I was in Falmouth Harbor, ready to begin a long risky voyage, and I did reach the conclusion that the chain of events that led to my being there began with the yearning aroused by the German chap who spoke at Woodstock and my reading, and the pleasurable aspects of my Jumna River initiation into sailing.

In the period between that initiation on the Jumna (it was in 1936) and my purchase of the boat that developed into *Tinkerbelle* in 1958, I went sailing no more than five times. But this was sufficient to magnify my love of sailing into something resembling a passion, which, in turn, made it inevitable that, as soon as we as a family could afford it, I would buy a sailboat.

Succeeding links in the chain were conversion of the boat into a more seaworthy craft, growing confidence in the boat's performance and in my ability as a sailor, studies that indicated an Atlantic crossing in the summer was feasible, an increasing determination not to let my long-time vision of an ocean voyage slip by unfulfilled and, finally, the granting by the *Plain Dealer* of a leave of absence which, coupled with three weeks of vacation, would give me enough time for the voyage.

In this way, in the early spring of 1964, my dream came into fortuitous conjunction with the opportunity to make it come true. That was what I had wanted, what I had longed for for so many years. It was, like my first sail and the day I got married, another great moment in my life. I recalled some lines by Thoreau: "If you have built castles in the air, your work need not be lost; that is where they should be. Now put the foundations under them." So I began in earnest to put the foundations under my air castle.

I must make it clear, though, that this was no one-man project; it was a family affair. Virginia and the children were in on it from the instant of the first firm decision to go. They helped in innumerable ways, but more than anything else, by just being there and letting me know I had their approval and support. They knew how long I had dreamed of a voyage and, bless them, they believed in the value of attaining one's dreams. I wouldn't have gone otherwise.

The main factor in my personal motivation, naturally, was my love of sailing, especially the type of sailing that goes under the heading of cruising, as distinct from racing. Sailing, for me, has been a way of achieving both companionship with my family in the healthful outdoors and much-needed solitude away from jangling telephones, auto exhaust fumes, too-eager salesmen and other unpleasant details of civilization. This love, this need, fundamentally, is a feeling in my bones, a pulsating in my viscera so personal it cannot be adequately explained. (I'm not trying to be mystical or mysterious. That's just the way it is.) Nevertheless, I'll try my best to account for it.

As every human does, I have expended a large part of my life searching, often blindly and sometimes painfully, for Truth. (But maybe searching isn't the right word because quite often the whole game's been reversed and Truth has found me, notwithstanding my kicking and screaming and panic-stricken efforts to avoid it.) The result has been that through the years I have collected a few miscellaneous chips from the Mother Lode; at least, I hope I have. These, insofar as human conduct is concerned, include the golden rule, Thomas A. Edison's axiom "Everything comes to him who hustles while he waits"; Socrates' adage "The beginning of knowledge is the awareness of ignorance" and Anglican Archbishop Richard Whately's postulate "A man will never change his mind if he have no mind to change." But in all my days on this earth I have come across no more than a handful of chips that, assayed for their Truth content, came anywhere near equaling the pure, unvarnished verity of what Water Rat said solemnly to Mole in Kenneth Grahame's delightful story *The Wind in the Willows.*

"Believe me, my young friend," said Water Rat, "there is nothing—absolutely nothing—half so much worth doing as simply messing about in boats."

Of course, I'm being half facetious. But also half serious. Water Rat's statement, to me, comes very close to being the revealed Word, the supreme Truth.

I find immense pleasure in the gurgle and splash of a boat propelled by a direct force of nature, the snapping of canvas and the humming of rigging in a fresh breeze, the rattle of ropes running through blocks, the crying of gulls, the lift and heave of a buoyant hull, the pressure of wind against my body, the sting of flying spray, the sight of billowing sails and the swirling foam of the wake. To me, nothing made by man is more beautiful than a sailboat under way in fine weather, and to be *on* that sailboat is to be as close to heaven as I expect to get. It is unalloyed happiness.

It is sheer delight to whisk myself off on a "small planet," as Joseph Conrad once described a boat, and, for a few hours or days, escape from the troubles and tensions of life ashore. Difficulties and stresses fall into perspective while you are sailing, for, in sailing, you are dealing with elemental forces of wind and water that have been here for aeons and are likely to remain long after we mortals are gone; forces that can be gentle and yet, stirred to fury, are so powerful they make all else shrink into insignificance. Sailing also helps to keep a man aware of his lowly place in the universe, especially if that sailing involves celestial navigation and its concerns with the sun and stars, for there is nothing to equal the astringent effect on one's ego of a long, thoughtful look into outer space. There is a challenge, too, in sailing; a summons to learn how to master wind and water and how to master yourself when you are in a crisis, balancing on the edge of panic.

My life on shore, especially in India, conditioned me to enjoy sailing, I think, because a sailor must be somewhat fatalistic, as the Hindus are. He must be prepared to accept whatever comes, from flat calms to hurricanes; and he must, like the Hindus, train himself to enjoy the conditions he gets if he doesn't get the conditions he enjoys. From the Indians, too, I absorbed the patience that serves a sailor well, and an appreciation of the fact that there is a great deal more to life—and to a voyage—than mere movement from one place to another.

Sailing also has been a handy escape valve for the psychological pressures that tend to build up on the newspaper copy desk where I have labored for the last thirteen years correcting, insofar as I could, the facts, spelling, grammar and style of reporters' stories, weeding out possible libels and double meanings and writing headlines. These pressures go with the job as certainly as paint-spattered hands go with a career in art. They are a product of recurring press deadlines, sedentary work, occasional friction between divergent personalities and the ever-present consciousness that regardless of how knowledgeable one may be one's reservoir of information is never entirely adequate; that the only perfect copy-desk man would be one who knew all there was to know about everything. The pressures may at times build up to considerable intensity, but putting my hand on the tiller of a sailboat releases them as surely and almost as swiftly as touching a grounded wire frees my body of static electricity.

A fondness for large bodies of water, particularly bodies of salt water, is a last major factor in my love of sailing. The clean, saline tang of sea air is a powerful attraction. So is the awe inspired by the ocean's (any ocean's) enormous breadth and depth, by the ghostly presence of all the famous and infamous ships and men and women it has carried through the centuries, and by the mysteries hidden beneath its sometimes placid, sometimes stormy surface. Perhaps there is an inherited something in the protoplasm of my body cells that feels an agreeable kinship with the sea, where life on earth began and where it existed for such a long time before it took to the land. At any rate, the sounds of the sea, especially of breakers pounding on a beach, have a strangely soothing effect that I crave only slightly less than an addict does drugs.

Aside from my love of sailing, I looked forward to a small-boat voyage because of an inexplicable notion I had that a voyage was a kind of microcosm of life, a life within a life, if you will, with a birth (beginning), youth, maturity, old age and death (end), and that it was possible for a sailor to express himself in this miniature life—with his technique, responses to changing conditions and endurance—somewhat as an artist expresses himself with paint and canvas. It seemed to me, too, that in this abbreviated life a sailor had an opportunity to compensate for the blemishes, failures and disasters of his life ashore.

This was a curious idea. Where it came from I don't know. It may have arisen from an awareness of behavior I was ashamed of, of unlovely shortcomings in my life ashore, linked with a hope that in the compressed life of a sea cruise I could, perhaps, redeem myself. I had to concede that my voyage would benefit few persons other than myself, except insofar as it might, momentarily, lift some who heard of it out of the routine of their own lives, but it did give me a segment of existence that, God willing, I might fashion into something nearer to a work of art than my life on land had been. This idea gratified me strangely although I knew perfectly well that at sea, alone, I would of necessity be an unsocial being.

So I was there in Falmouth Harbor, ready to begin a transatlantic voyage in a midget sloop, because I loved sailing, I loved the sea, I had long wanted to make an ocean voyage and I had finally got the chance to make one. Contemplating all this, I decided I knew and understood the "Why" of the voyage, except for two final points: Why was I making the voyage alone? And why was I making it in such a small boat?

Actually, these questions were easily answered. I was sailing in *Tinkerbelle* because she was the boat I happened to have and I was confident she was equal to the task. And I was sailing alone because I felt *Tinkerbelle* was too small to carry the supplies of more than one person. If there was anything I was absolutely certain of, it was that I was *not* there to commit suicide or perform a stunt or set a record or advertise a product. No one had given me financial assistance and I wasn't sponsored by anyone, not even by the *Plain Dealer,* my own newspaper. Nor was I actuated by the expectation of vast monetary gain, although I did dare to hope that I might, by writing articles or a book, recoup the cost of the voyage and, if I was lucky, make enough more to help my children through college without going deeply into debt. All I wanted to do, basically, was to achieve the dream of an ocean voyage I'd been harboring for nearly thirty years by crossing the Atlantic to England, and I wanted to do it with as little fuss as possible.

Most people, I think, understand the urges that prompted me to take the voyage; at least, most of those I've spoken with about it, now that it is over, have been satisfied with my brief explanation of why I did it. Occasionally, though, a person will ask me "Why did you do it?" with an inflection that makes the query sound as if the person were asking "Why do you play Russian roulette?" The crux of it, of course, is the implied dangerousness of a voyage like *Tinkerbelle*'s and the inference that it is a bad policy, if not morally wrong, to do anything, ever, that is the least bit dangerous.

It seems to me there are two sides to the danger coin, two reasons for questions like this. One is that the values of comfort and safety are being overemphasized in our society to the detriment of other, perhaps more important, values for which it may be worth enduring a little discomfort, even danger. The other is that persons who are shorebound, who have had no opportunity to learn about boats and the sea, tend to exaggerate the dangers of a small-boat voyage. And, of course, for such persons to undertake lengthy ocean voyages themselves would, in fact, be highly dangerous. Not so for persons with experience, a levelheaded grasp of the prerequisites and adequate preparation.

Essentially, I believe, it is a question of familiarity, of what one is used to. The same man who quakes at the idea of sailing across an ocean will, paradoxically, drive a car from coast to coast with hardly a thought about the annual toll of deaths on United States highways. He doesn't dwell on the hazards of automobile travel because they are so near, so familiar; he faces them every day. If he were equally familiar with the hazards of the sea, I am sure he would accept them with equal equanimity. I accepted them with a fair degree of composure, not because I am more courageous (or more foolish) than the average person but because I took the trouble to familiarize myself with them and prepare ways of coping with them. I admit that luck played a part in the success of the voyage, but not so big a part as might be imagined. I feel that intensive and extensive planning reduced this element to an absolute minimum. I planned with utmost care, first, because I am a husband and father with responsibilities toward those who love me and depend on me, and, second, because I feel it is the height of thoughtlessness to voluntarily get oneself into a predicament necessitating a call for help that may endanger the lives of others.

The moral questions evoked by my voyage caused me grave concern. Did I have the right to endanger my life, even slightly, and consequently jeopardize the future of my family? And did I have the right to separate myself from all human society and, for two or more months, occupy myself solely with doing something I had longed to do for years, but which would be of little value to others; in other words, did I have the right to surrender unconditionally to hedonism? With much soul-searching I answered these questions in the affirmative, although I am willing to concede I may have been wrong in doing so.

Although I'm convinced the riskiness of the voyage was far less than many people believe, I still must confess it was this riskiness that made the voyage seem adventurous, exciting —a wonderfully far cry from the immobility, tedium and sometimes harrowing predictability of copy-desk existence.

I remember thinking that night about the uncertainties ahead, about what might be waiting for *Tinkerbelle* and me out in the open ocean. I wondered whether this watery world would be kind to us, allowing us to pass unscathed to our far-off goal. Or would it be cruel, taxing us beyond endurance, cutting our voyage short, perhaps even destroying us? And the more I thought about it, the more I realized I really didn't want to know the answers to those questions. Not in advance; not for certain. For it was the uncertainties, the surprises, the risks that added up to the challenge that made life—and a voyage— interesting and worth while. Without them the sources of hope would dry up and life would indeed wither into a monotonous meander from womb to tomb.

But because risks add zest to life doesn't mean that I advocate casual plunges into situations fraught with danger, the more the merrier; or that I believe a voyage can or should be made more zestful through the deliberate courting of peril. This is foolishness, if not worse. What I do believe is that a blanket policy of risk avoidance is unsatisfying, that there are risks worth taking, provided you are aware of them and prepared to cope with them.

The key factor, obviously, is preparation. And, for a voyage, this preparation must be founded on a brutally realistic appraisal of the qualifications of the boat, its equipment and its skipper. Wishful thinking here can be fatal. I want to make that unmistakably clear because I stay awake nights worrying that the newspapers' detailed coverage of my voyage may induce others to attempt similar cruises without proper preparation. I would be greatly saddened if my voyage became the indirect cause of a sea tragedy.

Lying there in *Tinkerbelle* on the eve of departure, I was mindful of the extent of my preparations and it gave me a feeling of assurance. I didn't have the sensations of a man about to step off a cliff, as I had expected to have. My mood was one of calm inner confidence. And yet, remembering my Jumna introduction to sailing, I was only too aware that confidence is often that quiet faith, that euphoria, that pervades your being just before you fall flat on your face. So I held my feelings in bounds, well on this side of bravado.

Sleep was a long time coming that night. Being on the verge of a dream cruise was too exciting. The sounds of the harbor and surrounding area fell too insistently on my ears. Even though I couldn't feel it inside the cabin, I knew a gentle breeze had sprung up because the ripples it roused made clicking sounds as they hit the crevices in *Tinkerbelle*'s lapstrake hull. The air currents also, now and then, made the halyards bang against her mast—clack, clack, clack, clack.

I heard a dog bark a couple of times somewhere off the port beam and then the garbled sound of boys' voices—teenagers', I guessed—too far off to decipher. But soon the voices drew closer and I could make out a word here and there. It seemed that the boys had been fishing down near the harbor's mouth and were now, at about midnight, on their way home. I couldn't decide how many there were; probably no more than three.

When they came to the spot where *Tinkerbelle* was tied up, one of the boys said, "Hey! Look at that!"

Footsteps plunked out on the dock. There was a brief pause, and then *Tinkerbelle* heeled over as someone stepped onto the cabin top.

"Whatcha doin'?" one of the youths said.

"Just wanna look in her," the boarder replied.

I heard him kneel. Then his silhouetted head, upside down, moved into the open hatchway from above. I could feel his eyes trying to pierce the darkness.

What to do? I was sure he didn't have the least suspicion

that anyone was in the cabin. If I spoke or moved, he might be so startled he'd fall overboard. I didn't want that. So I froze, and tried not to breathe.

He was breathing so heavily himself I needn't have worried about his hearing me. He stayed there for what seemed like a couple of minutes. I wondered if he could make out my face or the outlines of my body under the dark-gray blanket. He gave no indication that he could.

Finally the head withdrew and *Tinkerbelle* rocked silently when the boy stepped back onto the dock.

"Gee!" he said. "Never saw a boat that small with a cabin on it. You s'pose someone goes cruisin' in it?"

"Nah," came the answer. "It's much too small."

7   The alarm clock jarred me awake. It was already
9 A.M., broad daylight, and the sun was beating on
the deck and cabin roof. Soon the interior of the boat would
be an oven. It was time to get moving.

I washed, had breakfast, attended to a few last-minute
chores and said a quiet goodbye to Bill Litzkow at the marina.
Then, at about ten-thirty, I hoisted *Tinkerbelle*'s red mains'l
and white genoa and she and I set forth on our great sea adventure.

It was a beautiful day. The sky was dark blue overhead,
shading to lighter blue near the earth and sea; it was pleasantly
warm, and a gentle breeze caressed *Tinkerbelle*'s sails. There
was just one little flaw in the otherwise perfect picture: the
breeze was from the southwest, which meant we had to tack
out of the harbor. But that was a small price to pay for a blue sky
and warm sunshine. Fortune was smiling on us.

We skimmed from one side of the harbor to the other,
dodging between handsome moored craft, and with each jog we
drew closer to the exit into Vineyard Sound, about half a mile
away. As we moved along, I saw on our portside a sleek boat
owned by Joseph P. Kennedy, former United States ambassador
to the country to which we were headed, and off to starboard the
fine restaurant where Virginia, her brother and I had had our
farewell dinner a few nights before. In a few more minutes
we slipped through the rock-lined channel into the sound.

From here it would have been possible to follow the course
Crapo had taken in the *New Bedford* exactly eighty-eight
years and one day before and sail directly eastward to Chatham,

and then on out into the open ocean. But Crapo's account of the voyage mentioned his having run aground several times near Chatham, and the *United States Coast Pilot* for the area contained frightening notations such as: "The channel is used only by small local craft with a smooth sea; strangers should not attempt it. . . . The wreck of the steamer *Port Hunter* is on the southwestern side of Hedge Fence. . . . Because of the numerous shoals, strong tidal currents, thick fog at certain seasons . . . the navigator must use more than ordinary care when in these waters." Consequently, I decided not to follow Crapo's example.

Another possibility was to sail more or less southward and pass through Muskeget Channel, between Nantucket and Martha's Vineyard islands, to the sea. Here again the *Coast Pilot* dissuaded me. One ominous sentence said, "Although this channel is partly buoyed, strangers should never attempt it, as tidal currents with velocities of two to five knots at strength make navigation dangerous."

We couldn't sail directly east or south, safely. There was just one other possibility and, fortunately, the *Coast Pilot* had no scary remarks about that. We could continue tacking and go southwestward around the western coast of Martha's Vineyard and thus reach the open ocean approximately at the point where the meridian of 71° W longitude intersected with the parallel of 41° 22' N latitude. So that's what we did.

We beat down Vineyard Sound, passing Nobska Point and, beyond it, Woods Hole, in the early afternoon. I was intrigued by a peninsula on the chart called Penzance, which bore about the same geographical relationship to Falmouth, Massachusetts, that Penzance, England, bore to Falmouth, England.

We had the sound to ourselves all afternoon except for one small trawler that hurried by in the opposite direction as we approached the Elizabeth Islands, hilly and partly wooded mounds of sand rising from low shoreside bluffs off to starboard. These islands have fascinating names: Nonamesset, Uncatena,

Naushon, Pasque, Weepecket, Nashawena, Penikese and Cuttyhunk, most of them Indian.

I wondered if Cuttyhunk had been named by Bartholomew
Gosnold, the English adventurer and explorer who landed there
in 1602. It was he who had named Cape Cod and Martha's
Vineyard, the latter for his daughter and the grapevines he
found, so it seemed possible that Cuttyhunk was his idea, too.

It was pleasant, easy sailing, with a breeze of ten or twelve
knots, just enough to keep *Tinkerbelle* moving along contentedly without any fretting or straining. After a long starboard
tack across the sound we came about off Martha's Vineyard's
Cape Higgon in the late afternoon and headed toward Nashawena. Along the way *Tinkerbelle* rose and fell to the first big
swells coming in from the open sea, and showers of spray shot
up from her bow, drenching her foredeck.

"Here we go," I said.

I don't believe I had any strong feelings of trepidation. It
just seemed that we were out for an enjoyable sail. I knew
that probably many rough, uncomfortable days lay ahead, but
I felt sure my preparations had been adequate and, more important, I had tremendous faith in my companion, my friend,
Tinkerbelle. She was the main reason for my serenity.

A voyage made by a solitary person is sometimes called a
singlehanded voyage or a solo voyage, but neither of these terms
gives proper credit to the most important factor in any voyage,
the boat. Far from being a solo, a one-man voyage is a kind
of maritime duet in which the boat plays the melody and its
skipper plays the harmonic counterpoint. The performances of
the boat and the skipper are both important, undeniably, but
if it comes to making a choice between the two the decision must
be in favor of the boat. For there have been a few honest-to-
goodness solo voyages, and these have been made by boats, not
men.

I had read about dories from fishing vessels on the Grand
Banks occasionally breaking loose with no one aboard, drifting

all the way across the Atlantic and being found weeks later on the coast of Ireland or England. But I had never heard of a man accomplishing that feat without a boat.

And there was the famous case of the *Columbine,* a 50-foot sailing vessel used in the Shetland Islands toward the end of the nineteenth century for trade between the port of Grutness and Lerwick, about twenty miles away. One January day this ship, carrying its skipper, crew of two and a partly paralyzed woman passenger, was bound for Lerwick when the mainsheet broke and the heavy boom began swinging back and forth dangerously as the vessel rolled from side to side. The skipper and the mate tried to retrieve the end of the parted line but a violent lurch threw them into the sea. The mate managed to get back on board, however, and he and the other crewman, without pausing to consider the consequences, put out in the ship's dinghy to rescue the skipper. They never found him. And they never got back to the *Columbine.* They did manage to get ashore, however, and sound the alarm.

The invalid passenger, Betty Mouat, had expected a voyage of less than three hours; instead, she got one that lasted more than eight days. And all that time she remained below, unable, because of her paralyzed condition, to get on deck. The *Columbine* sailed herself all the way across the treacherous North Sea, finally running aground on the island of Lepsoe, north of Alesund, Norway. Betty Mouat was rescued.

So, remembering the incredible voyage of the *Columbine,* I had no illusions about the relative contributions of *Tinkerbelle* and myself toward making our cruise a success. *Tinkerbelle's* part would be the greater, by far. I was just there more or less for the ride and to keep her pointed in the right direction.

Near Nashawena we went over onto the starboard tack again and soon we were due west of Gay Head, the westernmost point of Martha's Vineyard. I could clearly see the headland's cliffs, topped by a lighthouse, reddened by rays of the magnified sun that was now setting far astern beyond the Elizabeth Islands. "Red sky at night, sailor's delight." If that old jingle was right, we'd have good weather the next day. We could use it. We needed it in order to get as far away from shore as possible, as quickly as possible, because, contrary to what many non-seafarers believed, the most dangerous thing about the sea was not the sea but the land. As long as a vessel was in the open sea, with plenty of room around her, she could manage quite well. But if she was unfortunate enough to be blown against the land, perhaps on a rocky coast, she would be smashed like an eggshell. We had to get far enough from land to prevent that from happening to us.

The day was dying in a blaze of glory in the west as we slipped gently out of the womb of Vineyard Sound into the open ocean. Our voyage was born. It was a singularly thrilling moment for me, as moments when dreams are coming true are bound to be. How long had it been since I'd heard that German adventurer speak at Woodstock, creating my vision of an ocean voyage? Twenty-nine years and eleven months, to be exact. That was a long time to cherish an ambition. But think how few of the ambitions of youth are achieved by anyone. One of the tragedies of life is the way teen-age boys and girls have to abandon their bright, happy dreams, one by one, as they grow to adulthood and are forced to cope with the harsh realities of existence. I was fortunate beyond measure.

As we sloshed and splashed out into the dark of the night and the immense space of the ocean, I was swept by a feeling of elation derived partly from the satisfaction of crossing the threshold of a longed-for adventure and partly from an eerie sensation that I was sailing along in the afterglow of history, in the wake of splendid, momentous, exciting events.

These same Cape Cod waters, it was said, had been plied by Vikings about the year 1000, and by French and Spanish fishermen in the fourteen-hundreds. Historians believed John Cabot, an Italian sea captain employed by England, probably sailed along the Massachusetts coast in 1498 and, after him, Giovanni da Verrazano, an Italian navigator and pirate, who entered what is now New York Harbor and discovered the Hudson River in 1524. Then came Gosnold, and then another Englishman, Henry Hudson, who was employed by the Dutch and who, in 1609, sailed his ship, the *Half Moon,* up the river that bears his name.

Still another Englishman, Captain John Smith, arrived on the scene in 1614, explored the Massachusetts coast and drew maps of it that seamen used for many years thereafter.

The waters we were passing through had been alive with whalers, packets, down-easters, schooners, and those beautiful, trim greyhounds of the sea, the clippers, in the eighteen-hundreds. But then came steam power to drive these lovely sailing craft out of ocean commerce. Praise be the Lord, though, sails had not been banished altogether from twentieth-century America. They lived on, mostly in pleasure boats of varying types and sizes, and I hoped they would continue to do so. I tried to picture a world without tall masts raking the sky, without gracefully curving, wind-filled sails, and what I saw was dismal.

Behind us now, on the other side of the Elizabeth Islands, was Buzzards Bay, where the doughty Joshua Slocum had taken his first trial run in the *Spray* before proceeding to Boston to begin his historic globe-girdling voyage. The waves of Buzzards Bay also had been parted by the 20-foot *Nova Espero* as Stanley Smith and Charles Violet neared the end of their voyage from London to New York, and by the famous 96-foot *Yankee* in which Irving and Electa Johnson had cruised the world with amateur crews. And New York, a short sail to the southwest, had been the terminus of one of the most nearly flawless small-boat voyages on record, the classic cruise from England of Patrick Ellam and Colin Mudie in the 19½-foot *Sopranino.* There, too, had ended fine voyages of the Frenchman Alain Gerbault in the 39-foot *Firecrest* and the Englishman Edward

Allcard in the 34-foot *Temptress*. In fact, that part of the ocean had been crisscrossed by the tracks of innumerable small sailboats, some of them participants in recent singlehanded transatlantic races.

In the midst of these musings I felt a pang of hunger and realized I hadn't eaten anything since breakfast. I reached into the cabin, got myself a meat bar and munched on it as we continued on our way. I didn't want to stop to warm up some food because we had to keep moving offshore as quickly as we could and also across the shipping lanes leading eastward out of New York. I knew I wouldn't be able to sleep safely until we were well south of these lanes.

As we sailed southeastward on a course of 157°, we had the wind just a few degrees forward of the starboard beam, so we were able to make good time. *Tinkerbelle* frisked along like an energetic colt and gave me my first clear view of the pyrotechnic display put on at night by phosphorescent plankton and other minute oceanic creatures. I watched bewitched, for it was a spectacular show. The water ruffled by the boat's passage glittered and shone with a starry fire. *Tinkerbelle* appeared to be floating on a magic carpet of Fourth of July sparklers more brilliant than any I'd ever seen, and trailing behind her was a luminescent wake resembling the burning tail of a comet.

Spray at the bow occasionally tossed onto the foredeck tiny jewels of light that winked for a few seconds and then went out, only to be replaced by other blinking gleams. An examination by flashlight of the spot where a kernel of radiance was last seen sometimes revealed a microscopic blob resembling a fish and sometimes a fibrous mass that looked like a tuft of matted wool from someone's sweater. How such unlikely organisms could produce bright glints of light was, no doubt, a mystery that someday would be unraveled. Perhaps the phenomenon had already been explained without my having learned of it. That didn't make it any less wondrous.

It was a dark night and it rapidly grew darker as a curtain

of clouds moved across the sky, screening off the stars' light; but I didn't mind, for the darkness made the phosphorescent sorcery of the sea appear even brighter, more enchanting. Although I couldn't see it, I knew from the chart that we were passing, off to port, the small island of No Mans Land. The breeze was holding up well and we were stepping along smartly. Soon the last lighted navigation aids disappeared from view

and we were alone in darkness relieved only by the warm glow of the compass light and the fireworks in the water. It was eerie. And it was beautiful.

We must have been well to the southeast of No Mans Land when I looked at my watch. It was 2 A.M. The new day, the second of our voyage, was already two hours old. It was Wednesday, June 2nd, my birthday, and I was forty-seven, ten years older than *Tinkerbelle*, who was no spring chicken. According to the statistics, I was headed down the sunset trail, past the milestones of middle age, but somehow I didn't feel ancient enough to be on that particular trail just yet. Life was supposed to begin at forty. If that was true, *Tinkerbelle* was beginning her life early and I was seven years late getting across the starting line. No matter. Better late than never.

We kept moving all night and through the morning of what

turned out to be a cloudy day. No land was in sight. I ate a cold breakfast so I wouldn't have to stop to prepare anything, but shortly after noon the wind died and we came to a halt anyway. The ocean was a gray sheet of glass. I'd never seen it so placid, so flat, so motionless. It had an otherworldly quality.

Since we couldn't move, having no wind, and since I was tired, having had no sleep for more than twenty-four hours, it seemed an appropriate time to get some rest. So, leaving the red mains'l up to render *Tinkerbelle* highly visible to any ships that might approach, I stretched out in the cockpit as best I could for forty winks. It wasn't a particularly comfortable place for a nap, but I was fearful of sleeping in the cabin. I thought I might sleep too soundly there and fail to awake promptly if a breeze sprang up suddenly.

I slept longer and more soundly than I wished. It was about 2:30 P.M. when I awoke and found, to my dismay, that we still had no breeze and, worse, that we were surrounded by dense fog. We couldn't move, and I couldn't see beyond a few feet. Nor could the red mains'l now warn passing ships of our presence. A ship could run us down without even knowing it. I hoisted the radar reflector to warn at least radar-equipped vessels of our presence, and I got out the oars to be ready to row for my life if a vessel should slice out of the fog directly toward us. I also got out the compressed-gas foghorn and sounded it from time to time. There were no answers. In fact, there were no sounds at all, except those we made ourselves. And the fog seemed to intensify these, reflecting them back to us. It was spooky.

In an hour or two a very light breeze came along and I put away the oars. We had just enough wind power to maintain steerageway. That was a slight improvement. And every now and then it rained for a few minutes, clearing the fog a little. That helped, too. But as soon as it stopped raining, the fog returned, becoming as thick as before. It gave me a closed-in feeling that must have been related to claustrophobia. I was decidedly uneasy, for we were obviously in a rather ticklish situation. And when I began to hear ships passing by it didn't help to calm my nerves.

I was surprised at the intensity and variety of the sounds produced by these passing ships, and by the speed at which they traveled invisibly through the fog. And most surprising of all, few of them blew their foghorns—at least, not regularly. Some of them throbbed by so close I could hear their bow waves breaking and, if they were traveling light, their propellers chopping the water. Several times I expected to see one come charging out of the fog on top of me, but I never even saw the dim outline of one; not just then, anyway. I'll never forget one of those ships, however. It passed by with music from a radio or phonograph, amplified through a loudspeaker, blaring out across the sea. That music was as effective as any foghorn. It was so loud it seemed entirely possible that even the people ashore on Martha's Vineyard, thirty-five or forty miles away, could hear it.

According to my dead reckoning, we were down approximately to the latitude of the Nantucket Shoals Lightship and about thirty miles west of it. This put us very close to the shipping lanes between New York and Europe, which was undoubtedly why I heard so many vessels going by. We were in an area where numerous shipping disasters had occurred and I hoped that we wouldn't be added to the list of casualties.

Somewhere in these waters, in January, 1909, the White Star liner *Republic* had been rammed and sunk by the Italian ship *Florida*. However, all but six of the *Republic*'s passengers had been saved by a CQD (this was before SOS came into use) sent out by the doomed vessel's wireless operator, Jack Binns. It was the first time radio had ever been used in a sea rescue.

Also nearby was the final resting place of the Italian luxury liner *Andrea Doria,* which, on July 25, 1956, had sunk with the loss of fifty-one lives after colliding with the Swedish ship *Stockholm.* I wondered if the ghost of the Genoese admiral after whom the *Andrea Doria* had been named was keeping watch over his sunken namesake. He had been a great sea captain; as great as that other son of Genoa, Columbus, some said. He was credited with making it safe for seamen to sail against the wind. In the early sixteen-hundreds hardly anyone dared to do so because whoever did risked being burnt alive as a wizard. Seafarers almost always waited for a favorable wind from astern before leaving port, but Admiral Andrea Doria flouted this prejudice. He tacked against the wind whenever he chose and his enormous prestige preserved him from the wrath of the superstitious.

The admiral, who lived to be ninety-four, must have been a grand old sea dog. If his spirit was in the vicinity, I hoped some of his strong character would brush off onto me. I wouldn't need much of his talent for going against the wind, though, because on a course for England the prevailing winds were westerlies. We wouldn't have to do much tacking.

Just then a mammoth black apparition with steel masts, funnel and hull slid out of the fog off our port quarter and, apparently seeing *Tinkerbelle*'s red mains'l, let go with a tooth-rattling blast on its steam horn that made me jump with such involuntary vigor I nearly fell overboard. What did a single blast on a ship's horn mean? And what was the appropriate reply? I wasn't sure and there was no time to look it up in my book. I thought I recalled, though, that the signal for a sailing vessel becalmed in fog was three blasts on the horn, so that's what I sounded. We weren't totally becalmed, of course, but we were so close to it that I thought we might as well ignore the difference and, anyway, at that particular moment I couldn't think of any other signal more suited to our circumstances. Luckily, it worked out all right; at least the ship, on a course to pass a comfortable distance astern of us, stayed on that course and didn't change to a course leading straight for us. A minute or two later, when it had disappeared back into the mist and my heartbeats had slowed to their normal pace, I got out my

book and found that the signal I'd given was for "wind abaft
the beam." I really hadn't made a liar out of myself, though,
because the wind (what little we had) *was* abaft the beam. However, it was plain to see that I needed to review the rules for
horn signaling in fog.

The skipper of that freighter, the only ship I saw all that day,

probably shook his head and said, "Why the heck do amateurs
have to clutter up the ocean?"

Shortly after nightfall the breeze picked up and we began
moving again at a more satisfying pace. At about 2 A.M. it rained
very hard, dispersing the fog. Off to port I saw bright lights
which I took to be ships, and one especially bright point of
illumination, which, since it was stationary, I decided must be
a large buoy serving to guide ships toward New York. *Tinkerbelle* and I passed several miles to the south of it and, soon
afterward, were overtaken by a violent thunderstorm. The
flashes of lightning and crashes of thunder made me thankful

for the lightning rod at the masthead, although I earnestly hoped it wouldn't be put to use.

The noisy commotion in the sky passed quickly, fortunately, but then the wind freshened and, almost before I could get the sails down, it was blowing at what seemed to me to be gale force, forty or forty-five miles an hour, and, again, raining very hard.

We were in for it. I crawled to the foredeck, holding firmly onto the bounding boat while I put out the sea anchor as speedily as I could.

Our sea anchor was an army-type canvas bucket. It was streamed from the bow on a hundred and fifty feet of half-inch nylon line, with a polyethylene float attached to it by another, much lighter line to keep it from sinking farther than fifteen feet below the surface. Its function was to act as a brake, and to hold the bow facing into the wind and the waves as the boat, its sails doused, drifted slowly sternward. This was the safest way for a small boat, especially a boat with *Tinkerbelle*'s underwater shape, to weather a storm.

Although I'm ashamed to admit it, I must state that this was the first time I'd ever had *Tinkerbelle* tethered to a sea anchor, so I was afraid she wouldn't respond as I hoped she would, by facing into the wind and waves. In less than a minute it became apparent that my fears were well founded; she didn't face the waves, she turned her side to them. That posture meant calamity, for she could be bowled over by a breaker. What should I do? I didn't know for sure; all I knew was that, whatever it was, it had to be done soon.

The rudder! It extended deep into the water; it must be the cause of the trouble, I thought. So I took it off and stowed it securely in the daggerboard-keel slot. That was the right thing to do, for *Tinkerbelle* immediately swung around and faced the waves. Her motion became less frantic, easier, smoother. She began to look after herself, enabling me to think about something besides the basic necessity of keeping her upright.

Since the wind was blowing from the northwest, we were drifting slowly toward the southeast, the same direction in which we had been sailing. That was providential, for we were moving farther into the open sea, away from the land and its terrible dangers.

Lights appeared astern and drew closer and closer as *Tinkerbelle* drifted. Were they buoys, or were they ships, or were they something else? I couldn't be sure because the pelting rain obscured my vision, but I thought most probably they were small ships. In any case, one fact was clear: it would be wise to avoid contact with them. So I got out an oar, put it into the oarlock I'd fixed at the stern for just such an occasion as this and, by rowing one way or the other, controlled the direction of our drift sufficiently to prevent collision with the lighted objects. I never did find out what they were, but in an hour or so we were safely through them with nothing but blessedly black ocean beyond. And to make the situation even better, the rain stopped. Glory be! Now I really could relax a little.

Sitting toward the rear of the cockpit and looking forward into the wind, I saw staggered ribbons of phosphorescent wave crests bearing down on us. The entire sea, from the port beam all the way around to the starboard beam, was filled with graceful, undulating, luminous forms. It was a spectacularly beautiful sight. It would have been a most enjoyable one, too, if it hadn't been for the danger; for as I assessed our predicament that night, as *Tinkerbelle* and I rode out our first full-fledged storm, any one of those waves could have been lethal if it had broken at exactly the wrong moment and had caught *Tinkerbelle* in exactly the wrong position.

Yes, every wave was a potential disaster, but I was relieved to discover that, in the midst of those acres and acres of crashing, thundering breakers, very, very few waves broke at precisely the moment when we were in their path. The great majority broke either before or after they reached us. And they came in cycles. We would ride up and down average-sized waves for several minutes and then along would come a group of four or six much larger waves. Then we'd have another few minutes of average-sized fellows, and then another batch of whoppers. It continued like that, on and on.

And *Tinkerbelle* always seemed to be ready for those few waves (maybe one every ten minutes or so) that broke at the wrong moment and slapped against her. She met them like a trouper, head-on, and rode over them with a jounce that gave me the impression of being in the saddle of a bronco.

Measuring the waves as well as I could against *Tinkerbelle*'s eighteen-foot mast, I estimated the biggest ones we met were ten or twelve feet high, from trough to crest. These were not monsters, as waves go, but they were definitely bigger than any waves either of us had experienced before at such close quarters. At the beginning of the storm they were especially ominous because they seemed to be steeper then than they were later on. As the wind continued, it seemed as though the waves grew bigger and, at the same time, more rounded, somewhat as if new, sharply pointed mountain peaks were, in an hour or two, ground down by the erosive forces of geological ages and at the same time elevated to new heights by diastrophic movement of the earth's crust.

At long last the sky began to fill with light and, at about the same time, the sea grew less tempestuous. It appeared that *Tinkerbelle* and I were going to get through our first big oceanic crisis without mishap. Well, not exactly without mishap because when I looked up I found that sometime during the night the radar reflector had been shaken loose from the masthead and was gone forever. I could have kicked myself for not securing it more firmly, and for not bringing along a spare. All right, so it was gone. We'd just have to do the best we could without it.

During the half-light between night and day I had a moment of fright when a small vessel, probably a trawler, passed too closely astern for comfort, apparently without any knowledge of our presence. No one appeared on the deck of the ship, which remained on an unswerving southwestward course and soon was out of sight over the horizon. *Tinkerbelle* and I once more had the ocean to ourselves.

My little boat rode the waves as gracefully as a gull: up, over and down, up, over and down, up, over and down. I was pleased beyond words, as proud of her as I could be. I patted her cockpit coaming and told her, "Good going!"

*

8 By mid morning the wind had fallen off sufficiently
to resume sailing safely, so I pulled in the sea
anchor, rehung the rudder at the stern and ran the sails aloft. It
felt good to be moving forward again, able to steer, instead of
drifting stern first with scant maneuverability.

During the brief storm we had drifted steadily, though
slowly, southeastward. I was sure my dead reckoning was highly
inaccurate, for any one of half a dozen good reasons, but I
wasn't especially worried about it because there was nothing
but open sea for hundreds and hundreds of miles to the southeast or east. Even to the northeast we had three hundred or
more miles of ocean between us and the coast of Nova Scotia
and that graveyard of ships, Sable Island. So why worry? As long
as we moved on a course between, say, 45° (NE) and 135° (SE),
we could keep on going for days, maybe even weeks, without
any danger of running against the land. We really didn't have
to know *exactly* where we were for quite a few days yet.

I had a hunch, though, that we were many miles to the south
of the shipping lanes; in fact, I believed we were some miles
south of the parallel of 40° N latitude, which was roughly ten
miles to the south of the more southerly of the two main
shipping lanes between New York and the English Channel.
I didn't want to go any farther south than this because it would
add extra miles to our voyage. My plan was to sail more or less
directly eastward until we reached the meridian of 40° W.
This would take us to the south of most of the foggy Grand
Banks area and what the pilot chart called the mean maximum
iceberg limit. Then, at 40° W, we would sail northeastward

parallel to, but well away from, the great circle shipping track between the Panama Canal and Bishop Rock in the Scilly Isles, at the entrance to the English Channel.

If the voyage became too difficult, so filled with hardships that I couldn't go on, I would make for Flores, in the Azores, and either rest for a few days before continuing or end my trip there. I had a chart of the island to use in case that became necessary.

In my mind's eye I pictured the voyage as a tremendous countdown in degrees of longitude from 71° W, the meridian at which we had entered the open ocean near Martha's Vineyard, to 5° W, the approximate meridian of Falmouth, England, our destination. I viewed this huge countdown as a series of ten-degree steps, except for the first one, which was eleven degrees (71° W to 60° W), and the last one, which was only five degrees (10° W to 5° W). I thought it would be useful, psychologically, if I divided my main objective of a transatlantic voyage into this series of lesser goals. The first of these to aim for, then, was the meridan of 60° W; and after that would come 50° W, 40° W, 30° W and so on.

After we reached 40° W longitude, we would also begin a single, ten-degree countup in latitude, from 40° N, my anticipated latitude at that time, to 50° N, the approximate latitude of Falmouth. In fact, I thought we had better begin a short countup immediately because, according to my hunch, we were some miles to the south of 40° N latitude. Consequently, when we started sailing, it was on a course of 50°; that is, just a little eastward of true northeast.

By this time I had gone without sleep for more than forty-eight hours, except for the nap I'd had in the cockpit the second day out, and although I'd been taking stay-awake pills to keep myself alert, my body's desperate need for rest (ashore it had been used to a full eight hours' sleep every night) was becoming acute, unmistakable. Or rather, it should have been unmistakable. Actually, I didn't recognize the symptoms immediately because the pills I was taking contained a chemical mood elevator that made me feel great even though I was on the borderline of exhaustion. The symptoms were so unexpectedly fantastic, so far removed from any previous experience, that I didn't realize their import until many days later, after I'd encountered them once or twice more. Lack of sleep may not have been the sole cause; the pills themselves could have been partly to blame. But, whatever the cause, I floated off in the early afternoon into a realm of wild fantasy, a strange world of mixed illusion and reality such as I had never known before. I lived through an hours-long hallucination.

It provided an interesting subject for contemplation, after it was all over, but while it was occurring it was most vexatious, decidedly unpleasant. It made me waste a whole afternoon sailing hither and yon about the ocean. And the incident was so unusual, so completely different from any earlier happening in my life, that I have great difficulty in describing it satisfactorily, especially for anyone who has not had a similar experience. I suppose, in a sense, I went off the deep end, out of my mind, into a Never Land where real things and dream things existed side by side without distinction; where reality and imagination merged, leaving no hints of which was which. I have attributed what took place to lack of sleep and stay-awake pills, but anxiety and, even more likely, loneliness, as my mother had feared, may have contributed to it, too. Like a person in a hypnotic trance, I simply began seeing and hearing things that weren't really there.

I became aware, gradually, that I was not alone; someone, a man, was on *Tinkerbelle* with me. This man had no face that I can recall; nor can I remember what he wore, although his clothing seemed to be appropriate for sailing. He was a quiet man with very little to say, and he was friendly. At first I reciprocated with equal friendliness, but later on his presence became inexpressibly annoying, intolerable.

It developed that he was on *Tinkerbelle* as a seagoing hitchhiker and I was taking him to his home, which was on a small island somewhere in our vicinity. (Of course, there really was no island in that part of the Atlantic.) But we had a terrible time finding the place. We sailed this way, and that way, and around, and back, and north, and south, and east, and west, trying to catch sight of a scrap of treeless land with a couple of houses on it.

Sometime during the afternoon I recalled the storm *Tinkerbelle* and I had been through the night before and, fearful that we might be hit by a southeast wind that would batter

us toward a lee shore, I decided I should try out the storm sails I'd made of heavy canvas to see if they would enable us to beat away from such a hazard. However, my phantom companion thought I should take him to his home before I spent any time experimenting with the storm sails, and we got into a slight hassle about it. My arguments prevailed, though, for at sea the skipper's word is law. I tried out the storm sails.

I replaced the white genoa with a minute jib and the red main with a small trysail. The heavy-weather suit of canvas seemed to fit the boat all right, but beyond that the tryout was a flop; there simply wasn't enough wind to move the boat with such small sails. The only adequate tryout would be in a storm.

So I reset the original sails and we continued our island hunt, to the great satisfaction of the hitchhiker. In fact, preposterous as it seems, my airy chum took over the tiller and I became the passenger. Such is the remarkable stuff of hallucinations. On we sailed. We never seemed to talk out loud; that is, we seldom actually moved our lips, but we did converse in a miraculous, soundless way. I kept pressing my shipmate for descriptions of the island and for clues to the course to be sailed to reach it, all the while straining my eyes to spot a bit of sand or rock.

My companion then admitted that the island would be hard to find because it rose only a few feet above the level of the sea and was mostly rocky, the rocks being a blue that blended almost perfectly with the color of the sea—camouflage par excellence. Several times I thought I'd spotted the island and cried out to the phantom to steer in that direction, but when we drew closer it became evident that what I'd seen was merely rock-like wave forms. It was discouraging and irritating. This bloke I had on board was wasting my time on a wild-goose chase. I grew more and more peevish, more and more impatiently eager to find his blasted rock pile and put him on it so that I could continue on my way. I had started out as a good Samaritan, but now I was entirely disenchanted with that role.

I guess he sensed my rising exasperation because he kept saying, "It won't be much longer. Just be patient, we'll soon be there."

By early evening I was in a frenzy. I'm reluctant to own up to it because of what it may indicate about my character, but I was ready to run amok and toss my unwanted guest into the sea. Then I could resume my own hunt, for England. But at that very moment, in the nick of time, he yelled, "There it is! There it is!" And, sure enough, there it was. I saw it too.

It was a solid patch no bigger than a city block, and if it was composed of anything besides sea-blue rocks I couldn't see what it was. No sand was visible anywhere, and no vegetation of any sort. There was nothing but rock, rock, rock. Even the two small houses at the center of the island were made of the same type of rock, which made it hard to distinguish between them and their surroundings. About the only way you could tell they were houses was by the windows and doors.

Some people came out of one of them and waved to us and we waved back. The hitchhiker (I never learned his name, unfortunately) wanted to sail right up to the shore, but I was determined not to risk *Tinkerbelle*'s life on such foolishness. Why, she'd be battered into splinters! So, to be on the safe side, I took over the steering again.

We sailed around the island looking for a place to dock, but there was no suitable place. Good Lord! Now what? Was I going to have to put up with this guy even longer? I'd had about all the delays I could take. I was on the point of telling him to swim for it or else when, through the magic that exists only in fantasies, he was suddenly ashore with his family, grinning and waving me on my way. I waved back happily, delighted to be rid of him at last, and without wasting another minute I resumed my original course of 50°. The daylight was waning fast and I wanted to get as far away from that island as I could before turning in for some badly needed sleep.

Except for the two-and-a-half-hour nap, I had now gone without sleep for about fifty-five hours and I was drooping dangerously. I couldn't keep my eyes open. I'd force them open and they'd stay open for a time, but inevitably the eyelids would grow heavy and slowly close. I'd go on sailing with closed eyes for a little while and then a wave would jolt *Tinkerbelle* and I'd start to keel over, all but dead to the world. I'd catch myself just in time to avoid cracking my skull on the deck or rolling overboard. Several times, in my somnambulistic state, I put *Tinkerbelle* into an accidental jibe that sent the boom zinging around with a murderous slash. The spar itself hit me only once, painfully. But another time it drew the mainsheet across the bridge of my nose, giving me a bad rope burn that took many days to heal.

It was perilous to continue while so near the edge of complete exhaustion; I still had enough of my wits about me to realize that. I simply had to have some rest; my whole being cried out for it. So, finally, somehow, I put out the sea anchor, struck the sails, unshipped the rudder and crawled into the cabin. Luckily, the sea was fairly calm, making it safe to risk sleeping in the cabin; but even if it hadn't been calm I think I would have slept there that night. I had to.

I lay down on top of my supplies on the starboard side, pulled the blanket over me and dropped into unconsciousness as if I'd been dealt a knockout blow.

*

9 When I awoke, the sun was shining brightly, dotting the undulating cobalt of the ocean to the east with diamond flashes of intense light, and *Tinkerbelle* was tugging good-naturedly at her bucket anchor, nosing into a docile, westerly breeze. Happiness, that morning, was a body replete with rest—a body gorged, crammed, satiated with sleep—and I was happy. It was great to be alive.

I cooked a breakfast of hot cereal and coffee, and, as I ate, ruminated on the events of the previous day. That seafaring hitchhiker, where had he come from and where had he gone? Was he part of a daydream? Or something else? Or was my mind coming unglued? It seemed possible that I *had* dreamed the encounter. In any case, it would do no good to worry overmuch about it. I knew that truck drivers who took pep pills to stay awake sometimes "saw" things, and even Slocum had been visited by an apparition—the pilot of Columbus's *Pinta,* so he, the shade, had said. Slocum had ascribed the visitation to cramps caused by eating Azores plums and white cheese. I hadn't had any cramps, so I had to look elsewhere for a cause. The hallucination, I theorized, must have been induced by lack of sleep and the pills.

Neither *Tinkerbelle* nor I had suffered a serious mishap, we were both in good shape, but the weirdness of the experience left me feeling uneasy—half fearful, half embarrassed. The whole affair seemed so unnatural, so preposterous. I was so sensitive about it that I refrained from mentioning it in my log. Not until much later, after I'd had other, similar experiences, did I write anything about the illusory events of that afternoon.

After breakfast I washed my saucepan, cup, fork and spoon in the sea and tidied up the cabin. Then I heated some water and shaved for the first time since leaving Falmouth; that is, I shaved all but my upper lip, for, in response to Virginia's urgings, I had decided to grow a mustache. I hoped that by the time I reached England it would be a luxuriant, sea-dogish growth. I'd never had a satisfactory mustache, although once before I'd tried to raise one. The in-between days, when the bristles were ample enough to make your lip look dirty and yet too puny to keep your friends from inquiring (if only with their eyes) why you hadn't shaved, were slightly discomfiting. But now I had a chance to escape all that; I would be out of sight for enough days. I could simply turn up on the other side of the ocean with a mature set of handle bars.

A gentle breeze of about ten miles an hour blew steadily from the west, so I rigged *Tinkerbelle* to steer herself. I had tested the self-steering arrangement on Lake Erie and it had worked well. It consisted of twin genoas winged out on either side of the forestay (the oars having been adapted to serve as whisker poles for that purpose), with sheets running back from the clew of each sail, through blocks on either side of the cockpit, to the tiller. The sails were adjusted to slant slightly forward from the forestay. Then, if *Tinkerbelle* veered a little to port, the portside genny caught more wind and the starboard-side genny spilled more, which, in turn, caused a pull on the port sheet and an easing up on the starboard sheet. That put the tiller over to port, making the boat return to her proper course before the wind. And, of course, it worked the same way, but in reverse, if she veered to starboard. As a matter of fact, by adjusting the sheets, the boat could be made to steer herself on a course that was a few degrees to port or starboard of the exactly-before-the-wind course. (However, I was never able to get the boat to steer herself on a reach or when the wind was forward of the beam.)

Tinkerbelle tobogganed along amiably, steering herself skillfully and, seemingly, without effort. She was a good girl. I delighted in her obedient behavior and in my freedom from the tiller. I could do anything I wished now without impeding our steady eastward progress. To be sailing without any effort whatever, without having to be concerned with steering, that was undiluted ecstasy!

But I couldn't spend all day glorying in ecstatic idleness; there were other things to be done. I brought on deck clothes and

blankets dampened by the humid sea air and spread them in the sun to dry. Then I took a sextant shot at the sun in an effort to get a clue to our position, but something went wrong with the shot or the figuring, for I wound up with a sun line that was too fantastic to be believed. At noon I tried again, this time for a latitude shot, but again something went wrong. The latitude I got was 45° N, which couldn't possibly have been right unless *Tinkerbelle* had flown three hundred miles or more during the night while I was asleep. She was a marvelous boat, no doubt about that, but a three-hundred-mile flight did seem a trifle beyond her capacities. Oh, well, tomorrow I'd try once more to pinpoint our position.

About five-thirty that evening a trawler hove into view and, seeing *Tinkerbelle,* churned over to within a few yards of us, its diesels clattering noisily. It was the *Major J. Casey,* American or Canadian, I couldn't tell which. I cupped my hands and shouted to two fellows at the rail, asking if they'd give me my position, but I guess they couldn't hear me above the strident din of their vessel. I needed a megaphone to focus and project my voice. Boris Petroff of the *Plain Dealer*'s library staff had urged me to take one along despite the valuable space it would consume. "It's a vital piece of equipment," he had said, and now this inability to make myself heard tended to confirm his opinion. Wait till he found out about that. I'd never hear the end of it.

I could understand the men on the trawler, however.

"Where you bound?" one of them yelled.

"England," I hollered back with all my lung power.

They didn't even flick an eyelid, so I imagine they either didn't hear me or thought I was having a little joke. Anyway, they swerved away right after that and sped off to the southeast. In a few minutes I was alone again. Not really alone, though; I had *Tinkerbelle* with me, and she was good company.

As darkness fell, the wind grew stronger and I had to discontinue the self-steering. (It turned out that I never used the twin genoas for self-steering again, as one of the pair was an old canvas sail that tore to shreds in a hard blow a few days later. The surviving genoa was a dacron sail I had made myself. I should have made two of them.) I returned to my post at the tiller and we went on under a single genny at four or five knots until nearly midnight. Then I "parked" *Tinkerbelle* to the sea anchor, secured the anchor light between the mast and starboard shroud and turned in for some sleep.

After breakfast the next day, Saturday, June 5th, I experimented with different sea-anchor setups to determine which worked best. One rig I tested had the regular Danforth anchor and the canvas bucket drogue linked in tandem at the end of the hundred-and-fifty-foot nylon anchor line. I studied the boat's behavior for about an hour, eventually deciding this arrangement wasn't a success, for instead of sloping off from the bow, the line hung straight down and didn't keep the boat headed squarely into the waves. Several times she nearly turned broadside. When I started to pull the line up to test another setup, I found that either the Danforth was a lot heavier than I had thought or it had snagged a fish or some other heavy object. It was hard work getting it on board. I finally hauled it up, though, and when the bucket broke the surface I got a terrific shock; it was filled with sand! No wonder it had been heavy. There was only one possible explanation: we were in a shoal area where the sea was no more than a hundred and fifty feet deep and possibly a good deal shallower than that.

This threw my dead reckoning for a loop since, according to it, we were supposed to be in water that was more than a mile deep. How could I have gone so far wrong? I couldn't answer that question, but in view of the circumstances it seemed reasonable to conclude that the time had come to obtain a better indication of where we were.

Just before the sun reached its zenith, I got out the sextant and, summoning forth my best efforts, took as accurate a noon latitude sight as I could, using the natural horizon rather than the bubble. When I worked out the sight, I got another shock; the figures said our latitude was 41° 2′ N, about sixty miles north of my dead-reckoning latitude. I got out the chart and deduced from this latitude figure and the shallowness of the water that we were probably at the southernmost edge of Cultivator Shoal, some ninety miles east of Nantucket Island. That made our longitude roughly 68° 32′ W, not nearly so far eastward as I had imagined.

This blunt exposure of my shortcomings as a navigator left me shaken. Had I, in attempting an Atlantic crossing, bitten off more than I could chew? Was I likely to sail into, say, Brest, France, thinking it was Falmouth, England, or do something else equally ridiculous? I earnestly hoped not. But if the navigational clumsiness that had just been laid bare continued, it seemed possible that I would. Of course, there were important lessons to be learned from this chastening experience, the principal one being not to put much faith in dead reckoning (the boat's speed over the bottom and the influence of currents were too difficult to assess), but that didn't make me feel any better. Here I'd thought we were south of the shipping lanes and, actually, we were still thirty miles or so north of them.

I re-examined the chart, reread the *Coast Pilot* and sent my mind ranging back over the days since we had left Vineyard Sound, trying to find clues to how our actual course had varied from my dead reckoning. What about those bright lights I'd seen in the early morning darkness on the third day out? I had supposed they were on a buoy, but now I had doubts. Soon I found a paragraph in the *Coast Pilot* that appeared to solve the mystery. It said, "A Texas tower with lights and a fog signal surmounted by radar and radio towers, is in 41° N and 69° 30' W, near the southwest side of Fishing Rip. The entire structure is floodlighted at night."

So that's what had made that "buoy" seem so bright; it had been floodlighted.

Fishing Rip was a shallow area at the southern end of Nantucket Shoals, southeast of Nantucket Island, and the Texas tower on it was about twenty-five miles from the island. What *Tinkerbelle* and I had done, then, was to sail between the tower and the Nantucket Shoals Lightship, which was roughly twenty-seven miles due south of it. When the storm hit us, right after we passed the tower, we had drifted fifteen or twenty miles southeastward, and the next day, while I was in the grip of that hallucination, we had cruised around aimlessly, getting nowhere. Then, after those sublime hours of sleep, we had steered the 50° course that brought us to the southern tip of Cultivator Shoal, where the bucket startled me by scooping up sand from the bottom. Now I had an inkling of where we were.

Late in the day, after more sea anchor experiments, I tethered

Tinkerbelle to what seemed to be the most efficient rig, the canvas bucket used by itself with a float and line attached to keep it from sinking more than fifteen feet below the surface, and took a short nap in the cockpit. Afterward, I fixed myself a tasty dinner of curried beef, potatoes and peas, lit the hand warmer John Place had given me, for it grew uncomfortably chilly when the sun dropped below the horizon, and set off on a southeastward course of 150°. I was determined to get to the south of the shipping lanes before heading directly eastward.

We sailed all night at a delightful wave-slapping pace and shortly after dawn arrived smack-dab in the middle of the lanes. There were seven or eight ships in sight, some headed east, others west; and as one left, another would appear to take its place. Two identical black-hulled trawlers came up over the sharp rim of the horizon and one of them picked up its skirts and hurried over to examine *Tinkerbelle*. As it drew near, I heard music blaring from a loudspeaker. So that's what had passed by invisibly but far from soundlessly in the fog on the second day of our voyage—a trawler. When it got closer, I saw that it was Russian, as was its sister ship. And its music reverberated just as deafeningly as had that of the phantom ship in the fog. It was wonderful classical music, mind you; there was nothing wrong with it except that it was so loud it made the atmosphere quake.

Russians must be avid photographers because when the trawler drew to within fifty yards or so every member of the crew seemed to be on deck with a camera pointed at *Tinkerbelle* and me. Shutters clicked at a great rate. It reminded me of the time Virginia, Robin, Douglas and I had been becalmed in the channel to Presque Isle Bay at Erie and tourists in passing excursion boats had snapped us. This time, however, I decided to join the fun: I got out my own cameras, a 35-mm. still camera and a 16-mm. movie job, and clicked right back.

"*Tovarish!*" I yelled, using up with that one word fifty per cent of my linguistic resources in conversational Russian. And even that was a failure, apparently, for I got no response. The Soviet fishermen smiled in a friendly way, though, and when I waved they waved back. Then they raced away.

It was a perfect sun-drenched day, with a cloudless turquoise sky and a lustrous blue sea. The waves were just large enough to make things interesting and the wind strong enough to keep us moving along briskly. To all appearances we could have been on a pleasant Sunday afternoon sail on Lake Pymatuning; as a matter of fact, it *was* Sunday—Sunday, June 6th. I told myself that if most of the days ahead were as pleasant as this, our trip would be a breeze, or, as the English say, a piece of cake.

About midday I hove *Tinkerbelle* to under sail and prepared a meal of dehydrated scrambled eggs and bacon, with coffee, and ate it out in the cockpit where I could watch the steady stream of ships going by to north and south. We seemed to be on the blue-water center strip of a multi-lane oceanic turnpike. Trawlers, freighters and liners passed in processions that were exciting to see.

After I'd finished off my meal with some canned pears, we got under way again, still headed southeastward, and in the early afternoon met another Russian trawler, this one white and much larger than the black trawlers I'd seen in the morning. It was slowly hauling what must have been a huge net through the water. No doubt the fishing was good, for the trawlers were on the edge of Georges Bank, a fishing ground that some authorities have rated next to the Grand Banks.

Tinkerbelle and I cut across the big ship's bow, about two hundred yards ahead of it, and continued toward the southeast. By the middle of the afternoon every ship was out of sight; we were alone again. Moving so rapidly from an ocean teeming with ships to an ocean without any ships in sight made the aloneness claw into my mind, creating a keen awareness of my, I hoped, temporary separation from fellow humans. It was an intense feeling, but not an especially unpleasant one. Who has not yearned with all his heart to leave the "rat race" and get away from it all for a while? I was a privileged character; I was actually doing what so many people longed to do. No more rat race for me for at least a couple of months.

During the afternoon I took another nap in the cockpit; then, when we started moving again, it was on a due-east course of 90°. That night I wrote in the log:

"I saw a school of about eight whales after I resumed sailing after my nap. They were too far away for pictures, though. I've also seen a lot of gulfweed. And quite a few birds, which always seem to be too far away to photograph.

"I still don't know exactly where I am although I presume (from my dead reckoning) I'm near 40° N and 68° W. I'll take some sextant sights tomorrow and try to pinpoint it.

"I haven't seen a ship since leaving the lanes. The ocean is a vast empty expanse. I'm beginning to find out what real loneliness is.

"My nose is a bit sunburned and the backs of my hands are getting raw from being wet so much and chafing against my cuffs. But my biggest problem is my bumteratum, which is getting awfully sore from the dampness and constant jostling. I'm sitting on the life preserver cushion now and that helps, but tomorrow I'll have to render some first aid.

"Otherwise I'm in good shape. Have been eating and drinking less than I allowed for.

"But the cabin is a shambles. Everything is piled helter-skelter. The trouble is, when I want something it's usually under an assortment of other things and I have to get everything else out of the way to get at it. And it goes on and on like that. When I've eaten some of the food and drunk some of the water there will be more room and, I hope, less mess.

"The barometer has been holding steady at 30.8. I hope that means several days of good weather.

"Everything on board is now damp as can be, even these pages.

"At dusk we got into a tide rip, probably a tributary of the

Gulf Stream. Some dolphins, the first I'd seen, had been following us, but they left us at the tide rip, unfortunately.

"I hove to with the sea anchor at 11 P.M. (Eastern Standard
Time) and got about six hours' sleep."

My log notations for the next day, June 7th, were:

"Had a nice big breakfast of hot cereal (cereal bars crumbled
into water and heated) hot coffee, fruit, etc.

"Then got moving. It was a glorious day of sailing: blue sky,
sunshine, wind and waves just right. *Tinkerbelle* just scooted
along.

"Best of all, I finally got some good sun sights and established
our position—40° 4′ N and 67° 31′ W. This is not as far along
as I had hoped to be at this time, but I had a couple of bad days
there at the start and maybe I can make up for them now.

"I'm a little north of my planned route, too, but that may
be an advantage.

"Sighted quite a few whales—all far off.

"Also sighted a ship to the north, which made me fearful
that I was too near the shipping lanes, so I turned south for a
couple of hours. Then hove to to sleep."

I remember that night well. I was worried because it was
fogging up and I no longer had a radar reflector with which
to warn ships away. That made it difficult to rest. I lay awake
in the cabin for a long time, fretting, but in the end I dropped
off to sleep. What helped was that I was warm. It was the first
night I'd been warm since putting to sea, probably because we
had moved out of the cold coastwise currents from the north
into the warmth of the Gulf Stream.

That night I didn't shiver and shake as I had on all the
previous nights. I was cozy in the cabin. It was a welcome change
and a very pleasant way to end my first week on the ocean.

*

10   In the morning of the eighth day, as I lay asleep, a sound insinuated itself into my unconscious mind and tugged me toward wakefulness. It had the tone and timbre of a chorus of shouts—men's shouts. But that was absurd. Men's choruses simply didn't go about the Atlantic shouting. I must have dreamed it. I squirmed into a new position under my blanket and began to drift back into sleep. Then suddenly I was exploded into wide-eyed consciousness by:

"Ahyouuuuuuuuuuuga! Ahyouuuuuuuuuuuuga!"

That was no dream! Such a dreadful, ear-busting noise could mean only one thing: my time on earth was up. And when I identified the accompanying roar as that of diesels I was sure of it. Without a doubt a big ship was bearing down on *Tinkerbelle* and noticing her at the last minute, too late to swerve aside, it had sounded its klaxon in a desperate bid to save the life of whoever was aboard her. Any second now there would be a grinding crash as the ship plowed us under. My one chance of survival was to abandon *Tinkerbelle* at once and swim for it. If I moved fast enough, I might get out of the ship's path in time.

When I realized what I had to do and that my life depended on it, I sprang into action. I must have been hitting Mach 3 as I threw open the cabin hatch and flew out on deck ready to dive overboard.

Fortunately I was moving just slowly enough to have half a second to notice that, really, there was no ship headed toward us, and pull myself to a halt before plunging over the side. We were not about to be run down, but what I saw nearly made my eyes pop out of their sockets. Lying alongside *Tinkerbelle,* so close I could almost have jumped aboard her, was an enormous submarine. And on its bridge, staring at me, were three or four men, no doubt the chorus I'd heard.

I felt foolish. To be scared out of my wits was bad enough, but to be scared thus in front of an audience was too embarrassing to bear. I tried to salvage my pride by deftly changing my expression of panic into an expression of nonchalant greeting,

which, I hoped, would convey the impression that, far from being hurried by fright, I was accustomed to shooting out of the cabin like that every morning, and equally used to meeting submarines on the high seas. It's a shame my performance wasn't caught on film, for it may have been worthy of an Academy Award. Or it may have served a useful purpose, later, as a medical-school exhibit on the muscular contortions a human face can achieve. Despite my histrionics, however, I had a suspicion the men on the sub weren't the least bit deceived, and I learned afterward the suspicion was well founded; they knew I was in a blue funk.

What should I say? What should I do? I was racking my brain for answers to those questions, and trying to decide what the sub might want or do, when one of the men on the bridge (I heard subsequently it was the captain) called out, "Do you need any help?"

So that was it. They thought I was in some sort of trouble. I felt a great load slide off my shoulders, for I had begun to have wild notions such as maybe war had been declared since I'd left shore, or maybe the Coast Guard had sent the sub out to stop me from making what it considered a foolhardy voyage. Actually, it had only stumbled onto me, thought I was in distress and wanted to help. That was all.

I appreciated the offer of assistance immensely, but in my startled condition I could think of nothing I needed. So I shouted back, "No, thanks!"

Whereupon we lapsed into numbed silence, for the men on the submarine undoubtedly were as astonished by the sight of *Tinkerbelle* and me as I was at seeing them. We couldn't think of anything to say. We just stood there looking blankly, unbelievingly, at one another as we slowly drifted farther and farther apart. Soon we were so far apart we couldn't have made ourselves heard, even if we'd wanted to, over the shuddering clangor of the sub's engines. (I had no idea submarines, even non-nuclear subs like this one, made so much noise while running on the surface.) As the sub's stern passed by, I saw markings which told me it was an American craft, the *Tench*, named after a Eurasian fish noted for its ability to survive out of water. Finally its propellers began turning and in a very short time it slid out of sight over the horizon.

When I had recovered my composure, I berated myself for two serious omissions: one of courtesy, the other of seamanship. I felt I should have invited the sub's skipper over for a gam and a cup of coffee, and I should have asked him for a position report against which to check the accuracy of my navigation. I managed to get along without the position report, but my failure in courtesy was not so easily overlooked. After my voyage was completed, I wrote a letter of apology to the *Tench*'s skipper, Lieutenant Commander James A. Bacon, and he replied, kindly, with his impression of our meeting.

"At 0800 on 7 June," he wrote, "*Tench* departed New London for sea. . . . On arriving at Nantucket Lightship in the early evening of the 7th fog and numerous fishing vessels impeded our progress. As a result I spent the night in the conn or on the bridge.

"First light found *Tench* some 150 miles east south east of the lightship with the fog clearing. As the sun rose we broke out of the fog and the lookouts [one of them was Yeoman Robert R. Rentschler, a fellow Cleveland suburbanite] spotted a very small mast on the horizon some distance to the south of our track.

"At first I thought the mast belonged to one of the trawlers we had been playing tag with all night, but as we approached it became apparent that it belonged to a small sailboat. At this point I altered course to pass close aboard in order to hail the boat.

"When the small size of the boat became obvious, I thought it probably had been blown out to sea and no one would be aboard. Until this time no one had been seen in the boat and now I decided to stop alongside and examine it in detail. As we approached within a few hundred yards, it could be seen that the boat was riding to a sea anchor and was provided with oars and other gear lying in the after section—the forward area being decked over and having a small cabin.

"I stopped *Tench* with *Tinkerbelle* about 10 yards abeam of the bridge, and we continued our examination. Although no one had been sighted on board, it now was apparent that someone could very well be in the cabin. Mustering all the lung power of the bridge watch and using a megaphone, we hailed the *Tinkerbelle* but to no avail. It became obvious after a few minutes that if there was in fact someone on board another means would have to be found to rouse them.

"The solution to the problem was readily available. I reached over and gave a long blast on the ship's whistle, and there you were, leaping out of the small cabin as if you thought you were about to be run down by the *Queen Mary* or some equally large ship. I must now admit that I found your reaction somewhat amusing.

"We exchanged greetings as you have already stated. After you gave a negative response to my offer of assistance, I was at a loss for words. Since I had been delayed during the night and there was a good chance I was going to be late arriving at my assigned station . . . I proceeded on at best speed. I came to the conclusion that you were where you wanted to be and little could be gained by *Tench* remaining in your vicinity. I entered your position (39° 46′ N, 66° 27′ W) and the name of your boat in the ship's log in case the Coast Guard should start looking for you.

"I thought at the time that you most probably were a sailing enthusiast on vacation and sailing to Halifax from Boston or some place in the Cape area. I am sincerely glad that I did not know what your true destination was. I am sure that if I had known what you were attempting, I would have had a guilty conscience on leaving you there."

I, too, am glad Lieutenant Commander Bacon was spared the pain of a guilty conscience. There really was no reason for him to have had one, even if he had known where I was bound, because, as he said in his letter, I was where I "wanted to be"; no one had dropped me off there against my will. And, since I was there of my own choice, I had won the right to experience whatever that entailed, good or bad. So far it had been mostly very good and I was optimistic about the future.

I have just one bone to pick with Captain Bacon: he called that noise he made with his submarine a "whistle." How euphemistic can you get? I've called it a klaxon sound, but even that falls pitifully short of being an adequate description. There simply is no word for the sound the *Tench* produced, a sound that seemed to be a nerve-jangling synthesis of the wailing of banshees, the booming of thunder and the screeching of all the demons of hell.

Tinkerbelle spent the hours of darkness after our meeting

with the *Tench* riding big waves to her sea anchor while I tried as best I could to rest in her cockpit. It was a chilly, wet, miserable, dragged-out night. I was still too afraid of a capsize to seek shelter in the cabin when the waves were ominously large, so I had to bear the discomforts of the cockpit. It wasn't easy to sleep in that exposed, perpetually joggling place.

The next morning (Wednesday, June 9th) the wind continued to blow at twenty-five or thirty knots and my bleary eyes got their first good look at the waves that, until then, had been partly hidden by the mantle of night. Some of them must have been seventeen- or eighteen-footers, the biggest waves we'd yet encountered. I watched them in awe and was mightily pleased and relieved to see how gracefully *Tinkerbelle* climbed to the summit of each one in turn, glissaded into the valley beyond and then climbed the next peak, on and on. My little craft performed her nautical functions with all the agility and stamina of a ballet dancer. I was delighted with her and praised her to the skies.

The threatening waves were not to be trifled with; I was sure of that. It was better to be wary of them than wrecked by them. It was equally true, though, that every minute we stayed tied to the sea anchor meant another minute added to the duration of our voyage, and a lot of those extra minutes could add up to one or more of several different crises that ought to be avoided, if possible. Consequently, I was eager to be moving.

Still, the waves held me transfixed with fright. I tried to envision what it would be like to brave them under sail and the only pictures that came into my mind were of disasters. Did Si Lawlor in his little *Sea Serpent* and William Andrews in his collapsible *Sapolio* sail through waves like these? That they might have done so seemed unbelievable, utterly fantastic. Yet Lawlor got across the ocean in only forty-five days, an astounding accomplishment for a boat only fifteen feet long. Andrews, in a boat half a foot shorter and with a greater distance to go, took eighty-four days, but he couldn't have achieved even that mark if he had spent much time hitched to a sea anchor.

I wrestled with fear through the whole morning as I studied the waves. Finally, in the early afternoon, the conviction grew that we should get under way. "After all," I wrote in the log, "the whitecaps are small even though the waves are big." So, marshaling all my courage, I decided to put up one of the small jibs and proceed tentatively under it alone. If conditions proved to be too hazardous, I'd get the sail down again immediately and go back to the sea anchor.

I steeled my nerves and we started moving eastward once more. I was sure that, even under just the one small jib, we would take off like a jet-driven aquaplane. But I was wrong. We barely crawled. I had to hoist the mains'l, too, to get *Tinkerbelle* to move at a satisfactory pace. (However, I'm happy to be able to add that as the voyage progressed my ability to size up sailing conditions improved.)

I tried to get some pictures of Mother Carey's chickens (storm petrels) the next afternoon, June 10th, but they moved so fast it was extremely difficult. They were fascinating to watch, though, because of their odd habit of walking on the water. I'd never seen these birds before, although I had crossed the Atlantic several times previously on ocean liners.

The book Virginia had given me said they were Wilson's storm petrels, migrants from the antarctic and the commonest members of the storm petrel family. Mother Carey, it said, was a corruption of Mater Cara, an appellation of the Blessed Virgin Mary, and storm petrel was derived from Saint Peter, who also walked on the water, according to the Bible, until his lack of faith brought on a ducking. The Maoris of New Zealand had a poetic term for the birds, *"takahi kare moana,"* which meant "dancing on the waters." I thought that was a particularly apt description.

Wilson's bird was a little smaller than a robin, brownish-gray and black, with a white spot at the base of its tail. Sometimes it seemed to hop along on the water, sometimes it used its feet

like skis and sometimes it simply walked. Two or three times
I was amused by a bird that just stood on the water flapping its
wings, as though it were trying to pull its feet out of hardening
cement.

Not once did I see Wilson's storm petrels *in* the water, floating and resting like other water birds. They were always flying,
beating their wings without letup, moving erratically like but-
terflies and usually very close to the water's surface. They must
be tireless creatures, or else embarrassed to have anyone see
them inactive. The bird book said they occasionally alighted on

the water, but I never saw one do so, although I watched them
intermittently all the way across the ocean.

One other variety of bird accompanied me almost all the
way to England, the greater shearwater, a brown-and-white bird
about twenty inches long, with a wingspread of more than two
feet. I also saw, occasionally, pretty black-and-white terns and,
of course, gulls.

The greater shearwater was a lovely bird to watch in flight,
it rode the wind so elegantly. It, unlike the storm petrel, was
frequently to be seen bobbing on the water, resting or feeding.
However, it never accepted the tidbits I offered.

One day I came upon an oceanic melodrama, a tragedy of the

sea in which the innocent victims were little fishes, probably herring, and the villains were giant tuna and ravenous shearwaters. The poor herring found themselves in a terrible fix: if they stayed in the water the tuna got them, and if they jumped out of the water in their frantic efforts to escape the tuna followed right on their tails; besides which, in the air or near the surface, the shearwaters got them. They were trapped between two devils and the deep blue sea: doomed, no matter what they did.

I watched this battle for survival with something approaching horror-stricken fascination. The greedy tuna and shearwaters gorged themselves on the hapless herring. But as *Tinkerbelle* and I drew within twenty yards or so all the shearwaters in the area, alarmed at the sight of us, took to their wings. All except one, that is. This particular bird cut loose with a great squawking and flapping of wings, but, try as it would, it couldn't get airborne. At first I thought the squawks and the inability to fly meant it had been injured—by a tuna, perhaps—and was in distress, so I headed toward it with the intention of seeing if I could render first aid. However, in a very short time it became clear that the bird was simply cussing itself out in bird language for having eaten so piggishly that it was now too heavy to take off. And, believe me, that bird knew how to cuss. I am no prig and yet I was shocked! And so were the tuna, for, as the air turned blue, they left.

As we bore down on the bird, its cursing and wingbeats became more frenzied. Finally, goaded by fear into making one last, do-or-die, superbird effort, it flogged itself into the air like an overloaded cargo plane and lumbered away. I don't know bird language, so I can't say for sure what it said as it fought for altitude, but the tone and inflection sounded like "Gee-hookers! That was a close one!"

Shortly after sunset I noticed the barometer was down a tenth of an inch. That wasn't much of a drop, but sure enough it began to blow hard and I had to stream the sea anchor again.

"Wow! What a night!" I wrote in the log the next morning (June 11th), "I hope I don't have to go through any more like that, but I probably will. It was cold, too, as the wind had shifted from west to north."

The wind relaxed a little at about 12:30 P.M., however, and then the sun came out for the first time in three days and we had a gloriously sunny, warm afternoon of sailing. I hove to contentedly in the moonlight at about ten that night and, just before going below to sleep, saw a big liner rumble westward a few miles north of us, its portholes agleam and its decks bathed in soft light.

The next morning, I awoke at about sunrise after a full seven hours of warm, relaxed sleep, and lay there in the cabin luxuriating in the pleasure of being rocked gently by the waves. Sounds of water had enchanted and soothed me all my life: the roar of a fast-flowing stream in a valley of the Himalayas; the patter of monsoon rain on the tin roof of our home in Landour; the crash and hiss of breakers hitting the beach at Ventnor, New Jersey, where our family had thrice vacationed; the slap and gurgle of Lake Erie fresh-water waves around the breakwall at Wildwood Park harbor and now the happy laughter of Atlantic salt-water billows as they toyed playfully with *Tinkerbelle*.

It was Saturday, June 12th, and one of those "God's-in-His-heaven-all's-right-with-the-world" mornings that come along every once in a while to give you a taste of how wonderful life can be. And then, just as I was beginning to slip into utter harmony with the delights of the environment, I became conscious of a subtle something. I heard nothing whatever that could be termed alien or out of place and yet, gradually, imperceptibly, I was infused with an eerie feeling that *Tinkerbelle* and I were not alone, that we had company. It was an uncanny sensation, as if I were on the receiving end of a telepathic message.

I opened the hatch and went topside. Good Lord! There was another vessel!

This one was much larger than the *Tench*. It towered above us, its tremendous bow jutting higher than *Tinkerbelle's* mast-head. It was a Canadian naval vessel and to me, then only twenty-five yards away, it seemed large enough to be a battle-ship. However, I found out later it was a destroyer escort, H.M.C.S. *Columbia*, a beautiful light-gray ship with a well-cared-for look about it.

At the *Columbia's* rail, when I emerged from the cabin, was an officer in a smart white uniform. He had an electronic megaphone in his hands and, when he saw me, he used it to project his voice across the water between us.

"Good morning," he said cheerily.

His friendly tone and casual manner seemed to imply that the sole mission assigned to the *Columbia* by Royal Canadian Navy Headquarters was to conduct a genteel wake-up service for singlehanded Atlantic yachtsmen.

"Hi!" I yelled back, attempting to sound just as casual and cheery as the naval person at the rail above me.

"Are you all right?" he asked.

"Everything's AOK here!" I shouted.

Then I remembered what I had neglected to ask the captain of the *Tench* and added, "But I'd appreciate it if you'd give me a line on my position."

"Will do."

As we waited for the *Columbia's* navigator to work out the position, the officer asked me where I had come from and where I was bound and what my craft's name was. I yelled back the replies and asked him if he would report *Tinkerbelle* and me to the Coast Guard in Boston and he said he would. Then the position report came. We were at 40° 17′ N and 63° 7′ W. That was great news! It showed that my navigation was reasonably accurate, for the position I had calculated was less than six miles from that given by the *Columbia's* navigator.

It was a tremendous relief to find out that my sun shots and calculations hadn't gone haywire; that, apparently, I had

got the hang of it and could now rely on my sextant and arithmetic to take *Tinkerbelle* and me where we wanted to go. I
grew confident that we actually would land at Falmouth, England, and not unexpectedly at some other port.

"Smooth sailing to you," called the *Columbia*'s blithe officer.
And I yelled back, "Thanks! Same to you!"

Then the big ship quietly pulled away stern first, turned
northward and moved off with an air of majesty, its red-and-
white ensign fluttering in the breeze. For the first time since
we'd met, I looked about the ocean. There were three other
warships in sight and off to the west airplanes were streaking
through the sky. I must be mixed up in some naval maneuvers,
I said to myself. It turned out I was right, but at that moment I
didn't know how right.

Later I learned that *Columbia,* commanded by Commander
P. R. Hinton, was participating in Exercise Polestar as a member of the NATO Matchmaker Squadron, which was composed
of four ships, one each from Great Britain, Holland, the United
States and Canada. The three other ships I'd seen undoubtedly
were those of Britain, Holland and the United States.

"On the morning of 12 June at 0615," Commander A. C.
McMillin of the Royal Canadian Navy wrote to me, "*Columbia*
was patrolling her station when ordered to investigate a small
radar contact. This contact turned out to be the *Tinkerbelle,*
and at first sight it appeared to be derelict, as there was no sign
of life. As *Columbia* came alongside *Tinkerbelle* you appeared
and spoke to Sub-Lt. E. J. Kelly, who was the officer-of-the-watch
at the time."

I learned, too, that Exercise Polestar was an antisubmarine
exercise in which units of the United States and Canadian
Navies and the NATO squadron were divided into teams and
pitted against one another. In fact, the *Tench* was a participant,
but on the side opposite the *Columbia,* as the "enemy."

Meeting both "friend" and "foe" in a naval exercise was a
thrilling experience, one I shall remember always. But I feel

mortified about the way *Tinkerbelle* and I blundered like bumpkins into those war games and diverted two vessels, for some minutes, from their important assigned duties. Here and now I want to thank the officers and men of the *Tench* and *Columbia* for their solicitous concern for our safety and, humbly, beg the Navies of Great Britain, Holland, the United States and Canada to pardon our intrusion.

The next night, following our encounter with H.M.C.S. *Columbia,* we had another beautiful, easygoing sail in the moonlight until about 11:45 P.M., when I turned in.

On Sunday, June 13th, I awoke to find a stiff breeze blowing so I kept *Tinkerbelle* tethered to the bucket drogue and utilized the time that gave me away from the tiller to rearrange the stowage of my supplies. I was getting more and more fed up with having to root through nearly everything I had to find what I wanted. I also took the opportunity to write some letters, to Virginia and others, which I hoped a passing ship might eventually pick up and mail for me when it reached port. We were hove to for seven or eight hours, altogether, not counting the night hours when I was sleeping. It was a pleasant time, on the whole, for the waves were not quite big enough to scare me out of the comfort of the cabin, but I was impatient and fretful because we weren't moving eastward. In fact, we were falling behind on the schedule I'd set and if we didn't get cracking soon it would take more than three months to reach England instead of the two months I had estimated.

Fortunately, the wind abated a little at about one in the afternoon. I hauled in the sea anchor, put a tuck in the mains'l and then *Tinkerbelle* spread her red-and-white wings. We took off at top speed.

11 All through the night of June 13th and into the next day *Tinkerbelle* raced along before the strongest wind we had yet encountered. It was exhilarating, and it was exhausting, for the sea grew heavier every hour. Waves slammed into our starboard side without warning, and it was all I could do to handle the sheet and the tiller and stay on course. But I was determined to hang on, tired, sore and scared though I was, in order to make up for lost time; and so we kept driving on through the day and into the cold night.

It was no time for exuberance; we were perched too precariously on the thin line between maximum speed and minimum safety. To remain on that perch demanded senses tuned to their greatest receptivity. It called for unwavering alertness; instant detection of the slightest change in conditions and swift, appropriate responses. A moment's inattention could be disastrous. ·

I knew all this well, but it didn't help. The wind pulled a diabolical trick. It increased in force so stealthily I failed to perceive it until whammo! a puff caught the mains'l at the same time a wave struck the stern and *Tinkerbelle* spun around a full eighty degrees, paying no attention whatever to my frantic yank on her tiller. She wound up stopped dead in her tracks, facing into the wind, her sails flogging ineffectually with snapping sounds like firecrackers going off that meant the fabric might soon be ripped to shreds.

Fortunately, she started drifting backward almost at once and the rudder drew her stern around so that she went over onto the port tack and the flogging stopped. The sails were saved. I kept the genoa jib sheeted to the weather side and fastened the tiller and mainsheet on the lee or starboard side to heave her to. A reduction of the sail area was overdue.

A few minutes later the big red mains'l was down and lashed to the boom and we were continuing on our way under the genny alone. Even so, we sped along almost as fast as before, for the wind in those few minutes had increased markedly. It also had veered toward the west.

By the time the first lightening of the eastern horizon signaled the approach of daybreak and the longed-for blessing of the sun's warmth, the wind had moved all the way around to the west and now blew from directly astern. For a while the sea was confused. Then the waves, by degrees, adjusted to the changed direction of the wind. They grew higher and steeper as they bore in from behind, rank on rank, flinging us forward in spasms of breakneck speed. Clutched in a welter of sizzling foam, we surfed giddily down the forward slope of a breaking wave, paused for a moment in the trough as the wave raced ahead and then, when the next one grabbed us, repeated the maneuver. And so it went, on and on. It was exciting. It was also dangerous.

The chief hazard was that we might broach; that is, slew around broadside to the waves. A breaker striking *Tinkerbelle* in that position could knock her down, even roll her over and over. It might dismast her or inflict other dire injuries. It was a catastrophe to be resolutely avoided.

So, favoring discretion over sailing valor, I decided the time had come to put out the sea anchor again. I hated to end our eastward gallop, but consoled myself with the knowledge that even while riding to the sea anchor we would continue moving eastward, drifting at less than a knot, perhaps, but still that was better than drifting toward the west or even the north or south.

As soon as I got the bucket anchor out, the rudder off and the genny down, the strain on my nerves eased up and I could almost relax. *Tinkerbelle* seemed to appreciate the change, too. For a little while her motion was less violent; water sluiced across her deck less often. But the waves continued to grow. I could see them clearly in the brightening daylight. They were huge. They resembled rows of snow-capped mountains marching toward us. The mountains themselves weren't especially terrifying, or even their snow-capped tops. What really made my hair stand on end was the sight of one of those snowy tops curving forward and falling, carumpf! sending an avalanche of tons of frothing, hissing water cascading into the valley. What if one of those avalanches rammed into *Tinkerbelle* broadside? Oh, brother . . . !

I was tired. So far I'd gone more than twenty-three hours without sleep and goodness only knew how much longer I'd have to go. The skin of my face felt stretched taut. It burned from the protracted buffeting of wind and spray. I was shocked to discover my eyelids were beginning to droop and my head to nod. I even had some trouble focusing my eyes.

This is no good, I said to myself. I've got to snap out of it.

Quickly, I opened the cabin hatch, leaned inside, rummaged in my medical kit until I found a stay-awake pill, downed it with a swallow or two of fresh water and closed the hatch again. I moved fast, for I didn't relish the prospect of maybe having *Tinkerbelle* flipped over while the hatch was open.

The pill took effect swiftly. In a minute or two I was bright-eyed and bushy-tailed, the need for sleep seemingly banished. That was better, much better.

I thought how wonderful it would be to crawl into the cabin and at least get out of the reach of the wind, but I didn't have the courage or the faith in *Tinkerbelle* to do it. I feared she might be capsized, trapping me inside her, and I imagined that that wouldn't be much fun. So I remained outside in the pitching, bounding, rolling, yawing, dipping, swaying, reeling, swiveling, gyrating cockpit, exposed to the merciless clawing of what by then was either a full gale or the next thing to it.

Hanging on to avoid being tossed overboard by my little craft's furious bucking, I offered up prayers to God, and Neptune, and Poseidon, and all the sprites who might be induced to lend a hand in my hour of need. And then, just to be sure I hadn't overlooked a bet, I prayed "To whom it may concern."

I hunched down behind the cabin to escape the worst of the wind and flying spindrift, but every ten minutes or so I popped up to take a quick look around the horizon to see if there were any ships about. It would have been a splendid time, while we were riding to the sea anchor, helpless, unable to maneuver, for a big freighter to come along and run us down. We made a dandy target with that hundred and fifty feet of line stretched out from the bow. A picture flitted into my mind of *Tinkerbelle* and me being chopped into little pieces by the slashing, cleaver-like propellers of an Atlantic juggernaut.

From the tops of the waves I could see four or five miles, maybe farther. A reddish glow in the east foretold the imminent appearance of the sun. How I yearned for its heat! It would make life worth living again. Banks of orange-looking clouds hugged the northwest quadrant of the horizon, making it seem as if there must be land there, although, of course, there wasn't. The sky had already turned from black to gray to white and now was turning from white to pale blue. Except for the northwest sector, close to the sea, it was almost clear. Only a few small billowy clouds dotted its vastness.

With the arm I didn't need for holding on, I beat my chest and rubbed my legs in a frantic effort to generate warmth. I wriggled my toes and, as well as I could under the circumstances, made my legs pedal an imaginary bicycle. The exercise and the friction helped. It produced a mild internal glow that dulled the icy sting of the wind. It also gave me something to do, which, for the moment at least, relieved the mounting apprehension aroused by the incessant crashing of breaking waves and raving of the wind.

In another twenty minutes or so, at about 4:30 A.M., the sun bobbed up and so did my spirits. The red-gold rays burnished the varnished mahogany of *Tinkerbelle*'s cabin and sent waves of radiant relief deep into my chilled hide. The sight of my own shadow made life appear ever so much brighter and, somehow, this deep blue ocean of the day didn't seem nearly as threatening as the inky black one of the night had seemed.

What happened soon afterward happened so fast and, believe it or not, so unexpectedly, that I still don't have a clear picture of it in my mind. I remember I was reveling in the growing warmth of the sun and in the improved prospects for the day when a wall of hissing, foaming water fell on *Tinkerbelle* from abeam, inundating her, knocking her down flat and battering me into the ocean with a backward somersault. One moment I was sitting upright in the cockpit, relatively high and dry, and the next I was upside down in the water, headed in the direction of Davy Jones's locker.

I flailed my arms and legs, fighting to gain the surface. I wasn't exactly frightened; it had all taken place too fast for that. But the horrible thought of sharks passed through my mind and I was gripped by the awesome feeling of being suspended over an abyss as I recalled that not long before I had figured out from the chart that the sea was about three miles deep at that spot. No use trying to touch bottom and push myself up to the surface.

I struggled harder as pressure began to build up in my lungs and behind my eyeballs. I hoped I could get my head above water in time to avoid taking that first fatal underwater breath that would fill my lungs and, no doubt, finish me off.

My lungs were at the bursting point when, at last, my head broke out of the water and I gasped for air. I expected to find *Tinkerbelle* floating bottom up, her mast submerged and pointed straight at the ocean floor, but she had righted herself and was riding the waves again like a gull. We were no more than eight or ten feet apart.

I reached down, caught hold of the lifeline around my waist and hauled myself back to my loyal friend. Then, gripping the grab rail on her cabin top, I tried to pull myself on board. I couldn't do it; the weight of my wet clothes made the task too great for my limited strength. Nevertheless, I tried again. Still no go, so I rested a moment.

There must be an easier way, I thought as the boat and I rose and fell to the waves in unison. Of course, I could have taken off my clothes, put them on board and then climbed aboard after them, but I hoped there was a quicker way. And then it

came to me: hold the grab rail with one hand while floating close to the surface, get a leg hooked over the rub rail and onto the deck, and then pull up. I was given extra impetus by the mental image of a vicious, snaggle-toothed shark possibly lurking nearby and preparing to take pounds of flesh out of my quivering body, so, on the next try, I made it.

Puffing heavily, I flopped into the cockpit and lay there clutching the handhold above the compass as my breathing slowly returned to normal. The situation, to state the case mildly, could have been a lot worse. I had been given a bad scare and was soaked through, but nothing really calamitous had happened. *Tinkerbelle* was still right side up and clear of water, and neither she nor I had suffered so much as a scratch. And, best of all, I now had evidence of exactly how stable she was. That one piece of empirically gained knowledge transformed the whole harrowing experience into a blessing in disguise. There would be no more torturous nights in the cockpit; from now on I would sleep in comfort in the cabin, even in the foulest weather, with the assurance that my boat would remain upright. No longer did I need to fear being trapped there by a capsize. This discovery made the remainder of the voyage immensely more enjoyable than it would otherwise have been.

The steepness and dangerous size of the breaking waves remained undiminished, however, so I had to remain alert. There was no telling when we might be bowled over a second time. Although sopping wet, I was reasonably comfortable because my rubberized suit kept out the wind and the rising sun was beginning to produce the warmth I had longed for all night. It was a beautiful day, in fact, with white, cottony clouds flecking the inverted blue bowl of the sky, and white, foaming wave crests flecking the undulating, deeper indigo platter of the sea. If it hadn't been for the force of the wind and the size of those waves, it would have been a perfect day for sailing.

*

12   With *Tinkerbelle* doing her stuff, I bore up well under the waves' onslaught, but I began to have troubles of another sort, for by this time, about 10 A.M. *Tinkerbelle* time, I had gone without sleep for nearly thirty hours. As it had done the day I picked up that "hitchhiker," my mind began to play strange tricks on me.

During the next hour or so, as closely as I can recall, my being was gradually permeated with the inexplicable feeling that *Tinkerbelle* and I were accompanied by other people in other boats, none of them identified specifically, and that we were there to search for a small dock and community known as Ada's Landing. I didn't know why the other sailors had to find the place, but I had a clear understanding of why I had to do so: I was to meet Robin and help her overcome some sort of serious trouble she was in. I didn't know exactly what her problem was; all I knew was that it was extremely serious and that a solution was essential for her future happiness.

I took in the sea anchor and, sailing under genny alone, began to hunt for the landing. We sailed and sailed and sailed; and now, looking back on it, I realize the sailing I did that day, through those giant waves, must have been remarkable, even fantastic. Or maybe the magnitude of the waves was itself a part of the hallucination.

Eventually we got to a part of the ocean called the Place of the Sea Mountains, an aptly named spot, for the waves there were as lofty as snow-capped Alpine peaks; so enormous, in fact, that I realized, even in my hallucinational state, that for safety's sake *Tinkerbelle* should be returned to her sea anchor.

So I streamed the bucket again and we resumed our roller-coaster ride, slowly drifting eastward, stern first.

As we climbed and slid over those aqueous peaks, the notion seeped slowly into my mind that we were in a kingdom of the sea ruled by a crusty old Scotsman named MacGregor, a man with scraggly white sideburns, plaid tam-o'-shanter, knobby knees showing below his kilt and an even more knobby cane in his hand. And for some unknown reason he was determined to do me in.

Of course, I wasn't going to let him knock me off if I could avoid it, but he *did* seem to have a rather unfair advantage in the form of a demonic choir of evil-faced, surplice-clad cut-throats. This horrendous assemblage of gravel-voiced killers had the miraculous power of controlling the size of the waves by the loudness of their singing. They were singing their lungs out, goaded on to ever-increasing volume by vociferous tongue-lashings administered by MacGregor. Louder and louder they sang, and bigger and bigger grew the waves. It seemed as though my hours, maybe my minutes, were numbered.

During all this (and it went on for several hours) I had strange visions of MacGregor and his choir in the sky that appeared very much like the double exposures one sometimes sees in a movie or on television, where two or more images are super-imposed on the same background. And as the minutes passed, old MacGregor grew increasingly enraged by his choir's inability to sing loud enough to put an end to me. He raved and stormed all over the heavens, threatening his dealers in *a-cap-pella* death with horrible punishments if I survived their vocalizing. Meanwhile, I waxed more and more confident that, with *Tinkerbelle*'s help, I would be able to hold my own. Perhaps I even became overconfident because, even though the waves had not diminished in size, I felt I had to go on and find Robin. I was sure she was in desperate need of my help.

So I drew in the drogue again, set the genny and, with that single sail, started to swoosh up and down and around the wave mountains as if I were crossing the Rockies by bobsled. I did some of the fanciest sailing of my life, swishing around the edges of those huge waves, dodging the breaking crests and, sometimes, planing down their forward slopes at breakneck speed.

But I never seemed to get anywhere, much less to Ada's Landing. And neither did the people in the other boats accompanying me. We all seemed to be trapped in a maze, unable to find the way out. That's what the trouble was: the Place of

the Sea Mountains was a maze-like ocean realm, set entirely apart from the regular ocean we had been on the day before. We had to get out of it before we could get to Ada's Landing.

Eventually, after hours of struggling to find our way out, *Tinkerbelle* and I came upon a little elfin character who looked like a cross between a leprechaun and Gunga Din.

"How can we get out of this place?" I asked him in a tone of intense urgency.

He stood there on the water studying me for a long time in an impish way that I couldn't fathom. Then he scratched his bald head, threw out his arms, palms up, in a gesture of sad amazement, and said:

"Sir, the trouble is you have been sailing clockwise. If you want to get out of here you must sail counterclockwise."

And with that he was gone.

I put *Tinkerbelle* about and started moving on a counterclockwise course. It seemed to be the correct maneuver, for soon we came to a place where the sea descended in a gigantic staircase leading off to the eastern horizon. The whole world seemed to be tilted and yet, marvel of marvels, none of the water in the sea ran down the staircase and off the edge of the horizon.

Tinkerbelle and I now did some even fancier sailing than we had done already; we went down that mammoth staircase lickety-split. What we were actually doing, I guess, was to surf-ride the waves, which, through some sort of perceptual distortion induced by the hallucination, appeared to be great downward steps in the sea. The thrills of the downhill runs were electrifying, far more stirring than any I'd had before in all my life. They warned of danger, but I was in no condition to heed them.

We charged down wave after wave as if we were on a toboggan and then along came a wave we couldn't handle. It flung us forward so fast we broached and over we went. I found myself in the ocean a second time. I wasn't knocked as far from *Tinkerbelle* this time, though, because I had kept a firm grip on the tiller. I was back on board in a jiffy.

Two more times that afternoon *Tinkerbelle* broached and I was knocked into the sea by waves slamming into us from abeam. I held firmly to some part of the boat each time and got back aboard quickly, but the repetitious way in which I was being dumped overboard was as exasperating as my boat's self-righting accomplishments were gratifying.

Late in the afternoon we got to the bottom of the wave-formed staircase and again met the Gunga Din pixy. He told me Ada's Landing was off to starboard, not much farther, and so I turned and headed in the direction he indicated. In a few minutes I began to "see" bits of land ahead that I took to be the landing, but they always disappeared before I got right up to them. It was most perplexing, and equally infuriating.

I came to the conclusion—reluctantly, because he seemed a nice fellow—that Gunga Din was having prankish fun at my expense and that I had better not rely further on anything he said. I'd simply have to do the best I could on my own. I felt that I was bound to get out of the Place of the Sea Mountains, sooner or later, but I was assailed by painful shafts of doubt about whether I would be able to reach Robin and help her. The search for Ada's Landing began to seem futile.

My misgivings and anguish increased with each passing minute. My very soul was on the rack, tormented between the desperate ardor of my desire to help my daughter and the accumulating suspicions that I would not be able to do so, that I would fail her at this time when she needed me more than she ever had before. It was agony.

At about sunset *Tinkerbelle* and I (alone now, for our sailing companions had vanished) came to what seemed to be the brow of a long, easy slope off to port; and at the bottom of it was the "regular" ocean. This was the way out of the Sea Mountains. We'd found it, at last.

Tinkerbelle, still sailing under genny alone, all but flew down that ocean hill and rushed happily out into the normal, unjinxed, unbewitched sea. Oh, what a relief it was to be in it again! The face of our predicament was transformed from a frown into a smile, as though we had moved with one leap from hell to heaven. Goodbye, MacGregor! Goodbye, you sinful singers!

I had a queer feeling that Ada's Landing was nearby and that maybe we'd find it after all. But I needed sleep; every cell in my body cried out for it. So I decided to rest and go on to the landing in the morning, hoping that Robin would be able to wait that much longer. I put out the bucket drogue, took down the genny, hoisted the anchor light in the rigging, unshipped the rudder, changed into dry clothes (those I had on were still wet from my dunkings) and climbed into the cabin, closing the hatch (all but a crack left open for air) after me. It was good to pull that blanket over me and close my eyes!

I now had no qualms whatever about sleeping in the cabin. In any case, the sea had settled down considerably; it wasn't making nearly as much fuss as it had during the daylight hours. Conditions seemed ideal for sleeping, but just before I dropped off, the boat jiggled violently in a way that, I felt, couldn't possibly have been caused by wave action. I stilled my breathing and strained my ears for some clue to what was going on outside. I thought I heard someone, or rather, two people, holding onto the boat and whispering. And then the boat jiggled again in that peculiar way. It was clear what was happening. Two jokers had swum out from the landing and were jostling the boat to annoy me, to keep me from getting the sleep I needed and to see how far they could go before I flew into a rage.

I tried to control my temper, but it steadily became more and more difficult. When I heard my tormentors pulling themselves around the boat, hand over hand, and, in low voices, planning more trickery, I could hardly contain myself. Then they jiggled *Tinkerbelle* again.

"Cut that out!" I yelled in as threatening a tone as I could produce.

Quiet reigned for two or three minutes and then I heard more whispering. Soon the boat began to rock. Those damnable swimmers were hanging onto the rub rails, one on each side, and seesawing the hull with fiendish delight. I could stand their impudent maliciousness no longer. Adrenalin gushed into my veins, making me hot with anger, and I stormed out of the cabin ready to beat my harassers to a pulp.

"Dammit! You bastards are going to get it now!" I roared.

But nobody was there.

13 In the morning (Tuesday, June 15th), after more than ten hours of sleep, I awoke to find *Tinker-belle* again riding mountainous waves. But I wasn't worried; I knew she'd stay upright. All day the wind blew hard, too hard to do any sailing; so I remained within the shelter of the cabin, going out on deck only occasionally to see if any ships were in sight.

It was a huge relief to be myself again, to realize that Robin really wasn't in any difficulty, that all my fears about her had been part of a nightmarish hallucination. Robin wasn't in trouble, there was no Ada's Landing, no Place of the Sea Mountains, no MacGregor, no sinister choir, no Gunga Din, no staircase or hill in the ocean and no aquatic pranksters. O.K., granted. But what about those duckings? Were they hallucinatory, too? Had I or hadn't I been washed overboard four times?

The clothing I'd worn the previous day was tucked away in a corner of the cabin and it was still sopping. It couldn't possibly have got that wet unless I had actually been *in* the sea at least once. And if I'd been in the sea once, and knew it was for real, then the other times must have been real, too. Besides, the flashlight I'd had tied to a line in the cockpit was now gone. The knot must have come loose, allowing it to slip away when it, too, had been washed overboard. Yes, I really had been knocked into the sea four times. No doubt about it. (Fortunately, I had a spare flashlight, as well as a marvelous signaling spotlight a friend had presented to me as a bon-voyage gift.)

Describing the previous day in the log, I understated the case somewhat when I wrote, "This was one of the most unusual days of my life." Then, after telling about everything I'd "seen" and "done," I summed it up with, "This was a weird experience. It must have been at least partly hallucination, but part of it must have been real because I *know* I was sailing around, was swept overboard four times, and used up a whole day. I must have just slipped a cog.

"I must say that I have had the most uncanny feeling of having someone with me most of the time. It's not always the same person. Sometimes it's Virginia, sometimes Doug, sometimes Robin and sometimes John (John Manry, my brother). I'll have to get a psychologist to explain all this."

Perhaps this feeling of having members of the family with me was a technique my mind had of coping with loneliness, for I did at times feel extremely lonely. However, I didn't miss human companionship in a broad, generalized way, probably because I am inclined to be an introspective, self-contained sort of person, lacking strong inclinations toward gregariousness. I missed my family and close, personal friends intensely, but as for mankind in the abstract, no. I got along without human company (considered simply as human company) very well. And, after all, I knew from the very beginning that I wasn't going to be alone for more than three months.

Besides feeling that I had members of my family with me, I sometimes heard voices in the wake. This was in the first part of the trip before any weeds or barnacles had attached themselves to the hull, and *Tinkerbelle* could sail quite fast, leaving a bubbling wake behind her. To me, sometimes, the bubbles sounded as if someone were talking down there under the water and once I imagined that someone under the boat was calling for help and I even went so far as to look down over the stern to see who it was. I didn't see anyone.

To help face the loneliness I kept one of my watches set to Eastern standard time, the time of Willowick and Cleveland, so that I could visualize what might be happening at home. At

7 A.M. (E.S.T.) Doug would be getting out of bed, I knew, for he was the earliest riser in the family. As soon as he was dressed (if it happened to be Saturday), he would go out to the living room to watch the cartoons on television; otherwise he'd have a hasty breakfast and depart for school.

Robin, girl-like, spent the time between getting out of bed and leaving for school fixing her hair and making sure she was dressed to suit herself. And Virginia would have to keep urging her on so that she wouldn't keep her friend, Jean Perkey, waiting. Then the two girls would go on to school together.

After the children had left, if I was at home, Virginia would spoil me outrageously by serving me coffee in bed and then she would sit beside me and we'd have the most wonderful conversations. How I missed those talks and cups of coffee. The talks I had now were rather one-sided and the instant coffee I made for myself wasn't nearly as flavorful as the coffee Virginia brewed.

All day long I had only to look at the Eastern standard time to picture what was probably happening at home at that moment. It made the family seem much nearer than it might have seemed otherwise. I hoped that at the end of the month Virginia wouldn't have trouble paying the bills, a chore that previously had been in my province.

Wednesday, June 16th, dawned with *Tinkerbelle* bobbing gently on a smoothed-out sea. I ate a hasty breakfast and we got going as quickly as possible. It turned out to be a fine, sunny day, the highlight of it being that, finally, after sixteen days at sea, we crossed the meridian of 60°W, completing the first step in the giant countdown to England.

It was a wonderful feeling to have passed this first oceanic milestone, but it required very little arithmetic to see that if we continued to move at the rate we'd established in the first two weeks we'd require about eighty-seven more days to reach England, making the duration of the voyage more than a hundred days. And I was provisioned for only ninety days. It looked as though I might have to go on reduced rations.

I wasn't really worried, however, because I was consuming my provisions more slowly than I'd thought I would, and I was confident we'd move faster as I grew better acquainted with the ocean and with *Tinkerbelle*'s performance in relation to it. During these first two weeks I had been sailing cautiously, feeling my way, getting my sea legs.

About noon the next day *Tinkerbelle* almost slammed into a shark that was lallygagging at the surface with its dorsal fin sticking out of the water; I think it must have been sleeping. It was eight or nine feet long, not very big as sharks go.

In midafternoon we had our first serious mishap: the rudder broke.

The fiberglass covering of the rudder had cracked near the stock where the tiller fitted onto it, and water had seeped through the crack to the three-quarter-inch plywood underneath, causing it to soften. Finally, the enormous strain set up by the opposing pressures of water on the rudder and my pull on the tiller caused the stock to snap. I thanked my lucky stars that I'd brought along a spare. In less than five minutes it was in place and we were moving again.

We were becalmed for about four hours on June 18th and again for most of the morning of the next day. Shortly after noon, however, a breeze sprang up and, as it veered from the north all the way around to the south, it increased in force. *Tinkerbelle* soon was zipping along, headed due east.

"About midafternoon," the log says, "we were racing along at a great rate on the starboard tack when a large tanker popped into view over my right shoulder, no more than 25 yards away. It had sneaked up on me without making a sound and gave me quite a start. I must make it a practice from now on to scan all around the horizon from time to time to prevent this sort of thing."

The tanker was the S.S. *Otto N. Miller* of Monrovia. Crewmen at the rail waved and cheered as it sped past, and I waved back as well as I could while holding the tiller and mainsheet in my hands. The ship seemed to be going at terrific speed and the huge waves it sent out from its bow and stern gave us an exciting bouncing around. It didn't even slow down as it passed and was soon out of sight.

Captain Orlando Rolla, skipper of the *Miller,* told me later of his experiences that day. His ship had left St. John, New

Brunswick, Canada, the previous day and was bound for Bandar Mashur, Iran, via the Suez Canal.

"In the afternoon of June 19," he wrote, "Chief Officer Salvino Gallinaro was on watch. We had showers all around and our radar was working.

"Mr. Gallinaro advised me that a little object, not well defined, was showing on the radar screen. It was about 60° on our port bow and some three-quarters of a mile away. The horizon was clear of showers in that direction and, with binoculars, we saw a small red sail.

"We immediately headed the ship in that direction to investigate. We steered as close as possible so that no particulars about the sailboat would escape our attention. In fact, we passed so close I was able to see clearly the number marked on the bow of your boat and I saw you sitting at the tiller, looking as if you were sailing on a small lake rather than the Atlantic Ocean.

"I told the U.S. Coast Guard of our meeting, giving it the number and description of your boat, and advising it that no assistance was required.

"The night following our meeting we had a moderate sea and often our thoughts ran to you, alone in the open ocean."

I'll have to agree that Captain Rolla's ship passed close to *Tinkerbelle,* so close the shock nearly made me jump out of my skin. But, as I noted in the log, it taught me an important lesson: keep scanning the whole horizon so that you'll know when a ship is approaching. It was very kind of the captain to report me to the Coast Guard and to think of me that night. Conditions probably weren't as bad as he imagined them, though.

"Toward dusk," my log says, "the wind grew too strong for the genoa so I stopped to take it in and put out the sea anchor. Just then a cloudburst hit. It rained so hard I could hardly see 10 feet away. But I managed to get bounding *Tinkerbelle* bedded down without mishap.

"I stayed in the cockpit for a long time watching her take the huge waves. She did very well, but I'll have to improve the jigger sail at her stern. [I had rigged this to help keep her pointed steadily into the waves.]

"I was fearful of getting into the cabin and going to sleep because of the brush with the *Miller,* but *Tinkerbelle*'s anchor light seemed highly visible, so, finally, I did go inside where it was quiet and dry and got some sleep."

At dusk the very next day (Sunday, June 20th) we met another ship, the S.S. *Exilona,* a 9,598-ton freighter commanded by

Captain Helgi Loftsson. We had been through some squalls earlier in the day, but now the wind was light, although huge swells were running. Dark, threatening clouds partly covered the sky and caught orange-red rays from the setting sun. It was a scene El Greco might have painted if he had painted seascapes.

The *Exilona,* when I first saw her, was to the north of us, headed west, and I thought she would go on by, but then she saw us and came lumbering over, rolling and pitching through the swells. As she drew near, Captain Loftsson stopped her engines, but even without her propellers turning she moved so fast, blown by the wind, that *Tinkerbelle* could barely keep pace with her. I shouted to men at the stern rail and they relayed what I said to Captain Loftsson on the bridge by telephone, and then, in turn, passed his questions and answers back to me.

I learned the ship was on its way from Beirut to Boston, and told the captain I was bound for England and needed no assistance. I added that I'd appreciate a position check and would like to give him some letters to be mailed when he reached port. He gave me the position figures promptly and they showed that my own were reasonably accurate, but transferring the letters wasn't so easily done as I was afraid to get closer than about a hundred feet to the *Exilona's* stern because of the danger of having my craft slammed against her and smashed. A husky crewman tried twice to span the distance between us with a heaving line, but failed. It was hopeless.

The captain said he'd report me to the Coast Guard so that it could keep track of my progress, and I yelled back, "Thanks!" I found out later the message he sent was:

"Latitude 40.57 north; longitude 58.04 west. Passed sailboat OH-7013-AR, 14-foot [How he came so close to estimating *Tinkerbelle's* length correctly I can't imagine] lapstrake sailboat with red mainsail and white jib.

"One person aboard bound for Falmouth, England, from Falmouth, Massachusetts. Nineteen days at sea. Requested notify U.S. Coast Guard, Boston, that all is O.K. Required no assistance."

After I thanked Captain Loftsson, we bade each other good-bye and I exchanged waves with the seamen at the *Exilona*'s stern. Then we turned back to our original courses and went our separate ways as darkness closed in. A little while later a wonderful, steady breeze sprang up and *Tinkerbelle,* with a reef in her mains'l, gamboled over the waves as if she were a spirited fawn out for a romp in the woods. It was glorious sailing and I wished that Virginia and the children could have enjoyed it with me. It was so pleasant, in fact, I took a stay-awake pill and went on all night.

Three more days of good sailing followed. On the third night, Wednesday, June 23rd, the ocean was as calm as a millpond. Hardly a ripple disturbed its glassy surface as *Tinkerbelle* ghosted along noiselessly on a shimmering cushion of phosphorescence. I lay on my back in the cockpit with my legs extending into the cabin, my head propped up on a cushion, the tiller in my right hand, steering by the stars that bejeweled the black velvet sky. What an enchanting out-of-this-world night that was, with the sparkling diamonds in the water seemingly competing in brilliance with the diamonds in the heavens.

It was so calm I hove to for sleep without streaming the sea anchor, by simply hauling the jib to windward and tying the tiller to leeward. I slept like a baby and, in the morning, had the pleasure of beginning a new day without having to go through the arduous task of hauling in the bucket.

We had been at sea more than three weeks now and I had a daily routine more or less established. I usually awoke at about 4 A.M., *Tinkerbelle* time, shortly before the sun popped up from below the eastern horizon, and I began the day in sheer luxury. I treated myself to a delightful experience that, at home, was reserved for mornings when I was indisposed or had done something extraordinary to merit extra-solicitous indulgence: I had breakfast in bed.

As a matter of fact, I also had dinner in bed, for *Tinkerbelle*'s cabin was too small to permit my dining within it in any other way. Of course, my use of the word "bed" is a slight exaggeration. It wasn't *really* a bed; it was a couple of bags full of clothing on which I sat and a rolled-up blanket to my right against which I leaned and rested my head.

Tinkerbelle's interior was too crowded with gear to allow me to stretch out at full length, so I had to experiment with other positions for sleeping. I tried out several, but the one that worked out best was this semi-sitting-up position in which I planted my stern on the bags of clothing and leaned to starboard against the blanket. Then, to have breakfast in bed, all I had to do was to straighten up and my food and canned-heat stove were within easy reach.

Breakfast usually consisted of hot cereal with raisins, canned fruit of some sort and coffee. Sometimes I had scrambled dehydrated eggs and dehydrated bacon or, about once a week, a dehydrated Spanish omelet. The first time I prepared an omelet, it wound up with a taste and texture resembling shoe leather, but, happily, I became more adept at omelet cookery later on.

After breakfast I washed my utensils in the ocean and brushed my teeth; and every other week I shaved my face, all except my mustache, which, by the third week, was beginning to look quite respectable. And once a week, if the weather was favorable, I took a sponge bath in the cockpit with sea water, afterward giving myself a rinse with fresh water. Water for shaving and bathing was warmed on the stove.

When breakfast and these chores were completed, I prepared to get under way. I took the anchor light out of the rigging. I removed the rudder from the daggerboard-keel slot where it had been stowed for the night and secured it in the cockpit, ready to be hung at the stern when I was ready. I also took down the improvised stern jigger sail, which helped to keep the boat headed squarely into the waves. Then I crawled to the foredeck and hauled in the sea anchor, stowing the line in the daggerboard-keel slot and lashing the bucket and float firmly in place aft of the mast. The next steps were to put the rudder on and, finally, to hoist the sails. We were then ready to go. In good weather the whole rigmarole took about twenty minutes, but if the sea was rough, forcing me to hold on tight to keep from being pitched overboard, it sometimes took twice that long.

When I got back to the tiller and we started moving, we kept it up until the sun (if not hidden by clouds) was at least ten degrees above the horizon. Then I hove to for the morning sun shot by backing the jib and lashing the tiller down.

Most navigators, I believe, take a series of sextant sights and strike an average, but since I had to stop the boat every time I used the sextant, I tried for the best possible single shot I was capable of and relied on that. For accuracy's sake I always used the natural horizon, except once or twice at night when I used the bubble to get our latitude from Polaris. After I had gained some experience, I found that I could usually tell whether a given sextant sight was a good one.

When the sight had been worked out and the position line recorded on a plotting sheet, we resumed sailing and kept it up until just before noon. Then we stopped for the noon latitude sight, which usually took me twenty or thirty minutes, longer than was required for the morning or evening sights. By bringing forward the morning north-south position line, in accordance with the estimated distance and the course we had sailed, until it intersected the noon east-west position line, I got a fairly good idea of where we were at noon.

After the noon sight we again set sail and I ate a snack as we sloshed along. I'd have biscuits, or a meat bar, or a candy bar, or a concoction of dried fruit and nuts called pemmican. And I'd top it off with fruit juice or a carbonated drink. (Ben Carlin had written that he developed a craving for carbonated beverages while at sea so I brought along a good supply and was glad to have it.)

When the sun was far down in the western sky, but not yet closer than ten degrees to the horizon, we stopped for the evening sextant shot, which gave me another north-south position line on the plotting sheet. Then, by drawing a line from our noon position, according to the course we had traveled, to intersect the afternoon sun line, I established our position with sufficient accuracy for my needs. This type of position finding is called a running fix. It is not as precise as a regular fix in which position lines taken from two or more celestial bodies, in quick succession, establish the location of the vessel; but it nevertheless served us well, for we were not moving very fast, our average daily run being about forty miles.

Following the evening navigational exercise, I had dinner (in bed, usually; although I occasionally "lived it up" and ate outdoors, in the cockpit). The menus had a great variety of entrées: beef slices and potatoes, turkey loaf, shrimp, tuna and noodles, stuffed cabbage, stuffed peppers, spaghetti and meat balls, corned-beef hash, chicken and noodles, ham loaf and others. Dessert was usually fruit or a candy bar, but once a week I treated myself to a tiny fruitcake. The beverage was coffee, most often, with an occasional switch to an orange drink or cocoa. Sometimes I added beef or chicken bouillon, and I always added a vitamin pill and an ascorbic acid, anti-scurvy tablet.

Dinner over, I washed the saucepan or frying pan and silver-ware in the ocean and got under way again. Usually I sailed until well after darkness had fallen, stopping for sleep between. 9 P.M. and midnight, *Tinkerbelle* time; but once in a while, as I've already reported, I continued all night. The all-night sailing came, generally, when I was trying to get across shipping lanes quickly and safely, or was battling an adverse current.

The procedure for parking *Tinkerbelle* for the night was the same as the procedure for getting her under way in the morning, except that it was done more or less in reverse. I hove her to under sail, put out the sea anchor, lowered and secured the sails, unshipped the rudder and stowed it in the daggerboard-keel slot, raised the jigger sail at the stern and hung the anchor light in the rigging. If it was a pleasant night, I sometimes stayed in the cockpit for a few minutes, facing sternward with my back resting against the cabin, enjoying the sights and sounds of the nighttime ocean. At other times I played the harmonica or listened to the radio, most frequently to programs of the Voice of America, the Armed Forces Radio and Television Service and the British Broadcasting Corporation. Then I descended into the cabin, closed the hatch after me (except for the crack left open for ventilation), got into "bed," pulled a blanket over me and went to sleep. I'll have to confess that I didn't observe such amenities as wearing pajamas and sleeping between sheets. I went primitive, to a certain extent, and slept in the clothes I'd been wearing all day—many times even when they were wet.

Usually I was so tired I had no trouble whatever getting to sleep; the sea rocked me as though I were in a cradle. (Luckily I have never been bothered by seasickness.) In rough weather, though, waves sometimes broke over the boat sending streams of water gushing through the ventilation crack left open in the hatch. This was annoying because it soaked the blanket, though it didn't seem to reduce its warmth.

Tinkerbelle's cabin was a marvelous refuge, now that I had learned it wouldn't, couldn't become a trap. I wasn't able to imagine how Dr. Alain Bombard, Dr. Hannes Lindemann, and George Harvo and Frank Samuelson had achieved their crossings in cabinless craft. They weren't ever able to get out of the wind's clutches, away from its buffeting and shrieking, as I was. How they stood the hardships of constant exposure to the elements is more than I can comprehend. In *Tinkerbelle*'s cabin I was able to shut myself away from the occasionally harrowing difficulties of the sea world of waves and winds and enter a world of cozy comfort and order, where there was a place for everything and everything (I hoped) was in its place. The snugness and enveloping protection of the cabin touched latent atavistic inclinations within me that, no doubt, had been passed on from long-gone ancestors who lived in caves. The cabin was a little world unto itself, safe and compact. There I could fall asleep to the music of the sea, the chuckling, giggling and laughing of wavelets strumming the laps in the boat's clinker-built hull. There I could wait out storms with ease, passing the time with reading, eating, letter writing, napping, navigation figuring, radio listening and harmonica playing. There, too, I could raise my braying voice to top volume and burst into song without fear of annoying a soul, except maybe the birds or fish.

I loved the smell of the cabin. It was an exotic compound of the odors of paint, calking material, a tarry aroma that came from I know not where, damp blankets and mold, the whole business being delicately seasoned with a faint scent from whatever type of food had been accidentally spilled into the bilge at the last meal.

June 25th (Friday) was a fine sailing day; so good, in fact, that I decided to keep going all night in an effort to catch up on our schedule. Sometime after midnight an amazing thing happened; at least, it was amazing to me. I wrote about it in the log, thus:

"We were sailing along at a good clip with the usual phosphorescent phenomena [you see, by this time I was getting rather blasé] when all of a sudden a big patch of ocean the size of a baseball field lit up as though it were illuminated by under-water floodlights. And there was *Tinkerbelle* sailing on a sea of light. It was one of the most spectacular sights I've ever seen."

This was a unique experience for me. I had never seen any-thing remotely like it before, although I had once read a little about similar occurrences. I certainly can't explain it.

It was a beautiful sight, but it made me so nervous I failed to appreciate it properly at the time. The thought darted into my mind that maybe a whale was under the boat, stirring up the ocean's luminescence, and that it might at any moment rise under the boat and smash it. I hung on, waiting for the fatal blow, but it never came; and in a minute or so I sailed out of the floodlit tract, awestruck and mystified.

Having sailed all night with the aid of pills, I should have sus-pected that something of a hallucinatory nature might occur the next day (Saturday, June 26th), but I didn't. My guard was down and I drifted right into another fantastic experience.

This one began at about sunset. I believed I was sailing in an inlet, close to the shore, and that I heard two apish men on a small wharf talking in conspiratorial tones.

"One shot between the eyes is all it'll take," one of the men said.

"But how'll I know it's him?" the other asked.

"You can find his boat without no trouble 'cause he always puts out that there anchor light."

Oh, oh! A couple of killers were obviously out to get me. I had to move far away from there, quickly. I sailed for my life, taking all sorts of devious routes in order to escape from the assassins. I even sailed into fog and stealthily circled back, hoping to lose them.

Sometime after darkness fell, I grew conscious of having Douglas and an elderly man on board *Tinkerbelle* with me. They were in the cabin, the man supposedly taking care of my son.

A little later we approached an island and, somehow, I knew

that if we got onto the island we'd be caught and killed, so I steered *Tinkerbelle* away from it. But no matter what I did, she seemed determined to put us ashore and wreck herself in the process, for the coast was a mass of jagged rocks against which the waves hammered with sickening thunder. My boat simply went berserk. She became gallingly cantankerous, impossible to control. Nothing I did diverted her from drifting toward those terrible breakers. She would come about and then get into irons, come about and get into irons, over and over. She absolutely refused to obey me and to sail as she should. It was maddening, and I grew very angry. I shouted at *Tinkerbelle* and scolded her unmercifully. It was the first time I had said a harsh word to her. (I hope I'll never do it again.)

I don't know how it happened, but finally, by some means, I swerved *Tinkerbelle* away from her compulsive determination to kill us and herself. We broke away from the island's threatening rocks and headed out to sea.

Then, gradually, the feeling crept over me that the man in the cabin with Douglas was not a friend at all. He was really one of the assassins, bent on disposing of us both. As Doug's father, it was up to me to save him from the clutches of the masquerading murderer.

The only tactical plan I could think of was to move slyly, silently to the cabin entrance holding the signaling spotlight at the ready, and then to turn it on in the killer's eyes. The blinding light and the surprise of the attack might enable me to get his gun away and save Doug. I'd seen men do things like that in the movies, so maybe I could, too.

I moved forward to the cabin hatch like a panther about to spring. I picked up the spotlight without a sound and then, zip! I switched it on and thrust it inside.

No one was there.

Undoubtedly it seems peculiar, but the revelation that I was in the grip of another hallucination jarred me considerably. I realized, as I should have done long before, that I needed rest. So I put out the bucket drogue and prepared *Tinkerbelle* to look after herself while I was asleep. I was just about to secure the anchor light in the rigging when I recalled what one of the assassins had said, "You can find his boat without no trouble 'cause he always puts out that there anchor light."

"O.K.," I said to myself. "I'll fool those lousy hoods."

I outsmarted them with devilish cunning: I didn't put out the anchor light.

*

14

From the log:

"Monday, June 28—It's blowing up a bit this morning. I can't get going yet, anyway, because I've two chores to do. I've got to get the spare battery for the anchor light and fix up an aerial for the radio so I can get the WWV time signal. I couldn't hear it at all last night. If I'm left without the time signal I'll be in a bad spot; won't be able to tell my longitude.

"After monumental rooting around, while being tossed about in the boat, I found the battery. I also have an aerial rigged as the topping lift and I got the 9 A.M. (Eastern standard time) time signal from WWV. I think I'll just wait here another hour for the noon sight and then I'll get going."

Sometime during the day we completed another ten-degree step in the big countdown toward Falmouth: We moved to the east of 50° W longitude.

Again from the log:

"Wednesday, June 30—The last day of June and I'm only about one-third of the way. I don't think the rest of the trip will take two months, but I think it will take me until Aug. 15, all right.

"I was becalmed for a couple of hours. Lay out on deck and snoozed a bit. When I looked around again the ocean seemed full of dolphins, in widely separated groups. I wonder how those far in the rear kept from getting lost.

"Later in the afternoon *Tinkerbelle* was visited by some very colorful fish, three or four feet long, with dark iridescent blue bodies, two forward fins of lighter blue, and bright yellow tails. They cruised back and forth under the boat as I was having

⚓ 148

supper and wouldn't take any of the juicy morsels I offered them. [I learned later they were probably dorado.]

"Sailing in the dark, later, I was 'pursued' by a couple of thunderstorms. Lightning flashes lit up the entire sky, although they were too far off for me to hear the thunder.

"Finally, at about 1:30 A.M. (*Tinkerbelle* time), I decided to bed down and, wouldn't you know it, that's when the first ship

I've seen in days appeared. Fortunately it passed well to the south."

The next day (July 1st) I got my first good shots at the sun in four days and discovered that we were about ninety miles south of where we should have been. There are places in the Atlantic where the Gulf Stream meanders, even doubles back on itself, and I think we must have run into one of these places. The current, then, began taking us south at the same time that we ran into cloudy weather, which prevented my taking sun sights that would have revealed what was happening to us. As soon as I found out, I headed *Tinkerbelle* northeastward and we sailed hard to regain the latitude we had lost.

On Friday, July 2nd, we went right through the center of what I took to be a cyclone, or rather, it passed by us. The wind was coming from the southeast and, as the center of the low passed over, it shifted a hundred and eighty degrees very quickly, in no more than five or six minutes, to the northwest. And it rained very hard, both before and after the shift.

"Saw what I can only describe as a giant sea worm," I wrote later in the log. "It was about the same color as an ordinary garden worm, but about 10 feet long and fatter in proportion to its length than an ordinary worm."

We got back up to the latitude we should have been at on Sunday, July 4th, and the next day I awoke at about 5 A.M., *Tinkerbelle* time, had a good breakfast and got under way.

The sun was peeking through clouds and it looked as though the day could go either way: cloudy and dreary or sunny and cheery. It went sunny, at least for most of the day. And I went cheery. The breeze was perfect, ten to thirteen knots, just the right force. And it was out of the south, which made it easy for me to steer our course of 67°. We made good time. The fine weather, the blue beauty of the sea and the easy, smooth rolling of the swells put me into a wonderfully happy frame of mind.

"The only thing that could make this day more perfect," I said to myself, "would be for a ship to come along and pick up my mail."

About twenty minutes later I took my eyes off the compass and looked around the horizon and there, over my right shoulder, steaming toward me like the answer to a prayer, was a ship. It turned out to be the 12,640-ton cargo vessel, S.S. *Steel Vendor,* bound from India and Ceylon to New York.

Its master, Captain Kenneth N. Greenlaw, maneuvered the big ship very well, making it easy for me to bring *Tinkerbelle* in close, to within fifty feet of its starboard beam. The day was so calm, and the 492-foot *Steel Vendor* and the 13½-foot *Tinkerbelle* were so close to each other that Captain Greenlaw and I had no difficulty making ourselves understood. He wanted to know if I was lost and I assured him I wasn't, but that I'd appreciate a check on my navigation. So he gave me our position: 40° 53′ N and 47° 2′ W.

"Do you need any provisions?" he asked.

I assured him I had all the provisions I needed, and yet he looked skeptical, as though he just couldn't believe it. He seemed to be a big man, and he had a friendly face and a warm manner about him.

He readily agreed to take my mail aboard and soon a crewman heaved a line to *Tinkerbelle*. I had a bundle of ten letters all ready in a waterproof plastic bag and attached it quickly to the end of the line. Then the crewman hauled away. The letters were aboard the ship in a jiffy, on their way to my family and friends ashore.

"Thanks!" I yelled, waving to the captain and all the crew. "Have a nice trip."

"You have a nice trip!" the captain shouted back.

We all waved again, slowly drew apart and then turned stern to stern and resumed our separate courses. In a few minutes I was alone again on the restless sea.

Three days later, at one in the afternoon, we were becalmed at the center of a flat disc of blue. I used the time to bathe, dry blankets and clothing, write in the log and play the harmonica. *Tinkerbelle* had a small forest of gooseneck barnacles clinging to her bottom by then, for she had been at sea more than five weeks, so I also reached down as far as I could all around her and pulled off as many as possible. I think my efforts enabled her to sail a little more jauntily for several days afterward.

It remained calm until long after dark, the lengthiest period of calm we had yet encountered; but when I awoke in the morning a nice breeze was agitating the surface of the ocean. We started moving eastward again. Although it was rainy and dismal, we had good sailing all that day and the next.

"Looks as if it's going to be another dull, cloudy day, and the wind seems a bit strong for comfort," I wrote in the log shortly after awaking Sunday, July 11th.

This was an important day to me because sometime during the next ten hours (if the sailing was good) I expected to pass the meridian of 40° W, the next step in the longitudinal count-down to England. Passing this meridian would put me very close to the halfway point in the voyage, which, for my purposes, I decided was the meridian of 37° W. Since the winds were mostly westerlies, 40° W also was what I considered to be the point of no return; that is, the point from which it would be as easy, or easier, to sail on to England as to return to the United States, although, in case of trouble, the Azores still offered the closest haven. So I was hoping to have a good, long day of swift sailing.

"During the night the wind shifted from west to northwest," I continued in the log. "The shift has made it considerably cooler, but now we'll be able to reach rather than run. I just hope the wind doesn't get so strong we have to quit and put out the sea anchor.

"Well, now, up and at it."

The wind *was* strong and the waves seemed huge (some of them, I thought, were twenty-footers, the biggest yet), but I kept *Tinkerbelle* boiling along under genny only.

Conditions continued like this, teetering on the verge of being too obstreperous to handle, until just after twelve o'clock. Then, dramatically, the sky cleared and we were presented with a lovely sunny afternoon.

My spirits were beginning to soar when, crrraaack! the rudder snapped, rendering *Tinkerbelle* unsteerable.

It took me a few minutes to collect my wits and formulate a plan of action to deal with this crisis, but eventually I got organized and started to repair the original rudder, the one that had broken first, as it seemed to be the more reparable of the two. While I was pulling myself together, a breaking wave crest caught *Tinkerbelle* beam on and knocked her down, plopping me into the ocean for the fifth time. The boat righted herself at once, good girl that she was, and I scrambled back onto her very quickly, for by that time I had amassed considerable boarding experience (I knew exactly what to do to get back on her with the least effort and loss of time) and I immediately threw out the drogue so that the knockdown wouldn't be repeated.

It was desolating to have such a fine day and not be able to sail, but the cruel fact had to be faced—and dealt with. I gathered together my tools and, with pieces of oak, brass bolts, fiberglass and waterproof glue, went to work on the rudder in the relative comfort of the cabin.

Late in the afternoon I took a sun shot. It indicated we were only three or four miles away from 40° W longitude, but the news cheered me scarcely at all. I wasn't in despair, for I knew I could fix the rudder. I was as confident as ever that we'd reach England safely. But the enforced halt for repairs and the slowness of our progress made me melancholy. I missed Virginia and Robin and Douglas, and I didn't want to be delayed and cause them unnecessary concern.

"*Tinkerbelle* and I will make it all right," I wrote in the log, "but I hate to be so far behind schedule because I think V. and the kids may worry."

By nightfall I had stewed myself into a state of severe depression. For a few frantic moments I even considered swinging southeastward, once the rudder was serviceable again, and making for Flores, in the Azores. But after dinner that evening, as I was writing of the day's events, I spotted the tip of a piece of paper sticking out from between the pages of the spiral-bound notebook that served as my log. I pulled it out. It was a leaf from a little booklet that only Virginia could have put there. It said, in part:

"Charles A. Lindbergh, flying the Atlantic alone, came to the point where he could go no farther. He was exhausted. His hands were so tired they refused to obey his mind. Then he said he made this simple prayer: 'God give me strength.' From that moment on he declares that he sensed a third part of himself. It was 'an element of spirit,' which took control of both mind and body, 'guarding them as a wise father guards his children'."

Finding this message at that moment of utter dejection was a bit of a miracle, for I desperately needed something or someone to snap me out of it. Despite my having been reared by missionaries, I have never been able to get on intimate terms with God (not that I wouldn't like to), so I cannot attribute its appearance on the scene to divine intervention. Nevertheless, it satisfied a keenly felt psychological hunger. The content of the message was helpful, of itself, but what did most to lift my sagging spirits, I think, was the realization of the loving devotion that led Virginia to slip the message into my log. That gave me strength and elevated my mood. Before long I was back on an even keel.

The ocean was calm the next day (July 12th), so calm we couldn't have moved even if the rudder hadn't been broken. That was O.K. with me, for it meant we weren't missing out on a favorable breeze.

I finished the repairs and all that remained was to wait overnight for the waterproof glue to harden. We'd be able to sail in the morning. I felt like my old self, and that evening I took a sextant shot at the sun that made me feel even better. It showed that while I'd been working on the rudder the Gulf Stream had carried us eastward past the meridian of 40° W longitude. We had completed another giant stride toward our journey's end and had passed the point of no return.

*

15 On Tuesday, July 13th, after nearly two days of drifting to the sea anchor while working on the rudder, we started sailing again and it soon became evident the repair job would hold up. The rudder was now as strong as iron; I expected no further trouble from it.

That day and the next the weather was cloudy. Then came July 15th, a wonderful, sunny day, and my sextant sights revealed we had passed 37° W, the halfway mark. That evening I celebrated the occasion by eating, with delicious hard-sauce topping, the plum pudding I had brought along for that specific purpose. I felt we were getting somewhere at last. It would be a downhill run the rest of the way.

But there was a tinge of sadness in this fact, too, for it meant the voyage was now middle-aged, moving closer and closer to old age and, after that, "death." I didn't think I'd want it to go on forever, yet, whether I did or not, its end, no matter how happy or how longed for, would be accompanied by sharp twinges of pain, an undercurrent of profound regret. For then the voyage—and all it meant to me in happiness—would have moved from anticipation through realization into the past, where events, once lodged, existed only in the limbo of memory and could not (no matter how hard we tried) be relived. I consoled myself with the thought that there would be other challenges to face, other dreams to fulfill, even though none in the future could compare with this one.

When darkness descended on us, a fairly gentle southwest breeze was blowing, so I decided to wing out the small twin jibs for self-steering and let *Tinkerbelle* continue moving eastward, taking care of herself, while I slept. The small jibs didn't perform quite as well as the twin gennies had, since their smaller area meant less force exerted on the tiller and less responsiveness to changing conditions. They allowed the boat to weave from side to side somewhat, but nevertheless kept her headed in a generally eastward direction. I managed to get six hours of sleep. However, the possibility that the wind might increase dangerously while I slept made me so nervous I never again tried the self-steering stunt. I didn't even try it during the day, when I was awake, because the twin jibs were so small they couldn't keep *Tinkerbelle* moving at her best.

Between noon, Saturday, July 17th, and noon the next day, *Tinkerbelle* made her best day's run of the entire voyage: eighty-seven miles. To achieve that mark I had kept her going all night, but it was worth it, for it made the step from 40°W to 30°W the briefest of the whole countdown: only nine days. In comparison, the first step, from 71° W to 60° W, had taken sixteen days; the second step, to 50°W, had taken twelve days, and the third step, to 40° W, had taken thirteen days. (The next two ten-degree steps in the countdown were to take, in succession, eleven days and twelve days; and the last step, a five-degree hop, was to take five days.) By July 18th, too, we had moved along more than four degrees in the ten-degree countup from 40° N to 50° N.

Three days later, in the early afternoon of Wednesday, July 21st, we were becalmed for several hours. I lowered the sails, secured the boom in the boom crutch and sat in the cockpit, leaning back against the aft end of the cabin, resting and thinking. The ocean in a dead calm must be the quietest place on earth. Not a sound was to be heard except that of my own breathing. There were no birds to be seen or heard, and no chuckling of ripples against the lapstrakes of the hull, for there were no ripples. The ocean was flat and round like a gigantic blue coin, and it was as silent as a motionless penny. The scene was eerie and yet so peaceful, so soothing, so soul-refreshing. I reveled in it. It seemed almost as though I had achieved the blessings of the Buddhist's nirvana, the Moslem's paradise and the Christian's heaven without having gone through the qualifying preliminary travail. I was fortunate indeed.

At about five o'clock a westerly breeze started to blow, and the sea's surface stirred as if it were a counterpane on the bed of a sleeping giant. I didn't feel the breeze right away; I heard it first, or rather, I heard the breaking wavelets it caused. When the little breakers approached to within half a mile (or maybe it was closer than that), they sounded—amid that vast stillness —like lions roaring. My ears made them seem frightening, but my eyes told me they weren't worth worrying about.

Soon the breeze reached us and with it the midget breakers. The usual sounds of the sea resumed; the chuckling, gurgling, sloshing, hissing, bubbling that had grown so familiar in the weeks since we had slipped out of Vineyard Sound. I hoisted the sails and we got under way again.

Observed from the high deck of a liner, the sea had seemed rather drab and monotonous; nothing but unbroken stretches of water and sky divided by the horizon. But on board *Tinkerbelle,* down close to the water, the sea became immensely more interesting; first, because of the seemingly infinite variety of wind, wave and sky combinations, and, second, because down low it was easy to see things in and on the water that could seldom be seen by anyone from a fast-moving ship.

The waves, of course, were formed by the wind; and their size depended on the force of the wind, the length of time it had been blowing in a given direction and the distance it had traveled over the sea during that time. A moderate westerly wind blowing for, say, four hours over a hundred miles of ocean might start six-foot waves marching eastward. This, for *Tinkerbelle,* meant a relatively uncomplicated run before the wind; enlivened, perhaps, by some surfboarding down the forward slopes of the waves. Good enough. But now imagine the wind backing forty-five degrees into the southwest and starting other waves marching northeastward. This sort of change occurred frequently and kept things from getting dull, since the two different sets of waves periodically got into step, reinforcing one another and producing waves considerably bigger than those that came before or after. That was why, so often, bigger-than-average waves came in definite cycles, with smaller waves in between. Then, gradually, as the original waves lost their energy and subsided into swells, the newer waves grew and, if the wind continued blowing from the same direction long enough, erased all traces of the earlier waves.

But this was just the beginning of the possible variations. Sometimes eastward-moving waves met platoons of northward-moving cross-waves or even northwestward-moving waves. Sometimes a gentle northwesterly breeze pushed *Tinkerbelle* northeastward while the waves, marching out of the southeast, moved directly against the breeze. Sometimes the swells moved in one direction, the waves in another and the wind in still another. And once, unforgettably, *Tinkerbelle* was becalmed in the midst of rows of steep swells moving south while other equally steep swells moved north. As these opposing ranks of swells met, they shot up into sharp peaks that made our presence among them interesting, to say the least.

On another occasion *Tinkerbelle* was ghosting along before a very light westerly breeze, against big swells coming toward her from the east. Each swell was so big that it pushed a great mass of air in front of it, creating a breeze in opposition to the light westerly. And that produced a maddening afternoon of sailing for me. *Tinkerbelle*'s mains'l was swung out to starboard to catch the light westerly, but when a swell came along the breeze it made backwinded the sail and sent the boom flying toward my head. As the swell moved astern, the gentle westerly took hold of the mains'l and pushed the boom back out to starboard. And then, of course, along came another swell with another counter-breeze to shoot the boom at my head again. It went on like that for four or five hours, during which

I got a number of nasty knocks on the noggin.

There was no need to worry about *Tinkerbelle*'s relationship to the waves as long as there were no breaking crests. As the waves grew, they broke, first, in a gentle, sliding manner which allowed the foam of the crests to remain on the rear slopes of the waves; but then, as they grew bigger still, they broke with a definite curling forward which made the crests fall and thunder down the front surfaces of the waves. When the waves began to break in this forward-curling way, *Tinkerbelle* had to watch her step. And when the breakers got too big to sail among safely— usually when the wind was blowing at thirty-five knots or more —she had to be tethered to her bucket drogue to keep her headed straight toward them, so as to take them bow on.

The waves we encountered always seemed to be perfectly straightforward creations of the wind. Even the complicated patterns of waves, cross-waves and counter-cross-waves were born of the wind, and the steps in their genesis usually could be deduced from observation of their behavior. We never, that I know of, encountered "freak" or tidal waves one hears about occasionally, which are caused by undersea earthquakes or similar disturbances; but we did meet, fairly frequently, a peculiar type of wave that differed markedly from its fellows in deportment. We'd be moving along at a brisk pace, minding our own business (I, paying no attention whatever to the waves which were approaching, say, from the starboard quarter), when all of a sudden a chunk of frothing wave top the size of four basketballs would break off from a whitecap and come charging diagonally across the established path of the waves and give *Tinkerbelle* an impudent swat on her behind as though chastising her for some sort of misconduct. Or maybe they were love pats; I never did really decide which. Anyway, *Tinkerbelle* got a lot of them.

Besides the variations produced by winds and waves, the expressions of the sea's face were constantly being altered by changes in the sky. When the sky was an inverted bowl of translucent blue, unblemished by a single cloud, the sea, too, was a brilliant blue; deep, rich, so saturated with azure pigmentation it seemed as though *Tinkerbelle*'s white hull would be stained. At the other extreme, when the sky was blotted out by gray clouds, the sea also was gray, gloomy, foreboding. There were numberless variations between these extremes, of course, and the clouds themselves—cumulus, stratus, cumulo-nimbus, alto-cumulus and cirrus, varying in shape, extent and degrees of darkness—added a whole new set of possible combinations to keep the sea environment from becoming dull. No two days were exactly the same.

Sometimes cumulus clouds lay in banks right on the surface of the ocean, making it look as if they marked a nearby shoreline. At other times they spaced themselves in tiny clumps that made the sky look as if it were polka-dotted wth cotton balls. And at still other times they grouped themselves in huge, miles-long canopies that took hours to pass by. I remember one of these gigantic canopies that passed overhead. *Tinkerbelle* and I had been sailing under it all day and then, shortly before sunset, I looked back and there was its end a few miles astern, with clear, blue sky beyond. It was delightful to watch the sharp, trailing edge of that cloud blanket pass over us and move on ahead, leaving us under a cobalt dome with golden sunlight cavorting on a pathway to the west. It was like coming out of a cave into the daylight.

Objects I saw in and on the sea also helped to keep the trip from becoming tedious. I saw whale, dolphin, dorado, sharks, tuna, storm petrels, shearwaters, terns, flying fish, gulfweed and a sea worm, which I have already mentioned. In addition, I saw odd, translucent things drifting through the water, just below the surface, some of them rectangular, like shoe boxes, but about half that size. Each one of these had a bright orange patch on one side that, I guessed, could luminesce. And I saw countless Portuguese men-of-war.

I began seeing the Portuguese men-of-war as soon as we got

into the Gulf Stream and kept on seeing them almost all the way across the ocean, although the nearer we got to England the smaller and scarcer they became. They were most numerous in the area between 40° W and 20° W. While in this part of the ocean, I amused myself one afternoon by counting those I met; I spotted thirty in half an hour. Since I saw one a minute in the narrow strip of sea through which we were traveling, the total number must have been fantastically large, probably well into the millions.

The Portuguese man-of-war is a strange-looking creature (some experts say it is three creatures) with a transparent, elongated balloon float, surmounted by a sail-like crest, showing above water; and with long, evil-looking tentacles dangling below it, sometimes to a depth of three or more feet. The floats of a few I saw were almost colorless, but most of them were pale blue, and some of these blue ones had violet-tinted sails. They were pretty but, as I found out, painful.

I awoke one morning to find a Portuguese man-of-war entangled in a jib sheet that had been trailing in the water through the night. When I pulled the sheet on board, some of the man-of-war's tentacles clung to it, without my knowledge, and I touched them. They caused a pain very much like a bee sting and soon red welts appeared on my fingers. I had read that anyone heavily stung by a man-of-war would be lucky to survive and, after having suffered one small sting, I could well believe it. I henceforth made sure trailing sheets were free of tentacles before I handled them.

Once we were moving slowly before a gentle breeze and I noticed that many of the Portuguese men-of-war we passed had small fish, five or six inches long, hovering under them and that some of these fish left the men-of-war and took up new positions under *Tinkerbelle*. Before the day was out, my craft had a troop of more than a dozen fish accompanying her. I suppose they felt *Tinkerbelle*'s red bottom would scare off bigger fish that might otherwise be tempted to gobble them up. I was glad

to let *Tinkerbelle* watch over them as long as the breeze was
gentle and we couldn't go any faster, but the next day the wind
picked up and we had to leave the little fish behind. I imagine
they found other men-of-war with which to hobnob.

Besides living things, there were interesting inanimate objects to see in mid-ocean. An empty fifty-gallon oil drum sped

by one day before a strong southeasterly wind. I also saw drifting mooring buoys, gasoline cans, glass fish-net floats, and
planks, beams and tree trunks of varying sizes, all heavily en-
crusted with gooseneck barnacles. I came across pieces of orange-
red fish net, too, the same sort of net I saw later on trawlers in
England. But the most surprising non-living thing I bumped
into was an electric light bulb. It was bobbing through the
waves, buoyant as you please, untroubled by the breakers and
seemingly capable of continuing indefinitely. Only the Lord
knew how long it had been afloat and how many storms it had
survived, but I'll wager it had been through more than one.

Well, I thought, that ought to prove something about the

strength and safety of small boats too.

While I was still becalmed on July 21st, I saw three ships, two of them at the same time. It was the first time I'd had more than one ship in sight since June 6th when I had seen the Russian trawlers. "Made the spot seem like Times Square," I wrote in the log.

One of the ships came up over the eastern horizon headed straight for us, moving at full speed on an unwavering course. I was beginning to think it didn't see us and that I had better dive into the water and swim for my life when it finally swerved off to port and passed with no more than twenty-five yards' clearance. It had a hammer and sickle emblem on its funnel, so it was Russian; and on the stern was its name, *Neptun*. There wasn't a single person to be seen on deck, but just after it passed, someone, possibly the captain, came out on the port wing of the bridge and studied us through binoculars. I'd have given more than a penny for his thoughts. Then the ship disappeared over the western horizon as speedily as it had approached from the east.

That night I was sailing along happily when suddenly I saw a phosphorescent streak in the water headed directly toward *Tinkerbelle*. Startled out of my wits, I thought, Lummy! We're being torpedoed! But almost at once, of course, I realized that was ridiculous. Nevertheless, I half shut my eyes and held my breath, bracing myself for the impact of whatever it was against the boat. But none came. A few seconds later I heard a peculiar popping and the sound of air being expelled. That gave the show away. The torpedo was a dolphin.

Several other times, later on, I saw these luminous streaks in the water and they never failed to excite me. Dolphin visited us frequently, both day and night, but they never stayed with us for long. I think their longest visit lasted all of thirty seconds. *Tinkerbelle* was just too slow to be interesting to dolphin, so they'd swim circles around her for a few seconds and then off they'd race about their own high-speed affairs.

The wind was so strong all day Thursday, July 22nd, that I kept the boat hitched to the sea anchor while I remained snug inside the cabin. I relaxed, did a few maintenance jobs and listened to the radio. In addition to the B.B.C. and the other stations I've already mentioned, I began to get a station in

Lisbon, Portugal, regularly, and a delightful place in Holland that called itself "The Happy Station."

On Friday (July 23rd) the wind was still blowing hard and I was sure many of the waves were twenty-footers, equal to the largest waves we had met, but we started sailing anyway because I was determined to reach Falmouth, if I possibly could, by August 15th. It was wet going; I was soaked from the waist down, in spite of the anti-exposure suit I wore, but nothing untoward happened. There were no knockdowns or other crises.

The weather was cloudy, with scattered rain squalls to contend with, but nothing more serious than that. I remember I felt extremely pleased with *Tinkerbelle* and with myself when we managed to maneuver between two squalls, thus avoiding the rain they were dropping onto the sea.

The twenty-fourth was a beautiful, sunny day, with fluffy white clouds in the sky and a breeze of just the right strength.

Then on the twenty-fifth the weather about-faced, as it did so often during the voyage. Here's what I put into the log:

"Overslept just a bit this morning. Didn't hear the alarm. It's now 6 A.M. *Tinkerbelle* time.

"The wind and waves seem O.K. for sailing, but it's a dismal, cloudy day. (Barometer's up, though.) The weather sure has pulled a switch."

Just before sunset the sky cleared and that evening I logged this:

"Soon after it cleared, the wind died out for a bit, then shifted to the west for about an hour, still very light. Then it shifted to southwest, closer to south than west, and picked up in force. The sky stayed clear most of the night and it was very pleasant sailing. The wind was just right, strong enough to move us at a good rate, but not so strong as to make me nervous. I spent almost all night listening to the B.B.C. I heard a fine discussion on acting by Noel Coward, a moving essay (with sound effects) on the seasons in Britain, news, music and commentaries."

During the first half of the voyage I hadn't used the radio for much besides getting the time signals since I didn't want to exhaust the batteries too swiftly (although I carried three sets of spare batteries). But in the second half of the trip, when I found the batteries were holding up extremely well, I spent many hours listening. The sound of voices helped to soften the aches of loneliness that occasionally wrenched my inner being.

July 26th (Monday) was a cloudy, gloomy day and at about 2 P.M. the wind grew so strong we had to heave to. The next day started out even worse, for in addition to being cloudy the wind had shifted to northeast, exactly the direction in which I wanted to go. We'd have to beat against it. I wrote:

"The day began cold, cloudy and miserable. I'm afraid I was quite depressed. It got very foggy later on.

"I forced myself to pull in the sea anchor and get going.

"And then, about 9 or 10 A.M. (T.T.), a remarkable thing

happened. All the fog and clouds disappeared. And *Tinkerbelle* and I had a day of restful, easy sailing under a blue sky and on a blue ocean.

"Took the opportunity to dry clothes and towels. My spirits rose again to normal and above."

This type of mood change occurred about half a dozen times during the journey. Cloudy and adverse weather, or other setbacks, would get me into a state of melancholy and then, just as my spirits hit bottom, along would come a magnificent, sunny day of fine sailing that made me the happiest, luckiest man alive.

July 28th (Wednesday) was memorable for three events. I described the first of these in the log like this:

"This has been quite a day. Started sailing with just the jib because the following waves were pretty big and the wind quite strong. But I didn't get much speed with just the jib, so I decided to add the reefed mains'l. That was a mistake, under the conditions. We started surfing down the forward slopes of the bigger waves and then, while doing this, we broached and I got knocked overboard for the sixth time.

"That wasn't so bad. I climbed back on board very quickly. But when I went over I was holding the tiller and the 'axle' part of the rudder fitting was badly bent. [I held fast to the tiller because I wasn't wearing a lifeline and didn't want to risk being separated from *Tinkerbelle*.] Luckily, though, I had brought along a spare 'axle' and I put it into place without the loss of much time."

The second memorable incident occurred immediately after the rudder had been repaired, before we got under way again. I'm embarrassed to admit it, but in the interests of making this an absolutely true account of *Tinkerbelle*'s voyage I'd better do so. The painful fact is that while I was moving about the deck, preparing to resume sailing, I lost my balance and simply fell overboard with a great splash. I came to the surface, furious at myself for being so clumsy, but by then, of course, it was too late.

The third big event of the day was recorded thus in the log:

"I was breezing along between 23° W and 22° W in the late afternoon and happened to look back and there was a big freighter hot on my heels. It was the S.S. *Bischofstor* of Bremen.

"I waved as it passed and got a lot of waves back. Someone inquired if I was all right and I assured him I was."

The ship didn't stop, as I was in no need of assistance, and soon was out of sight. I was thankful that it hadn't passed by any earlier, for it might then have witnessed my ignominious fall into the sea. My clothes were still sopping when it went by. An hour or so later, when I stopped for dinner and the evening sun shot, I got into relatively dry clothes.

Some weeks after the voyage was completed, I got the *Bischofstor*'s side of the story of our meeting in a letter from Lothar Steinhoff, third mate of the 8,487-ton vessel. He wrote:

"We had been at sea for 11 days, coming from Tampa, Florida, and bound for Rotterdam with 11,000 tons of phosphate. For the crew and passengers of the ship the 28th of July, 1965, will ever be unforgettable. The sky was overcast and poor visibility made navigation very difficult. According to our logbook, the sea was smooth; we noted veering westerly winds of Force 2. A sharp lookout was necessary because of the misty weather.

"At about 1800 GMT [Greenwich mean time] the visibility became better. At 1830 GMT a very small object was sighted on our portside. It looked like a buoy. Our true course was 75° and the estimated position 47° 14' N, 22° 37' W.

"Capt. [Wilhelm] Beck altered course to approach as near as possible. Some minutes later at about 1840 GMT we were surprised to make out a small red sail, which we thought must belong to a lifeboat; so we got ready to save shipwrecked persons. But then we noticed it wasn't a lifeboat, but a very small sailboat, with what was probably a one-man crew. It was certainly a memorable occasion for us.

"Capt. Beck asked the lonely man if he needed help. With

gestures he indicated to us that all was well. So we continued our voyage, and at 1913 GMT we notified Portishead Radio [in England] of the sighting."

Tinkerbelle was about seven hundred and fifty miles off Land's End, the westernmost tip of England, when she met the *Bischofstor*. Two-thirds of her voyage was behind her. Before much longer it would be over.

The very next day, July 29th, we met another ship. This is how its master, Captain Olav Viken, described the meeting in a letter to me:

"Our meeting was at 47° 30' N, 22° 00' W.

"When I saw your boat I thought it must be a lifeboat, so we changed our course about 90° to see if assistance was needed. When we found out that you needed no help I wired Rogaland Radio about our meeting and it said it would ask other ships in the area to keep an eye open for you. That was our duty.

"We were on a voyage from Liverpool to Hamilton, Bermuda, and Nassau, in the Great Bahamas, with a general cargo."

Captain Viken's ship was the 9,350-ton M.S. *Vardal* of Haugesund, Norway. It passed *Tinkerbelle* to starboard, going southwest. I thought it had disappeared over the horizon, but a little later I looked around and there it was steaming directly toward us. It had finally spotted us and had doubled back on its course to make sure everything was all right. Captain Viken certainly lived up to the very best traditions of the sea in going to all that trouble to make sure I was O.K. I appreciated what he did, and what Captain Beck of the *Bischofstor* did, more than I can say, for it meant loss of valuable time for both of them.

Two days later I wrote in the log:

"Seems like every time my morale sags sharply and I begin to feel I've 'had it' a good day comes along to put me on my feet again. Today [Saturday, July 31st] was such a day."

We had a marvelous sail and, to make this last day of our second month at sea even better, we passed to the east of the meridian of 20° W, completing another stride in the countdown to England. Falmouth was only fifteen degrees away.

I had hoped to continue sailing all that night, but at about 1 A.M., Sunday, August 1st, a thunderstorm hit us. I streamed the drogue and, buttoning *Tinkerbelle* up tight, got into the cabin out of the blustery, wet weather. All that day and through the night we remained parked to the drogue. It was comfortable enough inside, away from the wind and rain, but it was nerve-racking to have to stay put when I wanted so much to be moving and end our long voyage. And the whitecaps that slapped the boat every now and then didn't add to my peace of mind.

To help pass the time I decided to launch a bottle with a note inside, just for the fun of seeing if anyone found it. I wrote this message:

"To the finder: This bottle is being released in the Atlantic Ocean at about 48° 30′ N, 19° 10′ W on Aug. 1, 1965.

"If you will send this message with your name and address —with information on where you found the bottle and when— to Robert Manry, 31003 Royalview Drive, Willowick, Ohio, U.S.A.—he will send you $5 to compensate you for the trouble. Thank you."

I put the message in an empty plastic bottle that had contained part of my supply of drinking water, screwed on the cap and tossed it into the ocean. It floated so high in the water that the northwest wind got a good grip on it and blew it rapidly into the southeast. It was soon out of sight.

Two months later, after completing the voyage, I was back at my home in Willowick and had forgotten all about the message and bottle, when a letter came from Francisco Maria Baleizao, a resident of a suburban town near Lisbon, Portugal. The letter, in difficult English, said:

"Dear Sir: I find your message on 25th September at three o'clock P.M. in Praia Grande Beach, Sintra, Portugal. I wait, then you send me $5 to compensate. Thank you."

My message, tattered now, apparently from the beating it had received as the bottle in which it traveled rolled over and over on its way to Portugal, was enclosed with Mr. Baleizao's letter. I was surprised and delighted to receive both. The five dollars I had promised and a ten-dollar bonus were on their way to him in short order, and in a subsequent letter, written in Portuguese, he told me a little about himself.

"I was born in a picturesque village of Baixo Alentejo called Moura, on March 27, 1925," he wrote. "I resided there until the age of twenty, but because of the poverty of the area I moved into the surroundings of Lisbon, where I have been for the last twenty years. I am a mason by profession. I am married and my wife's name is Gracinda Pechoso Baleizao. I like all sports, but like bicycle racing the best. However, I practice none of them. My parents lived in the Hawaiian Islands close to seven years."

I was pleased that my message was found, but especially pleased that it was found by a man who apparently could use the token reward I offered. I was happy, too, that it was found by a Portuguese because some of the world's greatest seamen have come from Portugal: Prince Henry the Navigator, the stern bachelor who, although he never sailed himself, founded Europe's first school of navigation and sponsored numerous voyages of discovery; Bartholomew Díaz, discoverer of the Cape of Good Hope; Vasco da Gama, who, following on Díaz's heels, reached the riches of India, and, naturally, Ferdinand Magellan, whose fleet was the first to circle the globe.

In the evening on Friday, August 6th, six days after releasing the bottled note, I wrote in the log:

"This was a nice sailing day—sunny, with fluffy clouds. I can hardly believe I'm getting all this good weather. It's quite a switch. Hope it continues.

"We're about halfway to 14° W (it's now 6 P.M. T.T.). I've just finished a huge supper of curried turkey and peas. I'll go on sailing until it starts getting dark. Then I'll size things up and decide whether to stop for sleep or go on all night. This good weather should be used to the fullest.

"I hadn't seen a ship for days and, of course, thought I was

miles from the shipping lanes, which I was. But about 5 P.M.
I began hearing a sound that I at first thought was a plane.
Then I looked around and saw it was a ship, almost on top of
me. It was Italian, the *Sirio* of Palermo.

"It went by awfully close and fast. I was afraid the bow and
stern waves might tip us over, but we rode them all right. The
crew at the rail gave us a hearty cheer and, as usual, snapped
our picture.

"I continued all night. Saw about five more ships. They're
getting thick."

Later I heard from Livio de Manzolini, master of the M.S.
Sirio, which was bound for London from Vera Cruz, Mexico.
He wrote, in part:

"At 1630 hours [on August 6th] we met your boat in latitude
49° 12′ N and longitude 14° 16′ W.

"You didn't notice our vessel approaching, but when we got
close you turned around and saw us. And when we drew abreast
of you, you waved to us as if an encounter such as ours was perfectly normal.

"When I saw that you didn't need help, I continued my
course supposing that you were one of those men who are com-
pelled to cross the Atlantic Ocean alone. . . . I telegraphed the
English Coast Guard your position."

My thanks to Captain Manzolini for reporting my position
and for his kind concern.

On Sunday, August 8th, two days after our meeting with the
Sirio, we met another ship, the 556-foot, 18,000-ton tanker *Belgulf Glory* of Antwerp, probably the largest ship we spoke on
the whole voyage. And the meeting was one of the most memorable.

The big ship, skippered by Captain Emile J. A. Sart, was on
its way from Port Arthur, Texas, to London, when it overtook
Tinkerbelle at 1230 GMT at 49° 30′ N and 12° 45′ W, about
three hundred miles west of the English coast. Captain Sart, an
extremely friendly man with a wonderfully jovial face, stopped

his vessel and hailed me through an electronic megaphone.

"Are you American?" he asked.

"Yes."

"What is your name?"

"My name is Robert Manry, M-A-N-R-Y. I've come from Massachusetts."

"Where are you bound?"

"Falmouth, England."

The captain said he had heard on a B.B.C. news program the day before that planes of the Royal Air Force had been searching for me, but I couldn't believe that was true because, according to the voyage plan I had filed with both the American and the English Coast Guards, I wouldn't be considered over-due until after August 15th. So I'm sorry to say I disagreed with the good captain.

"I don't think they're looking for me," I said. "They may be looking for another man who left Florida in a twelve-foot boat a week before I left Massachusetts. He was headed for Ireland."

I was referring to Captain William Verity, master of the diminutive *Nonoalca* (a Mayan word meaning "mute ones" or "those who don't speak our tongue"), who had hoped his voyage would help to prove that Irish monks came to North and South America in the fifth and sixth centuries. I found out later that Captain Verity had been plagued by bad luck and had had to abandon his projected cruise, at least for the time being.

"Do you need any provisions?" Captain Sart called across the ten yards of water between us.

"No, I really don't need anything," I shouted back. But I could see he already had the food there on deck and might be disappointed if I refused to take it, so I added, "But I sure could use some fresh fruit."

The food was sealed in plastic bags and these were then secured in a larger canvas bag, which, in turn, was tied into a life jacket to keep it afloat. One end of a heaving line was thrown to me and the other end was tied to the food parcel, which was then lowered into the ocean. I soon had it aboard and was inspecting its contents. Captain Sart had given me a banquet, the entrée of which was still hot from the oven: a whole roast chicken and potato croquettes (Poulet Rôti and Pommes Croquettes from the ship's officers' Sunday menu). The bag also contained a huge loaf of freshly baked bread, apples, plums, lemons, a pound of Dutch butter, a huge slab of chocolate with nuts in it, two cans of a soft drink and two bottles of beer.

I had to eat the chicken and the potato right away because there was no refrigeration on *Tinkerbelle.* And what a meal it was! I was more stuffed than the turkey at our family's last Thanksgiving dinner. It was extremely generous of the captain to give me all that food, I appreciated it immensely, but I couldn't help worrying that maybe one of the *Belgulf Glory*'s officers didn't get enough to eat at dinner that day because of the captain's kindness to me. I sincerely hope not.

Even with its engines stopped, the tanker moved too fast for *Tinkerbelle* and soon was beyond shouting range. So it circled around and moved by again, and, after that, two more times; and each time it passed we got in a little more conversation. Captain Sart was extremely considerate.

"Is everything all right?" he asked again as his ship passed by the fourth time. "Do you need anything more?"

"No, I'm fine. Thank you very much," I said. "Thanks for the marvelous banquet."

The *Belgulf Glory,* chivalrous ship that it was, dipped its flag in salute as it returned to its eastward course, and then it gave *Tinkerbelle* and me a salute of three blasts on its deep steam whistle. I had no flag flying with which to return the dip, unfortunately, but I was able to return the big ship's whistle blasts with my small gas-operated foghorn. I let loose three gas screams that made the hair on my head vibrate but which, to those on the *Belgulf Glory,* must have sounded like the peeps of a baby chicken.

The hefty tanker churned off toward the English Channel and I followed after it as fast as *Tinkerbelle* would go. We took the course Captain Sart had given to reach Bishop Rock: 85°. I had one hand firmly on the tiller and the other on the chicken dinner. It was an unforgettable experience.

The captain later sent me a Christmas card and his best wishes. He said he was spending a brief holiday leave with his wife and two children at their home in Belgium; it was only the

fourth Christmas he had been able to enjoy with them in the last thirty years.

Events began to move swiftly after the meeting with Captain Sart and the *Belgulf Glory*. About 5 P.M. (T.T.) that same day, an R.A.F. Shackleton bomber found us (aided, no doubt, by a position report radioed by the *Belgulf Glory* to Lloyd's of London). It was flying quite low, under a layer of dark clouds, when the pilot spotted *Tinkerbelle*'s red sail and headed straight for us. It roared by overhead, circled and then roared by twice more, and each time I waved. On the next pass it came toward us very low, so low I thought it might clip off the tip of *Tinkerbelle*'s mast; but it didn't, luckily. Instead, it dropped two bright orange cylindrical canisters tied together with a buoyant line.

I sailed over and pulled the canisters aboard. They contained a wonderful supply of fruit, apples and bananas, and a very friendly message from Wing Commander R. A. Carson of the 42nd Squadron of the R.A.F., based at St. Mawgan, Cornwall, not far from Falmouth, our destination. The message said:

"Welcome to British waters! You are 'big news' and we shall be bringing gentlemen of the press to see you tomorrow, 9th Aug.—at approx. noon. Your present position is: 4845N 1220W. Good luck."

It was great to be welcomed so warmly to British waters by the R.A.F. Commander Carson's greeting was a wonderfully gracious gesture; but the thought of being "big news" and meeting gentlemen of the press gave me more than a moment of trepidation. As I tried to cope with that, the big four-engine plane zoomed toward us again and I gave it the hands-clasped-over-the-head salute as it swept by so close I could make out every detail of its construction. (Those R.A.F. chaps are great fliers.)

That night after dinner, as I sat in *Tinkerbelle*'s cabin listening to a Voice of America news broadcast in French, the plot thickened dramatically. I was taken aback when I heard the announcer say something about Robert Manry (only he pronounced it "Row-bear Maw-ree," of course), *navigateur solitaire,* and then some stuff that went too fast for me, with my high-school French, to comprehend. But the newscast was repeated in English a few minutes later, and that *really* bowled me over. It told practically all there was to tell about me and *Tinkerbelle* and our voyage. I couldn't imagine where the Voice of America had got all that information, or why it was interested in the first place. Somebody on shore must be doing a lot of talking, I decided, and the circumstantial evidence seemed to point to Virginia. But I knew she wouldn't be talking unless she was being asked questions; so it seemed probable that the

V.O.A. had heard of the voyage and had questioned Virginia about it. However the V.O.A. wouldn't have heard about it unless the *Plain Dealer* had run a story on it that the Associated Press had picked up and put on its wires. The *P.D.* was apparently more interested in the voyage than I had thought it was. And the reports from the V.O.A. and the R.A.F. seemed to indicate that other papers, besides the *P.D.*, were interested.

I hove to about midnight for some sleep and got up early the next morning, ate a quick breakfast and got moving again. The wind was just a few degrees south of due east, which made it impossible to steer directly toward Bishop Rock, on a course of 85°. The best we could do was about 57°, which meant we were moving northward of the direct course. So, at about 11 A.M. (T.T.), I went over onto the port tack to regain our southing.

Not long afterward I saw a trawler approaching from the south on a course that would bring us within hailing distance and I wondered what nationality it was and whether it would stop to exchange a few words. When it got closer, it became apparent that it was steering to meet us rather than just to pass by. It turned out to be English, the *Roseland* of Penzance, the port west of Falmouth and not far from Land's End, and standing at the rail was a man in a handsome turtle-neck sweater whose face looked vaguely familiar. And behind him stood another man who was operating what I took to be a motion-picture camera.

Gradually it dawned on me where I'd seen the face of the man in the sweater before; it was on the screen of our television receiver at home. Now I knew it; he was a TV newsman. I had heard his broadcasts hundreds of times, but at the moment I couldn't remember his name. And I couldn't imagine what he was doing there; surely he hadn't traveled all the way from Cleveland to see *me*. Undoubtedly he was there for some other reason and happened to bump into me by chance. But, incredibly, he said he really was looking for me and no one else.

That made our meeting what might be termed "an occasion."

All my instincts told me that now was the time for me to say something genuinely profound, something that would ricochet endlessly down the corridors of history, something with the adroitness, depth and impact of, say, "Dr. Livingstone, I presume." But all I could think of was, "Haven't I seen you somewhere before?"

The man finally had to tell me his name, but he took my mental lapse with good grace. He was Bill Jorgensen of Cleveland's Scripps-Howard Station WEWS, and the cameraman with him was Walter Glendenning. They had been cruising about on the *Roseland* for about thirty-five hours, looking for me. The spot where we met was roughly two hundred and seventy miles from Land's End.

As soon as I realized whom I was talking with, a question of newspaper ethics arose in my mind. Could I in good conscience report details of my trip to these men from WEWS, a competitor of my employer, the *Plain Dealer?* Well, I reasoned, the WEWS men apparently are very interested in the voyage, so interested they have gone to enormous lengths and expense to find me, so I think I should tell them whatever they want to know. I felt this way especially when I recalled that the *Plain Dealer* and national magazines I had queried before my departure (all of them at that time believing, because of what I had told them, that I was going on the voyage with another man in a 25-foot boat) had expressed only mild interest in printing stories about the venture. I'll have to acknowledge, frankly, that I didn't think *Tinkerbelle*'s smaller size would make much difference in the interest shown by the *P.D.* or other newspapers or the magazines. It's painful for me to have to admit it now, because my experience should have developed a keener insight into what makes news, but I failed to assess properly the news value of my own story. And this failure probably was the greatest miscalculation of the entire expedition. I'm afraid it brands me as somewhat less than perfect as a newsman.

So I spoke freely with Jorgensen; in fact, we talked steadily for three and a half hours while Glendenning took both movies and still pictures. It was good to see a familiar face, at last. That made it seem as though I was actually approaching the end of the voyage. And Captain Victor Watling, skipper of the *Roseland,* and his crew were most kind to me. They gave me some delicious apples and some wonderful, fresh hot coffee, the best I'd had since leaving Massachusetts. The captain also gave me a position report and a tide table that proved invaluable as *Tinkerbelle* and I approached the coast of England.

During our conversation Jorgensen showed me a copy of the Falmouth *Packet* dated August 6th, and right there on the front page was a story that nearly floored me. It said:

"A hero's welcome awaits 47-year-old American Newspaperman Robert Manry when he sails his tiny boat *Tinkerbelle* into Falmouth Harbour, a few days from now, at the end of his epic single-handed Atlantic crossing from Falmouth, Massachusetts.

"For nearly 70 days, since he set sail on June 1, Bob Manry has braved the elements, mastering loneliness and enduring as-yet-untold discomforts, because of the cramped conditions aboard *Tinkerbelle,* to make his dream of an Atlantic crossing come true.

"Yesterday newspaper reporters and cameramen from the United States flew into Falmouth to join those of the British press and international news agencies already in town ready to record the scenes as Manry completes his 3,200-mile crossing at Custom House Quay."

There was more to the story and there were even two pictures: a drawing of me and a photograph of *Tinkerbelle* that could only have been taken from the deck of one of the ships we met along the way. How the Falmouth *Packet* happened to have either or both was more than a little puzzling.

A "hero's welcome!" What on earth was building up there in Falmouth? All I could say to Jorgensen after reading the first three paragraphs of the story was "My goodness! Boy, oh, boy!"

Finally we talked ourselves out and it was time to go our

separate ways. Jorgensen and Glendenning, who had been my guests aboard *Tinkerbelle,* scrambled back onto the *Roseland,* which then headed back toward Penzance. The breeze was very light, so *Tinkerbelle* and I were soon left far behind.

A few minutes before the *Roseland* departed, the R.A.F. returned, as it had said it would, presumably with the "gentlemen of the press." This time there were two Shackletons and a third, twin-engine civilian plane that flew very fast and low, passing over us again and again, while the four-engine bombers circled on a broad radius. After the civilian plane had flown over about eight times, it sped away and one of the Shackletons came in low, just above masthead height. Then it wheeled and came back, this time dropping two brightly colored canisters, like those that had been dropped the day before. The R.A.F. fliers must have been using their fancy bombsight for dropping the canisters because they wound up in the water no more than ten yards away and directly in front of us. *Tinkerbelle* didn't have to change course a single degree to enable me to pick them up. The drop and pickup went like clockwork.

The first canister contained a bunch of English newspapers, no doubt so that I could catch up on the news I had missed while out at sea. I was glad to have them. Then I opened the second canister. It had another huge supply of fruit inside— oranges this time. The way things were going, I'd reach England with more food than I'd had at the start of the voyage. The gifts from the R.A.F., added to what Captain Sart of the *Belgulf Glory* and Captain Watling of the *Roseland* had given me, nearly filled the cabin. It had never been so crammed.

Also in the second canister were three notes. The first one said:

"Your position this time: 50° 12′ N-12° 17′ W—with the compliments and best wishes of No. 42 Squadron, Royal Air Force—Coastal Command—St. Mawgan, Cornwall."

It sure was nice of those R.A.F. fellows to keep track of my position for me; made me feel pretty secure. I knew I wouldn't get into any trouble with them there, shepherding me along.

The second note was a blockbuster. When I read it, the recoil nearly knocked me out of the boat. It said:

"Bob—We're waiting for you in Falmouth with Virginia and your children. Dangerous to sail in at night. This harbor is jammed with traffic. . . .

"You will see our boat somewhere out of Falmouth. Virginia and the children will be aboard with us. . . .

"Keep sailing. Good luck, God bless you, and we'll see you soon."

The note was signed by Bill Ashbolt, George Barmann and Russ Kane, three men from the *Plain Dealer*.

The news that Virginia and the children were in Falmouth was a real bombshell. I was simply overjoyed, almost delirious with happiness. And oh, how I wanted to get into the harbor quickly and meet my family. It had been a long time since we had been together—a long, long time.

It turned out that the third note was from Virginia herself. She wrote:

"Dearest Robert—Just think, in a very few days I'll be seeing you.

"The *Plain Dealer* has sent us all over and we've been here since last Friday.

"We've been living in luxury like royalty, but we surely do wish you were here. You will be soon.

"Lots of love. We'll be in a boat to meet you. Virginia."

This was so much more wonderful than anything I had dared hope for that I was struck numb. It was just too much to comprehend all at once. I had to take it in little doses to keep from becoming dangerously intoxicated with joy. Virginia and Robin and Douglas were in Falmouth. They were actually there now, at this very moment, waiting for me. Soon we'd all be there together, reunited. It was marvelous, terrific, super-colossal.

And how generous it was of the *Plain Dealer* to arrange it.

Thoughts raced through my mind. That guy Jorgensen! He

certainly was a sharp newsman, talking with me for more than three hours and not letting me know that the *P.D.* had three men in Falmouth to cover my arrival or that my family was waiting for me there. Not that I blamed him for keeping mum. In his place I'd have done the same thing because if he'd told me the *P.D.* men and my family were in Falmouth I might not have spilled the whole story of the voyage to him.

He was just being a remarkably enterprising reporter.

William A. Ashbolt, one of the *Plain Dealer* men, was the newspaper's director of news photography; George J. Barmann was a veteran of the paper and one of its ace writers, and Russell W. Kane was an assistant to the publisher and the *P.D.*'s promotion director.

All three men were good friends of mine and I was delighted to know that I would soon be seeing them again—and on the eastern side of the great Western Ocean, as Europeans often called the Atlantic. There was just one little point that worried me: the fact that Russ Kane was the *P.D.*'s promotion director. Did that mean my voyage was going to be turned into a promotional gimmick for the paper? I hoped earnestly, ardently, that was not so; for I had dreamed of a voyage for too long and it meant too much to me to have it spoiled at the end by being transformed into a commercial enterprise. If that's what Russ intended to do, I would oppose him with every resource at my command. But first I'd have to wait and see what he actually *did* intend to do.

Crewmen of *Belgulf Glory* heave line to *Tinkerbelle*. (*Belgulf Glory* photo)

R.A.F. Shackleton flies over on evening of August 8.

Television newsman Bill Jorgensen interviews me at sea on August 9.
(WEWS-TV photo—Walter Glendenning)

Virginia, Robin and Douglas study chart to pinpoint *Tinkerbelle*'s
position.   (*Daily Mirror* photographer—London)

Part of the Falmouth welcoming crowd of 50,000. (*Daily Mirror* photographer)

Falmouth's Mayor Hooper receives *Tinkerbelle*'s ensign.
(*Daily Mirror* photographer)

16

The fact that Virginia and Robin and Douglas had got to Falmouth ahead of me, were there now, made it hard to wait to see them and hear all about everything that had happened on shore since May 31st, when I had telephoned home from the Falmouth on Cape Cod to bid them and my mother goodbye. In some ways it seemed like years since then; in other ways it seemed like hours.

Naturally, I didn't hear about the things that had befallen members of my family until after I got to England and was reunited with them. However, this seems to be the appropriate place to tell that part of the story, so I shall do so. What follows is quoted from Virginia's diary, with my comments set off by brackets.

"*Tuesday, June 1*—Today Robert left. He called last night to say goodbye. Next time I hear his voice he will be calling me from Falmouth, England, to say he made it.

"*Wednesday, June 2*—We got up at 6:30 because Nana [my mother, Mrs. James C. Manry] had to catch an early bus home. It was pouring and the freeway was bumper to bumper. Then the bus was a half hour late.

"David Losh [one of Robin's classmates] brought a harness for Puff [Douglas's iguana] to wear. While he was telling me about it the phone rang. It was George Barmann of the *Plain Dealer*. Seems they had received Robert's letter telling them he was going alone and they wanted to know the details. George was so excited he had to call back a couple of times for more facts.

"Ray Matjasic [a *P.D.* photographer] came and took pictures of us toasting Robert in milk. The kids didn't like all the fuss, but they cooperated. On the 7 o'clock news Bud Dancey told about Robert.

"Thursday, June 3—At 7:30 A.M. the *Press* called and asked to use the story. A girl from the *News-Herald* came to interview me.

"The phone rang and it was Bill Litzkow of the Falmouth marina [from which I had embarked]. He sounded so concerned and wondered if I had heard from Robert. I said no, and he asked if he could tell anyone now. Bless his heart.

"A few more minutes and the phone rang again. It was John Hough of the Falmouth *Enterprise*. He promised to pass on any word he might come by.

"Monday, June 7—Just a week ago tonight I said bon voyage to my own dear Robert. He's never far away from my thoughts. Just sort of counterpoint to everything I say and do.

"Tomorrow is Douglas's birthday. Not much of a celebration without his Dad, but I'll try to make it a nice one.

"Robin said today: 'People speak about Dad as though he were dead.' Won't they be surprised when he turns up 75 days from now, tanned, lean and fit.

"The astronauts are back down. I wish Robert were across. I imagine he has begun to miss his nice bed, lumps and all.

"I can't seem to accomplish much. Lonesome, I guess.

"Friday, June 11—I've been working in the back yard all day. It's 9:30 and I've just crawled out of the tub and now I'm going to rest.

"I discovered some little rosebushes sprouting around under the trees. I've weeded around them and I hope they'll grow. I cut the grass and I felt like The Neighbor in Edna St. Vincent Millay's poem: I left 'the clover standing, And the Queen Anne's lace!'

"Funny the things I remember about Robert and me. While I was mowing around the lovely pink clover I remembered a field near a motel where we had stopped during a vacation trip. We were walking Chris [our German shepherd] and the smell of clover brought the whole scene back so clearly. Made me kind of sad.

"I cleaned his darkroom yesterday, too, and that brought him near.

"*Sunday, June 13*—Mother and John [Virginia's mother and brother] came today [from their home in Pittsburgh, Pa.]. Mother will stay with me for as long as she can take us. Poor Chris got a walk finally. She pestered John so he took her for a nice long one.

"*Sunday, June 20*—At about 10:15 P.M. the *Plain Dealer* called to tell me the Coast Guard received word from a Canadian freighter [the *Exilona*] that Robert was 500 miles out and needed no assistance. It was wonderful to hear he is all right. He's not making much time, 19 days out, but he will eventually, I'm sure. Perhaps I'll even get a letter next time. I'm glad Mother and John were here when the word came; they are so anxious. Mother is not too fond of boats, but she is being very brave about Robert. Of course, she has confidence in him and that means a lot.

"*Monday, June 21*—Fred [the family cat] seems to like her name even though she is a girl. She got out around 11:15 tonight and we had quite a time rounding her up.

"*Wednesday, June 23*—I couldn't sleep last night. All sorts of visions racing through my head. I do wish we had enough in the bank to take us all to England to meet Robert. That's been my dream for years, to visit England and see all I've read about.

"Seems Robert had gone 585 miles instead of 500.

"*Thursday, June 24*—George called to tell me he had been to New York to talk to the captain of the freighter. The captain thinks at his present rate of speed, it will take Robert 91 days to reach England.

"*Friday, June 25*—A quiet day. It's good to have one now and then. Since the excitement began I've had trouble sleeping. I know Robert will be all right, but when the captain said 91 days it conjured up all sorts of pictures. If it took Crapo 51 days, Robert should surely make it in less than 91.

"I hope he won't be too annoyed with all the publicity.

"I'm planning to go to Pittsburgh for the Fourth of July. I hate being away from home for so long. Chris seems sad to me.

"*Thursday, July 1*—If Robert were on schedule he'd be pretty close to eating his plum pudding. I wish he were halfway there.

"Poor Robert, I feel sorry for him, but then he may be enjoying it. [I was, most of the time.]

"Paid all our bills today and we're all set for another month, at least.

"*Sunday, July 4*—People are beginning to ask me if we are going to England to meet Robert. They're even talking about having a parade in his honor! I can't imagine him sitting on the back of a car waving. When I asked Robin if she would like to go to England to meet him she said that if she went the kids would think she was stuck-up. I can't imagine why.

"*Monday, July 5*—We're going to Pittsburgh tomorrow. John is coming for me. Douglas is disappointed. He wanted to take his vacation on a bus; says now it won't seem like one. Wish I could take him to England. Robin says she still wouldn't want to go to England because of the kids' attitude.

"*Wednesday, July 7*—John is trying to figure out a way to get me to Cornwall. He keeps giving me guidebooks to read, the rascal. One of them, *Rambles in Cornwall,* calls Falmouth 'The Happy Harbour.' I surely wish I could be there to meet Robert. Maybe if I wish hard enough I can.

"*Friday, July 9*—We heard from Robert again tonight. Jo Talladino [one of our neighbors] called [to Pittsburgh] to tell me someone had called when she was in our house feeding the menagerie. She said a Mr. Larick from the Isthmian Lines steamship company telephoned to tell me that the *Steel Vendor* had picked up 10 letters from Robert and that he was about

1,000 miles east of Boston. All was well aboard and he expects to make England about August 15.

"Last night before I went to sleep I looked at the full moon and thought that Robert was watching the same moon. I wished on it and said a little prayer that we'd hear from him. My prayer was answered.

"*Monday, July 12*—Today began with a bang. Three letters from Robert for me and two for the children. Then began a struggle between the newspapers as to who should print them. Of course, the *Plain Dealer* is his paper and they deserved first chance.

"The family scolded me for permitting even the *Plain Dealer* to use them. As they said, 'Dad won't like it a bit.' [They were right; I didn't like it.] I hope they don't use the entire letter, parts of it are personal. [They used the whole thing.] I should have typed out a passage and made them settle for that.

"Robin was interviewed for the second time. She sounded as though she had been doing it all her life.

"Everything is fine with Robert except he is lonesome. Says no more solo sails for him. Also, he's losing weight. Good.

"*Tuesday, July 13*—A very exciting thing happened today. A Mr. Davis from the London *Daily Express* called from New York asking for a story about Robert. I told him how we envied his seeing England and we would have to be content just to hear about it, and how he had orders to stop at Liverpool to pick up just any old piece of soil that the Beatles might have stepped on once.

"The battery in the car is dead again and the kids had a grand time pushing the car up and down driveways to Perkeys' [neighbors] for a booster for the battery.

"I'm collecting the rocks the neighbors dig up in their yards when they have swimming pools put in. I want to make a rock garden. Can't seem to do much else about it, though. Lonesome, I guess.

"*Wednesday, July 14*—Victor Davis of the *Daily Express*

called to tell me his paper carried the story. He's sending me a copy.

"I called the insurance company about extending Robert's special policies, in case he does take 90 days. Also the lawyer about my will.

"I blew myself to *Mary Poppins* tonight. I needed to get away from the house and get my mind off things. *Goldfinger* is coming on July 28, at last. Now Douglas can stop worrying about missing it. He is counting the days.

"*Thursday, July 15*—The editor of the Falmouth *Enterprise* tells me Falmouth, Cornwall, is planning a royal reception for Robert.

"*Friday, July 16*—Today started out badly. The washer hose broke and I had a regular geyser of steaming water shooting all over the ceiling and then onto the washing. What a mess. The place was like a Turkish bath. I got a new hose and installed it all by myself. Robert would be so proud of bumbling me.

"About 4:30 Ray Matjasic called to ask if I could hurry down to see a movie of Robert taken by the *Steel Vendor*'s cook. Douglas went with me. Robert was all in the shadow, but he looked so dear and familiar, waving just as we used to see him doing on Lake Erie.

"Next week Phil Porter [the *P.D.*'s executive editor] and Russ Kane want to talk to me about a possible trip to Falmouth!

"Julian Wilson, the Associated Press photographer, said: 'He doesn't belong just to us now, he belongs to the world,' and he formed a huge circle with his arms. Imagine, my husband! I'm glad he belongs to me, too.

"John Metcalfe said: 'You have to watch these quiet ones. They're the ones to stir things up,' or words to that effect.

"It's hard for us to realize how famous he has become. One thing is sure. Life can't ever be the same for Robert. With a taste of adventure, he's bound to want more; and so will we.

"*Monday, July 19*—Today was hectic. I'd rather have them that way, though; I don't miss Robert so much then.

"This morning I took Chris to the veterinarian's for a blood sample. Just as they thought, she has a serious infection and must have her uterus removed.

"Doug and I went to town for some school clothes for him, and some to wear to England. We're going there, it seems.

"This evening we got the television picture tube fixed: $33. Tomorrow I have to have my tooth fixed. More money. Chris's operation will be at least $50, plus the additionals. The bank account sure is disappearing fast.

"Tonight Mother called to tell me she has my birth certificate (needed to get a passport). I also splurged and bought two pairs of shoes, on sale, and a handbag and hose for my visit to the *P.D.* tomorrow.

"*Tuesday, July 20*—Hectic is no word for today. Fantabulous about fills it. I got in early at the *P.D.*, had a cup of tea and a cookie, talked to Mary Hirschfeld, who writes the 'Mary Hears . . .' column, and then met Russ Kane, Phil Porter and Russ Reeves, day managing editor.

"Well, Robert is to receive his pay for the entire six weeks he's been gone, praise be! They are talking about paying our way over, the whole family, and Russ Kane is even talking about returning *Tinkerbelle* by air freight.

"*Wednesday, July 21*—I finally got a little cleaning done. John is going to Miami for a few days and mother will come here while he's gone.

"I can't find Robin's birth certificate. I know we have one, but I can't find it. I sent for both hers and mine.

"We finally got to see *Goldfinger*. At a drive-in. James Bond is quite a fellow. Doug was in ecstasy!

"Wonder what Robert is doing now. Sleeping, I guess. Must not think past the present. It's too thrilling.

"*Thursday, July 22*—More phone calls. Phil Porter called to tell me a check for six weeks' pay will be here soon, with another one each week until Robert comes home. We surely can use it.

"*Friday, July 23*—Big day today. At about 8:15 A.M. Chris had her operation. Dr. [James F.] Robertson performed it. He saved her life once before, too.

"It's 90 degrees. I went with Douglas for a dip in Perkeys' pool.

"Chris came through her operation all right. I'm exhausted. Hope I can sleep.

"*Saturday, July 24*—I brought Chris home today. The doctor said she came through very well. It was 99 degrees today, not a breath of air stirring. I wish I could be out on the sea with Robert. I'll bet it isn't this hot there. A letter from Sheila Beveridge in Newcastle, England, says they think Robert will make it the third week in August. They do a lot of sailing, so they may be right.

"*Monday, July 26*—I couldn't sleep and finally took a pill.

"I'm sort of boiling under a tight lid most of the time. When things get too bad I sit down at the piano and play some hymns and any other simple music I can figure out.

"I have to shop for Robin's birthday present tomorrow.

"*Thursday, July 29*—We heard from Robert again today. A West German ship [the *Bischofstor*] sighted his red sail and reported to Lloyd's of London. He was 1,000 miles from Land's End.

"I got our passports today. Lucky Mother was along because my birth certificate wasn't right. It hadn't been recorded until I was 25. Mother had to sign a statement and swear I was born.

"*Friday, July 30*—Mother and I took Chris to have her stitches removed. She had taken all but one out herself.

"*Saturday, July 31*—The AP in Rotterdam is going to talk to the captain of the West German ship to see whether he was able to talk to Robert.

"Phyllis Verity wrote saying her husband has called off his voyage to Ireland in his 12-foot boat. The weather is too bad. He's had a terrible time.

"*Sunday, August 1*—I dreamed Robert came home last night.

He needed more film. Came in on a train. He looked nice and brown and had lost some weight. I don't remember whether he had a mustache. He told me he was 641 miles from England. [That was pretty close. I was actually about 650 miles from England.] We talked awhile and then he said he had to get back to *Tinkerbelle* and finish sailing to England.

"When I read this morning's paper, I saw that the Coast Guard in Boston says he was probably 635 miles from England when he met the German ship. Maybe Robert and I are still in tune with 2,500 miles of water between us. Or ESP, maybe???

"*Monday, August 2*—Boy, has this been a day! Falmouth, England, cabled that they sighted a boat with two men in it and they think it is Robert's. I said it couldn't be, unless he had picked up a hitchhiker, but everyone is all shook up. That boat is blue, too, and ours is red. Oh, well.

"The RAF will be going out to look for him at dawn and George [Barmann] will call London at noon to hear the results. I can't imagine he has picked up so many miles in such a little while.

"Russ Kane is off on vacation in North Carolina and they can't find him. He didn't expect to be leaving for a couple of weeks.

"My passport hasn't come yet and the wires have been burning between here and Washington. The phone rang almost constantly from 4 until 8 today. Washing, dry cleaning, shopping, house cleaning, all in one big jumble because of Robert's arriving early—if he is!

"*Tuesday, August 3*—Holy cow, what a day! First it looked as though we might not go until Thursday and Mother and John went home. Then I sort of went to pieces for the first time. Just nerves. One minute we're going, then we aren't, and still no passport.

"About 4 P.M. Ted Princiotto [the *Plain Dealer*'s city editor] called to tell me to begin packing. We're leaving at 6:30 A.M. tomorrow. They say Robert is practically there.

"My ear has a callus from talking on the phone so much. I called Beverly Banci [one of Virginia's very good friends] to come over because I was in such a state. She took charge and soon things began to even out a little.

"During all of this the assistant superintendent of the Willowick post office, Mr. [Charles] Rittenhouse, appeared at the door holding my passport. He had had every available person looking for it. I was talking to Ted Princiotto for the umpty-leventh time when it came, and I gladly put Mr. Rittenhouse on the line.

"In the midst of this chaos the dumb iron stopped working, and me with scores of things to iron. Lee Orpse [another neighbor] brought her iron over and while she was here told me that Frank is hard at it planning a reception to greet Robert on his return!

"Jean [Perkey] and Will [Hughes], friends of Robin's, were here to help Robin pack. They will take care of Chris and Fred. David Losh came for Puff yesterday.

"Russ [Kane] has been located and will join our little band in Washington. Surely broke up his family's vacation. I'll be so glad to see Robert.

"Poor Chris. She knows something is up and we can't explain that soon her beloved Daddy will be back. I do wish we could communicate better with animals.

"I really must stop, but to paraphrase Eliza Doolittle, 'I could just write all night,' and I very nearly have. It's 2 o'clock, and I have to be up and going in three hours. Such fun. I do wish Robert were here, but he soon will be. I miss him so at times like this. He is so levelheaded and plans seem to go more smoothly for him. I've never had to plan even a vacation without him and here I am trying to organize our departure for England. At least the *Plain Dealer* is handling all the important decisions and thinking.

"*Wednesday, August 4*—I haven't written a line in here until today. Everything has moved so fast I haven't begun to catch my breath.

"We left Cleveland at 8:55 A.M. Mike Roberts, a reporter from the *Plain Dealer,* came for us and drove us to the airport. Jean and Willie came to see us off at the house, and to clean up the mess we left.

"We flew to Washington and, since we were to be there a few hours, we got a room at the Willard. It was huge, almost as big as our whole house.

"We drove to Baltimore by taxi and then to Philadelphia where we left for London. I don't know why the change in plans, unless it was for secrecy. I'm being guarded like I was an atomic secret.

"It's a strange feeling to leave at dusk and see the sun set and a bit later see the sun rise from the same side. They say it's because of the earth's curvature.

"Russ was still wearing his fishing clothes, those being all he had. He had a plaid shirt, tan levis and suède sheepskin-lined hushpuppies. Hardly the outfit in which to arrive in London, but he had no other and no time to buy any.

"He and Bill Ashbolt spent almost the whole trip trying to fix a secondhand movie camera they had bought in Washington, and whose footage indicator wouldn't work. They never knew how much film there was left. Bill took some pix of us in the plane.

"*Thursday, August 5*—Our first day, the only one, really, in London, was a dilly. The minute we stepped off the plane, on which we had slept not a wink, there were about six photographers all snapping away. Interviews by reporters with those heavenly British accents, and then a drive to the Whitehall Hotel on Bloomsbury Square. Bloomsbury Square sounds so storybookish.

"Eric Piper, a *Daily Mirror* photographer, told Robin all about her beloved Beatles. He had even taken pictures of them!

"London is busy and exciting. I'd love to see it when we have all the time in the world. Everything we saw was through the windows of a taxi or the bus on the way from the airport.

"*Friday, August 6*—We were supposed to meet Russ and

Bill in the lobby at 8 A.M., eat and leave from Paddington Station for Falmouth.

"I slept as one drugged and when Russ knocked on the door I awoke as though I'd been raised from the dead. We tore around washing, dressing, packing. Then we found that with the new clothes we had bought on Oxford Street there wasn't enough room in our suitcase. Russ waved his magic wand and there were cardboard cartons for us.

"Russ and Bill bought us a huge bag of fruits and candy bars to eat on the train because it was a five-hour ride. After some confusion arising from uncertainty as to which track our train was on, we got in the compartment and slid through Paddington on our way to the Cornish Riviera, pulled by an engine called the Western Trooper.

"We felt as though we were playing parts in an English movie. As Robin said, we hardly dared to speak for fear of breaking the spell.

"When the train pulled into Truro, George [Barmann, who who had flown to England earlier] appeared. Seems he and Vic Roberts, a transplanted Londoner, had come from Falmouth to take us the rest of the way by car.

"I'll always remember our first glimpse of the Greenbank Hotel in Falmouth. We came into a conservatory-like entryway leading off a lovely flower garden in front of the hotel. From it we could look straight through the lobby onto a blue, blue harbor with sailboats anchored peacefully and sea gulls wheeling about, the sun streaming into the glassed-in lounge.

"The manager, Avon Tregenna, has arranged for Robert and me to have a lovely room at the top of the hotel overlooking the harbor. He said it is so quiet Robert will be able to get a good rest.

"Tom Reedy, the AP man from London, an American from Pennsylvania, by the way, told me over our tea: 'This will be another Dunkirk.'

"*Saturday, August 7*—Frank Goldsworthy of the *Daily Ex-*

press, London, has converted his hotel quarters into a chart room. We call him admiral and keep track of Robert on his charts.

"CBS television news and United Press called. The reporters say this is nothing to what it will be when Robert gets here. I do wish he'd come soon. It's so hard to wait now that we are actually here and it'll be more fun to explore Cornwall with him.

"Sunday, August 8—A Belgian ship [the *Belgulf Glory*] saw him today. The best guess now is a week from today, just as he said, on August 15.

"I guess his beard isn't too long. There seems to be some dispute about it. Some captains say he has one and others don't mention it. Just so he has a mustache.

"The crowd seems to be gathering; the dining room is more crowded. After dinner we took a taxi and visited Pendennis Castle where Bill [Ashbolt] took some pix of us hanging onto the battlements. Shades of King Arthur!

"Monday, August 9—Things are moving right along. Today some sailors [and Bill Jorgensen and Walter Glendenning] from Penzance saw Robert. Soon he will be meeting ships every day. Russ had Bill and Eddie Worth [an AP photographer] drop a letter from me to Robert today. [Actually, it was dropped by the R.A.F.]

"A man from the BBC named Robert Forbes came over from Plymouth to interview me. He also drove Robin and me [Douglas was shopping in town] over to Plymouth to be on TV."

*

17
Toward evening on August 9th *Tinkerbelle* and I were alone again on the ocean, the trawler *Roseland,* the R.A.F. Shackletons and the smaller civilian plane (which, I found out later, had brought out Bill Ashbolt and Eddie Worth) having departed to return to their bases. The wind died to a mere whisper, making it difficult to maintain steerageway. We rolled about in the swells for two or three hours before another breeze sprang up, this one from the south, enabling us to roll along right on course. We kept going in fine style until about 3 A.M. when we hove to. I had to have sleep.

The next day (Tuesday, August 10th) I awoke at 7 A.M. (G.M.T.) and we resumed our pace. The noon sight put us at 50° 19′ N. For the last two days we had moved steadily northward toward Ireland, which meant we were in the clutches of another current. According to the *Sailing Directions,* it was probably Rennell's Current, which flows at one to one and a half knots northward across the western approach and entrance to the English Channel. Our bumping into it indicated, at least, that we were getting close to the channel.

We struggled all afternoon and part of the night to get back down below 50° N, but a sextant shot at Polaris during the night put us even farther north, at 50° 25′.

On Wednesday, August 11th, clouds covered the sky, making it impossible to shoot the sun, so I couldn't be sure where we were, exactly. I just had to do the best I could with dead reckoning and hope the sun would come out again before we got into deep trouble.

That night, when I was putting out the sea anchor and taking down the sails, I lost the mains'l halyard up the mast. Fortunately the end of the halyard didn't run through the masthead sheave; the shackle that serves to attach the halyard to the head of the sail was too big to go through it. But how to get it down again, that was the problem. And I had to get it down or I wouldn't be able to raise the sail.

It was too dark then to see what I was doing, so I decided to wait until morning. I had a hard time getting to sleep because of worrying about how to go about retrieving the halyard end. I knew I couldn't climb up the mast since my weight would certainly capsize the boat. I wasn't panicky, for I knew that if worst came to worst I could unfasten the forestay and lower the mast in its tabernacle, which would make it simple to recover the halyard and shackle. But lowering the mast at sea would be a tricky operation and I didn't want to do it unless it was unavoidable. I hoped there was another way.

After some cogitation in the morning (August 12th) I decided the topping lift might be it. This consisted of a light dacron line that ran through a small block at the masthead and had both its ends attached to the end of the boom. With wire and a pair of pliers I improvised a little grappling hook, lashed it to the topping-lift line and ran it aloft.

It took about thirty minutes of flipping the line about to accomplish it, but finally I snagged the shackle with the grappling hook and, much to my relief, was able to pull the halyard end back down, shackle it to the head of the mains'l and then, joy of joys, hoist the sail. We were ready to get cracking again. It was a great pleasure to have escaped so easily from what might have been a rather sloppy situation.

We had to spend part of the morning riding to the sea anchor because the wind blew too hard for us to sail safely, but even so, sometime during the day we crossed the meridian of 10° W, completing the last full stride in the oceanic countdown to Falmouth, England. There were less than five degrees of longitude left to cover. We should reach our harbor haven (and possibly it would seem like heaven, too) in less than a week, maybe in as little as five days. The voyage was advanced in age now; it was old, full of "years." The end, with its mingled joys and sorrows, was near.

It was still quite cloudy. At midday, however, the sun came out long enough for me to get a good latitude shot. It showed we were farther north than ever, at 50° 33' N, and that meant we were within sixty-five miles of the coast of Ireland. Something had to be done or we'd make an unintentional landfall on Cape Clear.

The trouble was that besides the current we had a southeast wind to fight, and that meant tacking. And that, in turn, meant slower progress; and I wasn't in the mood for dawdling. I did everything I could think of to propitiate Aeolus and induce him to shift the breeze around to the south or southwest, but nothing worked. It came down to making a choice between tacking and landing in Ireland. I chose tacking.

I had nothing whatever against Ireland or the Irish; it was just that I had started out to sail to England and my family and newspaper colleagues were waiting for me there. So the only decent course of action was to do my level best to get there. We went over onto the port tack, heading southwestward on a course of 220°. This took us southward against the current all right, but it also took us *away* from England. It was only on the starboard tacks, if the wind held in the southeast, that we'd be able to head *toward* England.

Early in the afternoon, while still on the port tack, I heard a plane to the south; in fact, I continued hearing it for half an hour or more. I thought that probably it was the R.A.F. back, trying to find me, and later I learned the R.A.F. *had* been out looking for me and that its failure to find me had aroused considerable concern on shore. (I hoped Virginia wasn't worried. I had told her that small-boat voyagers were reported lost rather frequently, erroneously, and not to be unduly alarmed if I was so reported.) As I had feared, it was widely reported that

I was lost, but of course I wasn't. It was simply that nobody knew where I was except me.

About the time the sun dipped below the western horizon, the wind moved into the southwest, enabling *Tinkerbelle* to sail southeastward on a broad reach. We were on the home stretch, sprinting for the finish line.

The breeze was so good I decided to keep going all night and sometime after midnight we passed down the aisle between two long rows of trawlers, so brilliantly lighted they gave the ocean a festive look. We seemed to be rolling along the surface of a mammoth liquid birthday cake between two ranks of flickering candles. The experience put me into a happy, partyish frame of mind.

When daylight returned, I suddenly realized it was Friday the thirteenth and I wrote in the log: "I hope this isn't an unlucky day." It wasn't.

All that day and the following night we continued sailing southeastward, battling the Rennell Current, working our way to a lower latitude so that we could pass to the south of the Scilly Isles and into the English Channel. I believed that would be much safer than trying to go to the north of the Scillys because along the northern route lay the dangers of the Seven Stones, a mile-long group of exposed rocks, and Wolf Rock, a lighthouse-topped hazard some eight miles southwest of Land's End.

We continued moving southeastward throughout the next day (Saturday, August 14th) and through about half the night. Shortly before midnight we approached a particularly brightly lit trawler and I thought I had better go up and check our position. As we drew near, I saw what seemed to my unsophisticated eyes to be some sort of pagan rite, perhaps a ritual of initiation. Persons clad in yellow oilskins (and I'm almost positive some of them were women) were kneeling on the deck and then rising and kneeling again. Then they would disappear into the hold for a while, only to reappear and go through the whole rigmarole again. I simply couldn't understand what it was all about.

I hated to disturb whatever was taking place, but I hated even more to go without a check on our position. So when we got to within ten or fifteen yards of the trawler I yelled with all my might, "Which way to Bishop Rock?"

It was a silly question; I'll admit that freely because I knew the way perfectly well. (Bishop Rock was a navigation hazard near the southwestern edge of the Scilly Isles and on it stood Bishop Rock Light, a hundred-and-sixty-seven-foot-high granite lighthouse. It was used as a point of departure or arrival by most of the ships entering or leaving the English Channel, and it was about forty-five miles away on a heading of 20° from where we were at that moment.) So, O.K., it was a silly question, but surely it was good enough to serve as the opening gambit in a conversation. But do you think I got a reply, or so much as an acknowledgment that I had been heard? No, sir! Those yellow-coated figures kept right on with their ritual without so much as blinking an eye.

"Ahoy! Hey, there!" I yelled. "Can you tell an alien where to go to register?"

Still no reply.

I pulled myself together, filled my lungs and let go with a torrent of sound of sufficient volume to rattle *Tinkerbelle's* sails: *"Sprechen Sie Deutsch? Parlez-vous français?* How's the fishing? Catching any sea monsters?"

Nothing. No one on the deck of the trawler, if that's what it was, even looked in my direction. Everyone just kept on kneeling, rising, kneeling, rising and disappearing into the hold for a time. It was queer. It was the strangest thing I'd ever seen in my life, and I had seen some pretty strange things in my time. And I still don't have the faintest idea what it was all about.

By then *Tinkerbelle* was past the ship and moving out of voice range and, anyway, it was obvious that no one was going to pay any attention to us, so we kept on going. I had a lot of fun mulling the whole thing over in my mind, though, and I wondered what sort of headline I would have written if a story about the experience had come over the *P.D.* copy desk while I was working there. Probably I would have written something like:

SAILOR SLIPS;
GOES SILLY
AT SCILLYS

A couple of hours later, at about 1 A.M., I put out the bucket and got some rest even though we were very close to the shipping lanes. I reasoned that the dangers arising from exhaustion were greater than the danger of being run down. I was so tired that I had no trouble at all falling asleep. Knockout drops couldn't have accomplished it any faster.

In the morning (Sunday, August 15th) I woke up just in time to see a trawler (it looked exactly like the one of the strange ritual) moving off, apparently after having examined *Tinkerbelle* at close range. I popped out of the cabin and shouted after it. The response was the same: zero.

Listening to the B.B.C. during breakfast, I heard that Virginia was aboard a trawler searching for me; in fact, she had been out on the sea for several days. I wished that I had some way to let her know where I was. How I looked forward to seeing her again! No more solo voyages for me; that was for sure. Any future sailboat trips would be in a larger boat and with Virginia and the children.

The noon sun shot showed we were down to about 49° 40′ N, about twelve miles south of the latitude of Bishop Rock Light, so it was safe to turn eastward, or even a little north of due east, to head into the channel toward the famous Lizard Head that I had heard so much about in the accounts of other voyages. The Lizard, as it was called, was now about sixty miles away and Falmouth, our journey's end, was only twelve miles beyond that. It would all be over in a couple of days, three at the most.

It was a nice day, mostly sunny, with only a few small clouds in the sky. During the afternoon I saw lots of ships and at one point experienced another, brief hallucination. There was a trawler behind us and I imagined that Virginia was on it, trying to reach us. But *Tinkerbelle* and I had been caught in a whirling maelstrom and were in danger of being sucked under. The water was very confused and rough and, as I looked astern, I hoped and prayed that Virginia's trawler wouldn't be caught, as *Tinkerbelle* and I were, and dispatched into the depths. I even went so far as to yell at the trawler, "Stay out! Stay out! It's too dangerous here!" (I'm sure if they had been able to hear me they would have thought I had blown my top.)

The trawler skirted the terrible area where we were and finally went out of sight over the horizon. That seemed to snap me back to reality.

We kept on moving all afternoon on a course of about 75°. The sea seemed to be crowded with ships. There were lots of freighters and trawlers and once I even saw a big passenger liner. In the evening I had dinner and afterward, about the time the sun dropped out of sight, resumed sailing. There were some clouds close to the horizon in the northwest and others scattered about to the south, all tinged with red from the afterglow of the sunset. Then, all of a sudden, I saw a light flashing (seemingly from the clouds) in the northwest, off *Tinkerbelle*'s port quarter. It went: Flash, interval, flash, long interval, flash, interval, flash, long interval, flash, interval, flash, long interval. . . . Could it be true? Was that *really* it?

With trembling hands I got out my light list and turned to the proper place. In the column on "Characteristic and Power" were listed these facts: "Gp. Fl. W. (2); period 15s; fl. 0.7s, ec. 1.6s; fl. 0.7s, ec. 12.0s; Cp. 720,000." Translated into normal English this meant: Group, flashing, white (2 flashes); duration of total cycle, 15 seconds; first flash, 0.7 second; eclipse, 1.6 seconds; second flash, 0.7 second; eclipse, 12 seconds; candlepower, 720,000.

I timed the flashes and the intervals of darkness between them. There could be no doubt now; it was Bishop Rock Light. And it was exactly where it should have been, according to my navigation! That was the most amazing thing of all. If I hadn't been afraid of falling overboard, I would have jumped up and danced all around *Tinkerbelle*'s little deck! It was great to see something, at last, that I knew was on land, even though I couldn't see the land itself.

In high spirits I sailed on through the night on a course for the Lizard. It was a wonderful brisk sail in the moonlight, but as the first hints of dawn appeared in the east I grew so drowsy I periodically fell asleep at the tiller and, several times, almost put *Tinkerbelle* into a jibe. I decided I simply had to stop for some rest, so I hove to under sail, without the sea anchor, and dropped into unconsciousness in the cabin.

The next thing I knew, I heard voices shouting, "Matey, wake up, wake up! Yank, are you there? Mr. Manry, wake up!" I jumped out of the cabin and saw an English trawler with four or five men at the rail calling out between cupped hands.

I was surprised that they knew my name, but glad they had awakened me, for I knew I shouldn't be sleeping in those heavily traveled waters. And then, as I drew alongside I got another, bigger shock; they asked for my autograph! They must be daft, I thought. Why in the world would they, or anyone, want *my* autograph. But I obliged, happily.

It turned out that the skipper of the trawler, the *Trewarvenneth,* was a fine-looking Cornishman named Harry Small, and he was the brother-in-law of Captain Hunter of the *Excellent,* the *Trewarvenneth*'s sister ship, which, by sheer coincidence, was scouring the ocean for me with Virginia aboard. Captain Small soon had Captain Hunter on the radiotelephone, told him he had found me and gave him our position. And Captain Hunter replied that he was already headed for the *Tinkerbelle* and would arrive in about four hours. I was delighted to know that in just that length of time I would see my lovely wife again.

I thanked the captain and crew of the *Trewarvenneth,* which then went on about its own business, and pushed on for the Lizard. Soon things really began to pop.

An R.A.F. Shackleton flew over and dropped another canister, this one with a message saying, "Sorry we have not been with you since Monday. You have done well. Position now: 49° 32′ N, 06° 05′ W. Mrs. Manry aboard trawler PZ513. Will home her to you now. Cmdr. R. A. Carson, Royal Air Force." The big plane started circling about, sending out that signal for the *Excellent.*

Then a handsome Royal Navy frigate, H.M.S. *Brereton,* hove into sight and, after it got close enough, its captain and two sailors came over to *Tinkerbelle* in an inflated rubber boat powered with an outboard motor. We had a wonderfully pleasant little visit as we moved along side by side. The captain, Lieutenant Commander Nick Barker, gave me a bottle of fresh milk, the first I'd had in more than two and a half months. I'll never forget how delicious it was. He also gave me a sailor's hat ribbon with H.M.S. *Brereton* printed on it in letters of gold, as well as the pleasure and honor of signing my name in the *Brereton*'s guest book. Then he putt-putted back to his own ship, which also was emitting a homing signal for the *Excellent* and which began circling around *Tinkerbelle* like a mother hen watching over a chick.

"Wonderful welcome," I had written in the guest book, and it certainly was. It was so marvelous, so totally different from what I had expected, that it took on a sort of Alice in Wonderland quality, an out-of-this-worldness that left me numb.

Virginia's diary for the previous seven days tells vividly her side of the story.

"*Tuesday, August 10*—Poor Robert, the winds are practically gale force, and we heard tonight on TV that he had been swept overboard several times. Luckily, he has a lifeline around his waist. He must be exhausted. I do wish we could do something to help him.

"Bill Jorgensen hired a trawler and went out and interviewed him. Everyone in Cleveland knew it, but we didn't. Our boys are kind of put out. I told them if they ever go to look for Robert to take me along, too.

"*Wednesday, August 11*—We have chartered a trawler and Russ and Bill and Eric Piper, and Paul Hughes, a *Daily Mirror* reporter, and I are going out to look for Robert. It's all very hush, hush. I have to be up at 5 A.M.

"*Thursday, August 12*—We left the hotel at 6:30 and raced in Paul Hughes' car to Newlyn [near Penzance]. I'll never get used to English driving. It's terrifying. Paul says all it takes is 'a bit of dash and verve.'

"Our trawler is the *Excellent*, and this is my first time on the sea. It's a lovely day and I'm enjoying it.

"The captain is Ernie Hunter and the crewmen are Jock Skinner, Bob Sowden and Bert Morris. Bert is also the cook, and he gives us meals fit for any first-class hotel. He's really a whiz in the galley. I don't know how he does it.

"They all treat me like visiting royalty. Jock told me about Scotland and Bob drew me a sketch of the *Excellent*.

"*Friday, August 13 to Sunday, August 15*—Our trawler trip was more like a pleasure cruise than anything else. Sometimes I felt guilty for enjoying the cruise so much when poor Robert was alone in his little cockleshell in the vast ocean. I did acquire a sense of oneness with him, though, which was impossible to feel ashore.

"We searched the horizon so diligently I began to see red sails everywhere I looked. Looking out over the waves I could understand how it would be nearly impossible to find him without *Tinkerbelle*'s red sail.

"Paul and I had a tendency toward seasickness and we took all our meals at the stern of the boat. Luckily, as long as I stayed out of the galley I was able to keep my meals down. Bert told me to keep on eating, no matter whether I lost a meal or not. The seasick pills made me groggy, so I did a lot of sleeping.

"Paul, probably because of *his* pills, was always flopping down somewhere to sleep. One time he curled up in one of the fish nets and went to sleep, and Bob sewed him up in it.

"The *Excellent* has a terrific roll to it. It rolls so far over the sea comes in through the scuppers on one side and gets halfway across the deck. Then, when it rolls to the other side, the sea goes back out on the first side and in on the other.

"The boys are in constant touch with land by radio. And now and then Russ and Bill communicate with the *Plain Dealer* by radio and transatlantic cable. The fellows back at the newspaper can't seem to understand why we can't find Robert.

"We passed several trawlers. One of them we took to be French and among us we figured out enough French to ask if they had seen '*un petit bateau avec rouge* sail.' They stared at us in bewilderment and then gave us that peculiar sign, chopping the palm of one hand with the side of the other. It turned out they were Dutch!

"No sign or word of Robert and we have had to put back to Newlyn for more supplies and fuel. I still feel he's all right.

"*Monday, August 16*—I couldn't get to sleep last night. The bed wasn't rocking and it was too quiet. Guess I missed the sea. Anyhow, we got up early and made off to Newlyn once again. This time, hopefully, we'll find Robert.

"It was a sparkling, bright blue day and it felt good to have a deck under our feet again. We were all filled with high hopes.

"Bert gave us some old bread, which we crumbled and tossed to the scores of gulls following us. I couldn't help remembering the last time I had thrown bread to the sea gulls was when Robert was loading his supplies aboard *Tinkerbelle* in Falmouth, Massachusetts.

"Russ and I had a conversation about my feelings concerning Robert's safety. I told him I felt that when Robert left Falmouth, Massachusetts, he became one of the sea creatures and, since God watches over them, I felt sure He had Robert in His care, too. Maybe it was childish, but I felt I just had to have faith. And what is life itself but many acts of faith? I have believed from the beginning that worry would avail me nothing. It couldn't possibly help Robert and it could drive me mad.

"While we were talking Bert came out and said, 'The captain wants you in the wheelhouse.'

"I ran along the deck and climbed the little ladder into the wheelhouse. Captain Hunter said he had just heard by radio that his brother-in-law, the commander of another trawler, had found the *Tinkerbelle* a few miles southeast of the Scilly Isles. Robert had been curled up in the cabin, asleep.

"From that moment on a carnival air prevailed aboard the *Excellent* with dancing on the deck and slapping of backs. Soon an RAF plane flew over so close we all ducked and Captain Hunter, who had piloted a boat to help evacuate the British forces trapped at Dunkirk during World War II, thought for a moment that he was back there.

"Bert fixed us some sandwiches because there wouldn't be time for a proper meal, and we were too excited to eat anyhow. The *Excellent* moved at top speed to meet Robert and *Tinkerbelle*.

"I remember Eric came up to me, took my chin in his hand and said, "Are you happy, luv?'

"I felt tears of joy springing into my eyes as I answered, 'Oh, yes,' and said a little prayer of thanks.

"Dolphins, that had previously kept their distance, then began ducking underneath the trawler and diving from one side of it to the other. Then, as suddenly as they had appeared, they vanished.

"Russ, up on the observation deck, shouted for us to come up there. We all climbed up the ladder and saw what had become of the dolphins. There were two on each side of the bow, escorting us to Robert. What better sign of luck did we need?

"Captain Hunter kept scanning the horizon with his eagle eyes (no binoculars for him) and finally announced that he had spotted *Tinkerbelle*. I don't know about the others, but as for me, even using binoculars, it was a good long time before I made out that little red dot that was *Tinkerbelle*'s mainsail.

"But what a moment that was!"

In three hours the *Excellent* was in sight and in less than another hour it was alongside and I got my first glimpse of Virginia. She looked great; tanned and fit, as though life at sea were agreeing with her. And she had on slacks and a pretty blue jacket and hat that seemed just right. I don't remember what I said first or what she said. Everything was so exciting and happening so fast. My mind reeled.

I'm sure I must have said it was good to see her and, no doubt, she said she was happy to see me, but I can't remember. I was too dazed. I must also have said "hellos" to Bill and Russ of the *P.D.*, and Paul Hughes and Eric Piper of the *Daily Mirror,* to whom I was quickly introduced, and to Captain Hunter and his good crew. We were like a happy family having a wonderful time at a picnic.

"Well, *Tinkerbelle* got you to England after all," I called over to Virginia.

"Yes," she said. "Even got me here before you."

When *Tinkerbelle* was securely moored beside the *Excellent,* Virginia jumped down beside me and we hugged and kissed. It was marvelous to have her in my arms again, to be together. The photographers kept asking us to kiss and hug some more so they could get pictures and, of course, we didn't mind. We could have gone on for hours. Virginia said she liked the looks of my mustache and didn't mind its tickling. I was glad to hear that. She was also delighted with my slimmed-down looks. (We discovered later that I had lost forty pounds.)

We sat down in *Tinkerbelle*'s little cockpit with our arms around each other, but there was hardly any opportunity for a private conversation. The two photographers kept asking us to pose and the two reporters kept firing questions at us. All of us were spinning like tops in a scene of wild, happy confusion.

I found out later that Bill had told the Englishmen on the *Excellent,* "Wait'll you hear his laugh." And I guess they weren't disappointed, for I did considerable laughing and with as much gusto as ever. It seems to me that moments of happiness are times for laughing, and I have seldom if ever been happier than I was at that reunion with Virginia. Even the apprehension I had felt over Russ's being the *P.D.* promotion director disappeared, for I learned that there would be no brazen attempt to capitalize on my voyage. I deeply appreciated the *P.D.*'s forbearance. That made everything absolutely perfect. Maybe old Dr. Pangloss was right after all; maybe this *was* the best of all possible worlds.

Bert, the *Excellent*'s chef, handed me a nice big mug of oxtail soup, but I was kept so busy answering questions I only had time to take a few sips of it before someone shouted, "We gotta get going," and there was a mad scramble on the trawler to get Virginia back on board and return to Newlyn. Virginia, it seemed, had become the *Plain Dealer* team's "secret weapon." By getting exclusive stories and pictures of her high-seas reunion with me the *P.D.* men hoped to ease the pain of the

"Atlantic scoop" perpetrated by Jorgensen and Glendenning. So, at the first sign of an approaching boatload of rival newsmen, they whisked the soup out of my hands and leaped to pull Virginia up onto the *Excellent*. They had to start moving, anyway, to get the story filed in time for the *P.D.*'s deadline.

Well, getting Virginia back up on the *Excellent* wasn't nearly so simple as it had been to get her down onto the *Tinkerbelle*; but Bill and Russ were willing to try. They grabbed Virginia's

arms and pulled, thinking she would be able to help by getting a toe hold on the side of the ship. But there was no place for a toe hold; the hull was too smooth. So there she dangled, suspended two or three feet above the water.

Virginia said later she had visions of having to hang there all the way back to Newlyn, if Russ's and Bill's arms held out. Frankly, I didn't have that much confidence in their arms. I thought she'd drop into the water any second. And there I was, unable to help because *Tinkerbelle* had drifted too far away.

Suddenly Paul Hughes thought of a way to avert catastrophe and rushed forward. He reached down to grab my darling wife by what he later referred to as her "haunches," but then, at the last second, he saw the horrified look on my face and decided he'd better not go through with it. He explained afterward that he wasn't going to offend, knowingly, a man who had just sailed the Atlantic singlehanded.

The situation was becoming truly desperate when Bert, one of the crew (good old Bert, Virginia called him ever after), lunged low enough to grab her ankles, raised them, and then rolled her inboard over the railing like a sack of flour. Luckily neither of the photographers recorded the humiliating event.

There was no time to observe the amenities. We all waved quickly and then the *Excellent* sped away, Newlyn bound, just as the first boatload of rival newsmen arrived. This new batch of reporters shouted over questions and I shouted back answers for thirty minutes or so as *Tinkerbelle* continued on toward the Lizard. Then the boat headed back to harbor, to be replaced by another boatful of curious interviewers. It went on like that until darkness began to fall. There were five or six boats altogether, I think, and believe me, some of those English journalists were go-getters. Carl Dyer, a reporter for United Press International, wasn't satisfied with shouting back and forth. He stripped to his shorts, put on a pair of water wings and swam over to get a better look at *Tinkerbelle* and me. And there was another chap—I didn't get his name, I'm sorry to say—who tried to row over in his boat's dinghy but got dumped into the sea instead.

Finally it was night and *Tinkerbelle* and I were alone together once more. It was our last night alone together; our last night on the sea.

*

18 Soon after night cloaked the sea, and before the moon arose, I noticed the loom of a bright light brushing the sky to the northeast. I was pretty sure it couldn't be anything but the Lizard Head Light, but I got out the light list to make certain. The book said the Lizard Light was white, flashing, and had a period of three seconds, of which 0.1 second was flash and 2.9 seconds was eclipse. Its strength was 4,000,000 candle power. I hadn't known there were lights that bright.

I timed the sweeps of the loom. It was the Lizard Head Light all right.

A table in the front of the book indicated that the light, which stood on a cliff and was two hundred and thirty feet above the water, could be seen from a distance of about twenty miles. However, what I saw was not the light itself but its beam in the sky, so we were undoubtedly a good deal farther from it than that; probably closer to twenty-five miles away. It would be dawn before we got to it.

Tinkerbelle skipped joyfully over the waves, headed straight for the light like a horse galloping toward the barn. There was an extra little jauntiness in the spread of her sails, an extra snap in her step, an extra sauciness in the wiggle of her stern. I was proud of her. And happy.

She had guarded me well. Although being knocked overboard had been frightening, especially the first time, we had come through unscathed, thanks to *Tinkerbelle*. She simply wasn't the sort of boat to leave one behind (unless she was rigged for self-steering) because she had the admirable habit of facing the wind and stopping whenever the tiller and mainsheet were released.

Yes, *Tinkerbelle* had protected me. She had never allowed herself to be turned bottom up (as I had feared might happen) and even on those few occasions when one of the bigger breaking waves had flipped her over on her beam ends she had righted herself at once. If she had been able to steer herself all the way, I'm sure she could have crossed the ocean entirely on her own, without any help whatever from me.

Besides righting herself after each knockdown, she had stead-

fastly kept herself watertight and buoyant. I had expected that at some time along the way she might be filled with water, which I would then have had laboriously to pump out of her; but that calamity never even came close. Nor had there been any significant breakage of her gear, aside from what happened to her rudders.

Tinkerbelle never allowed me to get into a really serious predicament and, consequently, I never became panic-stricken or fearful that we might not reach England safely. I was confident of her seaworthiness before I started the voyage (I wouldn't have started otherwise) and grew more and more pleased with her capability as she demonstrated again and again that my faith in her was not misplaced. In my opinion she was, and is, a nautical gem.

There were some scary moments, some moments of sharp loneliness and some other moments of depression, but for the most part the voyage was a great, glorious, happy adventure. I wouldn't have missed it for the world. And as the fulfillment of a long-time dream, it had a special, deep significance for me that only those persons who have long desired and then achieved can fully appreciate.

It had been an eventful voyage, too. The log revealed that I had sighted about sixty ships in the vast expanse of ocean between Vineyard Sound and the Scilly Isles; and, of these, two had looked *Tinkerbelle* and me over to make sure we were all right, four others had exchanged words with me "on the run" and five more had actually stopped to converse. One of these last five had also picked up letters to mail when it reached port and another had given me a complete hot meal, the equivalent of a banquet. I had seen one or more vessels on thirty-three days of the voyage (which now was approaching the end of its seventy-seventh day) despite my efforts to stay away from the shipping lanes. The longest I had gone without sighting a ship was nine days, between June 21st and 30th.

All this, it seemed to me, pointed to the fact that the Atlantic was an exceptionally sociable ocean, and a crowded one. Apparently I was never more than a few days away from help if I had needed it and had used the Victory Girl emergency transmitter to summon it. The tradition of helping those in distress that exists on the sea was heart-warming to behold in action, and I hoped all those captains who had taken the time to rush over to rescue me, only to find that I didn't need rescuing, would forgive me for causing them concern and delay. I saluted them with sincere thanks and respect.

I also owed a debt of gratitude to the U.S. Weather Bureau and the U.S. Naval Oceanographic Office, as their reports on winds and waves to be expected on the voyage had proved astonishingly accurate. The largest waves had been twenty-footers, but we hadn't met many of them, fortunately. Most of the time the waves were under twelve feet high and the wind blew at less than twenty-five knots. We were forced to ride to the sea anchor thirteen times (not counting the times when I was sleeping) and were becalmed thirteen times for varying periods, the longest being about a day.

The moon had risen at about 9:30 P.M. and had now, just before midnight, added its magical touch to the channel scene as we continued slapping, sliding, sloshing toward the Lizard Light. The light itself was visible at last. It had a strangely hypnotic effect. A few minutes of staring at it made it seem very close, although the length of time required to reach it proved it was still many miles away.

As *Tinkerbelle* jogged along gaily at about four knots, I was enchanted by the sparkling moonglow in the water and the warm lights of far-off freighters. I had felt we were sailing through historic waters when we left Falmouth, Massachusetts, but now as we approached Falmouth, England, that feeling was intensified a hundredfold. What an utterly fascinating land this was.

Falmouth, up ahead, only a dozen miles beyond the flashing Lizard Light, was noted for many things. Long ago Phoenician, Roman and Greek traders had visited the site of the city seeking tin, corn and hides. Then came Danes and Vikings seeking conquests and, after them, Frenchmen seeking revenge. It was from Falmouth that Bartholomew Gosnold had sailed in 1602 on his voyage of discovery to Cape Cod. It was not certain that he landed at the site of Falmouth, Massachusetts, but at any rate he had sailed by, and when Cape Cod's Falmouth was incorporated in 1686 it took the name of the town from which he had begun his voyage. So the two Falmouths definitely were linked in history.

It was to England's Falmouth that the schooner *Pickle* brought the official news of Nelson's tragic death in 1805 at the moment of his greatest triumph, the defeat of a combined

French and Spanish fleet off Cape Trafalgar on the southern coast of Spain. It was from Falmouth that a British warship sailed to take Napoleon to his exile on the island of St. Helena. And it was into Falmouth that Captain Kurt Carlsen and his first mate, Kenneth Dancy, were brought in January, 1952, after being rescued from the freighter *Flying Enterprise,* which, after their heroic fourteen-day struggle to get it into port, sank off the Lizard. As a matter of fact, the trawlers *Roseland* and *Excellent* had participated in the dramatic *Flying Enterprise* rescue effort.

Falmouth Harbor also had been the jumping-off point or terminus of quite a few transatlantic small-boat voyages. The voyage of the 18-foot *City of Bath,* begun in Newfoundland, had ended there in 1881. So had the 1947 voyage of the 22-foot *Adventure,* which had begun at Miami, Florida. The voyage of the 17-foot raft *L'Egare,* sailed from Halifax in 1956, ended there, too, as did the 1960 voyage of the 26½-foot *Humming Bird,* which had started at Antigua in the West Indies. Headed the other way across the Western Ocean, Humphrey Barton and Kevin O'Riordon sailed the 25-foot *Vertue XXXV* from Falmouth to New York in 1950; Ernst Karulis and Jan Paltins sailed the 25-foot *Polaris* from there to Panama in 1949-50, and Patrick Ellam and Colin Mudie jumped off from the same place on their voyage in *Sopranino* in 1951. Other voyages begun at Falmouth were those of the 31-foot *Uldra,* 24-foot *Wanderer II,* 29-foot *Moonraker* (Dr. E. A. "Peter" Pye's famous cutter), 20-foot *Skaffie* and 25½-foot *Valkyr.*

I gazed at the flashing light ahead and wondered what *Tinkerbelle*'s voyage had accomplished. Well, for one thing, it had helped to make an honest man of me. When I had asked Virginia to marry me I had promised her two things: one, that we would travel, and two, that although I might be a headache I would never, never be a bore. Well, in fifteen years of marriage we had had a couple of vacation trips to Canada, but it could hardly be said that I was making good on the promise of travel. And as for the second pledge, after twelve years on the rim of a newspaper copy desk I was becoming a crashing bore, without even the relief of being interesting enough to be a headache. So the situation was critical. It was beginning to look as though I had lied and had married Virginia under false pretenses. But *Tinkerbelle* saved the day. She banished boredom from our lives and, although she sometimes became a bit of a headache, it only made her that much more interesting. And she made good on my promise of travel for she took me to England and in the process influenced the *Plain Dealer* to send Virginia and the children over to meet me, an exceedingly kind and gracious act on the *P.D.*'s part. Virginia appreciated it immensely, I knew, because for years she had dreamed of visiting England. So, *Tinkerbelle* made a dream of hers come true as well as one of mine.

What had the voyage achieved besides making dreams a reality? I think probably the most important thing it had done for me was to enable me to stand back, away from human society ashore, and look at life for a little while from a new perspective. In a sense, the Atlantic Ocean had been a personal Walden Pond on which I had lived simply, in close communion with nature, confronted by elemental dangers and necessities. It certainly had not been a place for trivialities and I think, perhaps, that fact may have done something to make me a better person inside than I had been before. Anyway, I hope it did.

Although I was lonely and discouraged at times, my primary feeling was of contentment and peace. My boat was my dearest companion and though the wind and sea were sometimes my adversaries, they were mostly friendly and even when they were not they behaved with straightforward honesty according to their inherent natures. To know them was to respect them.

I must confess that, seen from the peace and quiet of mid-ocean, many aspects of life on land seemed grim indeed. Well, we might as well face it; in some basic ways life ashore *is* grim, especially for underprivileged or underequipped persons. I couldn't help thinking of the gray flannel suit brigades in the big cities ashore, living in a kind of lock-step frenzy, battling noisy highway or subway traffic to get to work in the morning and to return home in the evening, existing on pure nervous energy in between, having to be ever alert to opportunities to get ahead and on guard against the encroachment of rivals.

Henry Thoreau said, "The mass of men lead lives of quiet desperation," and he was probably right. In my life, certainly, there had been many periods of quiet desperation, although I was sure my existence had been less harried than that of most men. I shuddered to think what those less fortunate than I were enduring.

One of the implications of these musings was that my voyage in *Tinkerbelle* had been prompted by an itch and was itself a form of scratching. That was true. The voyage was something I simply *had* to do, had wanted to do for a long, long time. In fact, I had wanted to do it so intensely and for such a long time that my natural timidity, the basic Walter Mitty– Caspar Milquetoast cast of my character, had finally been beefed up with a fair-sized dash of Captain Ahab. And that's when planning for the cruise had got under way in earnest.

The story in the Falmouth *Packet* had referred to me as a hero, but that was absurd. As far as I was concerned, I wasn't taking any great risks, and I was doing something I enjoyed intensely. I really couldn't understand why so much excitement was developing in Falmouth. I'd heard on the radio that a tremendous welcome was being planned and that the mayor had even postponed his vacation in order to be there to greet me when I stepped ashore. And there was talk of thousands of people being on hand to watch *Tinkerbelle* arrive. It seemed as though a real ordeal was shaping up for me and I'll have to admit that for a few moments I considered turning off to port and heading for Penzance in order to escape it.

A huge welcome by crowds of people and the mayor and all that sort of thing was a far cry from what I had expected. I had thought that since England was a maritime nation and had had her full share of adventurous sailors little attention would be paid to *Tinkerbelle* and me. Prior to my discovery of what was going on ashore, I had expected to sail into Falmouth Harbor almost unnoticed, moor my boat at a dock and go to a hotel for a nice bath and sleep. Then, in the morning, I would look for the Falmouth representative of the Associated Press, tell him that I had just sailed the Atlantic singlehanded and that I thought my newspaper back in the States might be interested in having a story about it. Now, it appeared, it wasn't going to work out quite like that.

The impulse to duck away from all the hoopla that was being prepared in Falmouth was strong, but then I thought of how wonderful the R.A.F. had been to me and how well I had been treated by the personnel of the *Roseland, Trewarvenneth, Excellent* and *Brereton* and that my family and *P.D.* colleagues were waiting for me in Falmouth, not to mention the mayor and the crowds, and that I was to be a guest in the country, anyway. It would be inexcusable to skip out and dash the hopes and expectations of all those people, so I decided to go on in as I had planned and face the music.

Dawn was approaching now. The stars disappeared as the inky blackness of the sky gradually changed to gray and then grew lighter and lighter with each passing minute. Up ahead the Lizard Light was still flashing faithfully with its regular three-second rhythm. It was not yet possible to tell how near or far it was, for judging distances over water was extremely difficult, especially when there was nothing of a known size to gauge by.

We kept going as we had all night before the southwest breeze, *Tinkerbelle* taking it over the port quarter, heeling pleasantly to starboard. More light filled the heavens. Finally, in another thirty minutes or so, the outline of a steep headland could be distinguished from the sea and sky. Land! At last! Land! Solid, firm, immovable land! It was Lizard Head rising steeply from the ocean; and rolling northeastward from it was the pleasant, green, undulating shoreline leading to Falmouth!

It was a breath-taking view, and it grew even more striking as the daylight increased in intensity and revealed the details of rocky cliffs, lovely green trees and even greener fields, attractively landscaped houses and interestingly winding roads. I consumed it with my eyes, spellbound, transported, enraptured. What a sublime sight.

"Only twelve miles to go," I told *Tinkerbelle*.

The thought brought on a faint stabbing of pain. The voyage was almost over. It was in its hoary old age, moving swiftly toward its end, its death.

19 This day, our seventy-eighth since leaving Cape Cod, promised to be momentous. There seemed to be a portentous tingle in the air, as if it were charged with electricity. I could feel goose bumps rising on my skin and spasmodic shivers running up and down my back. I hoped I could live through what was coming.

We were about four miles off the Lizard, as close as I cared to get because of what I'd heard about the dangerous rip tides that swept around its base. I didn't want *Tinkerbelle's* bones to be added to those of other vessels that littered the ocean floor in that area. So we stayed a comfortable distance offshore.

I backed *Tinkerbelle's* genny and lashed down her tiller to heave to for some breakfast. It seemed prudent to eat at once, while I had the chance, to build up strength for what might lie ahead. I also bathed as well as I could, shaved, got my mustache into the best shape possible and put on the cleanest clothes I had. And then I spruced up *Tinkerbelle* with Old Glory flying from a staff at her stern and the Union Jack fluttering from her starboard shroud. I must say she looked a gallant little lady with those flags snapping merrily in the breeze.

When all these preparations were completed, I looked shoreward again and found that the Lizard Light had stopped blinking; in the daylight it was no longer needed. About the same time the sun rose above the edge of the sea and, soon after, surrounded us with pleasant warmth. It heightened the colors and rolling configuration of the countryside: that beautiful, beautiful land. It revealed, too, that the sky today, August 17th, would be blue. It was going to be a wonderful day.

We started moving again, northeastward toward the fearsome Manacles, jagged rocks that reached out from the shore like the lower jaw and teeth of a gigantic monster. The wind had shifted into the west and had become several knots lighter, but we were still able to travel at a good clip. There were no other vessels in sight; we had this section of the channel all to ourselves.

I looked back over the stern toward the sea we were leaving behind and again I don't mind admitting I felt a few sharp pangs of regret. There was peace out there of a sort one could never find on land; there was quiet, too, and even more important, a challenge that brought out the best in one and focused it on basic, consequential things. I felt the experience had enriched my life; and I hoped that, through me, it might touch the lives of others.

I had become well acquainted with loneliness and I believe that gave me a greater comprehension of the value of human companionship. The sea had its drawbacks, though; there was no doubt about that. It couldn't give you a formal education (or even a well-balanced informal one), or love or a helping hand when you needed it. The sea was cold, disinterested, impartial. There was no real warmth to it, no sharing of knowledge or feelings. And yet there was one hugely wonderful thing to be said for the sea: it was always the sea—constantly, perpetually, invariably, uniformly, eternally the sea. It was the sea and nothing else. It couldn't dissimulate. It couldn't say one thing while thinking another. It couldn't flatter you and turn your head. There wasn't a treacherous or dishonest wave in its whole massive body.

Another thing I liked about the sea was that I could pit myself against it without fear of injuring another human being. Nothing I did mattered at all to the sea; nothing I did could hurt it in the least. But in the hurly-burly of life ashore, where people were pitted against one another in a furious scramble for success, it was almost impossible to avoid hurting others or being hurt by them. I wasn't much of a scrambler and that's why I liked that nice cozy seat on the rim of the *P.D.* copy desk. It was a relatively peaceful spot, like the eye of a hurricane.

We were approaching Black Head now, about halfway between Lizard Head and the Manacles, and as I looked toward the west I saw a sailboat disengage itself from the shore and head toward us. Then other craft, sailboats and motorboats, came into sight to the north, all moving in our direction.

The first sailboat, the one in the west, closed in fast and as it passed those on board waved in a most friendly way and called out, "Well done! Well done!" And I shouted back, "Thank you! Thanks for coming out to see me!" It was the first of hundreds of similar exchanges that took place that day.

As we approached the Manacles, I thought that we were probably sailing over the very same channel floor that the Invincible Armada had sailed over more than three hundred and seventy-seven years earlier while on its way to meet the British fleet off Plymouth. And no sooner had the possibility popped into my mind than another armada appeared on the scene, this one English and headed south, straight for *Tinkerbelle* and me. It came toward us fast, turned and then swept us up into its bosom to escort us the remaining few miles to Falmouth; and as it moved along it continued to grow. It was a fantastic sight.

One of the first boats to reach us was an R.A.F. launch carrying a few of the pilots who had so kindly watched over us as we neared the coast. Someone on the launch thrust a marvelous big sandwich and a nice cup of hot coffee into my hands. How good each tasted! It was about noon and I was getting hungry.

Shortly after that some Royal Navy helicopters arrived to form an umbrella over us as we sailed in. It was wonderful of them to come and I appreciated the honor immensely; the only trouble was that the backwash from the rotors whipped *Tinkerbelle*'s mains'l back and forth in an alarming way that prevented it from functioning properly. It behaved like a whirligig. I guess the choppers saw what was happening, for in a very short time they considerately moved off and things slipped back more or less to routine.

I think it was about one o'clock when we passed by the menacing Manacles, keeping well offshore for safety's sake. And then the boats really began to swarm around us. They were just like bees around a hive. It was absolutely astounding. I heard a newsman estimate that there were three hundred craft surrounding *Tinkerbelle,* which made this armada more than twice the size of the Spanish one, in numbers of vessels if not in total

tonnage. I think perhaps the man may have put the figure a little high in the enthusiasm of the moment, but, anyway, there were an awful lot of boats out there. I doubt if anyone had seen anything like it since World War II, when an enormous fleet of small boats helped to take three hundred and fifty thousand trapped Allied soldiers off the beaches of Dunkirk.

Many of Falmouth's commercial craft had gone to work ferrying people out to see *Tinkerbelle* and me as we neared the harbor. They were jammed to the gunwales and whenever one went by a chorus of "Well dones" would fill the air. And then I'd call out "Thank yous" and we'd all wave happily to each other. Americans often think of the English as being a little stiff and standoffish, but let me say at once that isn't true. I have never met more friendly, more warmhearted people than I met that day. They couldn't have been nicer.

And I must say those Englishmen were no slouches when it came to business. You can believe this or not, but postcard pictures of *Tinkerbelle* sailing along in the midst of that armada were being sold even before we reached the harbor entrance. How it was accomplished, I don't know. But I do know it was being done, because I got one of the cards while we were still miles from our goal.

Radio newsman Robert Forbes got in some pretty fast licks, too. He came aboard *Tinkerbelle* and tape-recorded an interview with me as we sailed along, then said "Thank you," got back on his own boat and churned off. A few minutes later, while we were still sailing toward Black Rock, at the mouth of the harbor, I heard the interview over a portable radio on an adjacent boat. It was a novel experience for me to be interviewed in the first place (as a former reporter, I was accustomed to asking questions instead of answering them), but to be interviewed and then to hear the interview within a very few minutes, that was really something!

Before we had progressed very far past the Manacles, the fishing boat *Girl Christian* came alongside and on it were Virginia and Robin and Douglas. It was wonderful to see the children, at last, and to see Virginia again. I could hardly wait until we were all together ashore. What a marvelous reunion it would be. The *Plain Dealer* and *Daily Mirror* newsmen were also on the boat and it was good to see them again, too. We all chatted like magpies for a few minutes and then the *Girl Christian* hurried back to shore. Those aboard her were to meet me when I docked at Custom House Quay.

By this time it was after 6 P.M. and although we were only about two miles from the harbor entrance it began to look as though *Tinkerbelle* wasn't going to make it in before nightfall. The wind had fallen off to almost nothing. We were held to an agonizingly slow pace. But then the harbormaster, Captain Francis H. Edwards, came along and offered me a tow. I had hoped that *Tinkerbelle* would sail in all by herself so I was reluctant to accept the offer, but then I thought of all the people waiting on shore to see us (including the mayor) and how disappointed they might be and, in fact, how disappointed I would be, too, if we didn't make it before dark, so I finally agreed.

We were soon moving again at a lively pace and the increased tempo seemed to accentuate the holiday mood of the escorting armada. Boats circled, crisscrossed and flocked all about us. Several times I thought we were going to be crushed. People cheered and shook my hand and gave me the thumbs-up victory sign and passed me things to eat. One young fellow in a small runabout stayed alongside for quite a while and gave me a couple of Cornish pasties. A few persons simply wanted to touch me, as if I had some magical power to impart. Others just shouted, "Well done!" "Good show!" or "Glad you made it, mate!"

I patted *Tinkerbelle* on the stern and said, "Well done!"

It was nearly seven when we approached Black Rock. Off to port the shore was a solid mass of people and behind them, at the top of a small hill, were the ruins of Pendennis Castle, ancient guardian of Falmouth, its ramparts crowded with more spectators. If I half closed my eyes, it was easy to imagine the spectators were Romans defending the castle against attacking Saxons. It was a spectacular sight.

We turned to port, moved past Falmouth's famous docks and shipyards and on to the Custom House Quay. People were everywhere: standing along the shore, perched on window ledges, leaning out of doorways, crowded onto jetties, thronging the streets, clinging to trees and cramming the inner harbor in boats of every size and description. The whole place was teeming with humanity. I heard later that fifty thousand people were there to see *Tinkerbelle* and me complete our voyage.

I was simply dumfounded, numbed by the enormity of it all

"Any perfumes, liqueurs, cigars. . . ?"

—JAK in (London) *Evening Standard*

and not a little bewildered. It was just too much to take in all at once.

I put down a couple of fenders to protect *Tinkerbelle* from the stone quayside and then, after seventy-eight days of living on a pitching, rolling, swaying boat, I stepped ashore. And almost fell flat on my face!

The quay seemed to be shaking, as if an earthquake were in progress. I wobbled about and staggered like a man who had had too much grog; and with all those people watching. It was embarrassing. I could see it was going to take a few days to get back my land legs.

Most of what happened after that is blurred in my mind. I was too stunned to comprehend fully, or remember. I do recall, though, that every boat and ship in the harbor let go with its horn or whistle and shook the whole waterfront with reverberating sound as the crowd yelled, R.A.F. Shackletons flew overhead in wigwagging salutes and a band on the quay (I heard later it was the St. Stythians Silver Band) played "The Star-Spangled Banner" and "The Stars and Stripes Forever."

I hugged and kissed Virginia, Robin and Douglas and then met Samuel A. Hooper, mayor of Falmouth, who looked most impressive in his scarlet robes and golden chain of office. He welcomed me to the city and I apologized for delaying his vacation. Then I knelt and kissed the stones of the quay in thanksgiving for a safe passage across the ocean and in gratitude for the warm welcome I was receiving.

The pier was a mass of faces. People waved flags, pointed cameras, fired flashbulbs, cheered. I waved and shouted back, "Hi, everybody!" When a newsman asked me what I thought of the welcome, all I could say was "I'm flabbergasted!" But I felt as if I had been elected President.

Then it was time to go. We were led through the crowd toward some autos on the quay and Virginia and I were asked to get into the back of one of them. Before I got into the car, I felt pricks of conscience at the thought of leaving *Tinkerbelle*.

I looked back to where I knew Russ Kane and the Falmouth police were looking after her, but she was hidden by the high side of the quay and by the crowd. I couldn't even see the tip of her mast.

It was all over now, all behind us. The voyage was dead. I felt a lump rising in my throat. I looked around at the thousands of people on the quay and on the shore, and I heard the "Well dones" and felt the handshakes of those nearest to me. And then I knew that, for *Tinkerbelle* and me, our voyage over, what Tinker Bell's friend Peter Pan had once said was true: To die *was* an awfully big adventure.

Labels within image: FALMOUTH, MASS.; MANRY'S TINKERBELLE; FALMOUTH, ENGLAND; KUEKES

—Kuekes, Cleveland *Plain Dealer*

Bob made it ! ! !

*

Comments for Sailors

Tinkerbelle's voyage, I believe, supports the theory that a boat's size has little or no bearing on seaworthiness (only on comfort) and tends to prove that very small boats, reasonably well designed and handled, are capable of crossing oceans. (However, I hope no one reading these pages will assume that *any* small boat is able to cross an ocean, because in that direction lies potential tragedy.) The principal factors that made *Tinkerbelle* capable of the voyage were, I think, her watertightness with hatches closed, her unsinkableness and her self-righting ability. Of course, many other factors also were involved, but these three probably were the most important, and the absence of any one of them might have resulted in insuperable difficulties.

My general advice to anyone contemplating an ocean cruise in a small boat is to get all the sailing experience you can, especially in the boat you expect to use, read all you can about the voyages of others and, most important of all, profit to the fullest possible extent from your experience and reading. Don't gloss over hazards that should be faced squarely. And don't take chances unnecessarily. By this I mean don't reason thus: Yes, I know the mainsheet halyard is badly worn in one spot, but it's probably strong enough to last through this voyage. Or: The bilge pump seems to be working all right, so I don't see why I should have to check its insides or take along spare parts. It is folly to leave a potential source of trouble uncorrected.

It is important to assume, I think, that at one time or another your boat will be completely submerged and/or capsized and, to be extra safe, that it will be filled with water. So you need a boat capable of coping with each of these possibilities. If you don't have such a boat, the risks you face will be correspondingly greater.

The cockpit or foot well should be small so that, if filled by the sea, it will not add a dangerous amount of weight to the boat, making it sluggish and lacking in buoyancy. *Tinkerbelle*'s foot well was reduced in size through the temporary installation of a box-like contrivance containing flotation material at its aft end and a storage compartment at its forward end. It was a worth-while alteration because the remaining part of the foot well *was* filled with water several times.

If a conventional keel sailboat weighing a ton or more is rolled over or pitchpoled (that is, somersaulted stern over bow) by an enormous wave, it will almost certainly be dismasted and suffer other serious damage. However, I think *Tinkerbelle* could be rolled over and possibly even pitchpoled without suffering grave injuries because she weighs only six hundred and fifty pounds, and her hundred-pound daggerboard-keel is not heavy enough to cause sufficient strain to break her mast while righting her. I can't prove this. It is simply a feeling I have acquired, partly through reasoning and partly through familiarity with *Tinkerbelle*'s usual behavior.

If I were to repeat the voyage, the only change I would make in *Tinkerbelle* herself would be to equip her with roller reefing or with an extra set of reefing points. I would also add a hacksaw, a pair of tinsnips, a small can of machine oil, a spare radar reflector and a second dacron genoa to my stores. I could have used the hacksaw and tinsnips in repairing the broken rudder. The machine oil would have helped to keep my tools from rusting, although I improvised machine oil by melting Vaseline on the stove. The radar reflector would have replaced the one lost overboard and the second dacron genoa would have allowed me to make *Tinkerbelle* steer herself more often. If I had been able to do that, I might have done more reading.

On a repeat voyage I would not take any cotton clothing whatever except possibly shoregoing clothes sealed in plastic bags. Everything else would be of wool, for wool retains body warmth even when it is wet. Wet cotton, on the other hand, becomes chilly and then, when it dries, the salt in it makes it stiff so that it chafes against your skin.

Incidentally, the plastic bags in which I packed my cans of food and many other items were sealed by folding a piece of Teflon tape over the open end of each bag in turn and going over it with a hot iron. I found the iron worked best when it was set for woolens, although some experimentation was necessary to get the proper combination of heat and time to secure an air-tight bond. Of course, the same piece of Teflon served to seal all the bags.

I had very few health problems. During the first month the prolonged contact with salt water made my fingers and toes swell rather painfully, but twice-daily applications of skin lotion and Vaseline cleared up this condition. Similar treatment, plus a course of achromycin antibiotic capsules, kept the salt-water sores on my buttocks from developing into anything serious. I found that the sores began to heal as soon as I switched to wearing wool next to my skin. Salt-saturated cotton underclothing tended to irritate them, causing me considerable distress.

When I began the voyage, I was somewhat overweight at two hundred pounds. All the way across the ocean I dined very well indeed, from the point of view of quantity if not quality, and so I expected to arrive in England weighing as much as I had at the start, if not more. But, very much to my surprise, I found I had lost forty pounds. (Possibly this means that a good way of losing weight is to go on a canned-food diet.) I suffered no ill effects, however, and at the end of the voyage I still had thirteen gallons of water and a month's supply of food.

Despite the periods of depression and the hallucinations, my mental health apparently remained good (unless you believe I was insane to make the voyage in the first place). I have been interviewed by three psychiatrists, two of whom specialize in the study of human reactions to monotony and loneliness, and have learned from them that my responses were predictably normal. It seems that sagging morale and hallucinations are experienced by practically all singlehanded voyagers, although not all of them admit it publicly in their books.

The lack of sleep and the drug I took to keep myself alert no doubt accelerated the appearance of the hallucinations, but the visions themselves were largely the result of my mind's efforts to cope with the solitude and danger. My mind invented people, both friends and enemies, so that I wouldn't be alone or without help in facing the hazards of the vast, empty ocean.

I wish now that I had done more with photography. It is not especially easy to sail a boat and take pictures, either stills or movies, at the same time, so I found that the high points of the voyage, periods of very rough weather or the moments when I was conversing with the captains of ships that stopped to see if everything was all right, went unphotographed. I was simply too busy doing other things at those times. Which makes this a good argument against singlehanded voyaging, because, if a second person had been present, he could have taken the pictures while I handled the boat, or vice versa.

The picture I most regret having missed is the one of the giant "sea worm" I saw. I wish I had taken the time to get out my cameras and go back to photograph it. Who knows? It might have proved to be some as yet uncatalogued creature of the sea.

Moisture and heat are the worst enemies of photographic film, especially color film, but the film aboard *Tinkerbelle* was not damaged to any great extent. Heat was no problem at all since the cabin temperature, out at sea, never got above seventy degrees; but moisture was another matter. Still, the only film that suffered moisture damage was 16-mm. movie film that had been left in the camera for several days. When the camera was not in use, I kept it sealed in a plastic bag, but apparently this did not prevent some moisture from reaching about twenty-five feet of film and altering the colors slightly.

The still camera, being designed for underwater as well as above-water use, protected the film from moisture very well; and as soon as a roll was exposed I popped it back into its sealed container. But the movie film wasn't as easily protected. It was all right as long as it was in its original package and, after exposure, when I resealed it in the package with cellulose tape. But while *in the camera* it was vulnerable.

In addition to being sealed in its original packages after exposure, all the film (both before and after exposure) was kept sealed in large plastic bags, which also contained silica-gel moisture-absorbing tablets.

Another minor disappointment of the voyage was that I never got to take any underwater pictures, even though I had an underwater camera. The homemade device I had for thrusting the camera below the surface and operating it from above contained a heavy brass plate and when the second rudder broke I had to use this plate as part of the material for making repairs. And that put the underwater picture device out of action before I got around to using it.

Now, about expenses. The total cost of the one-way passage to England, not including the cost of the boat and the expense of repairing and remodeling it, was roughly $1,000. Since it would have been possible to fly to England in June for approximately $400 (first class) or $270 (coach), the voyage was actually a rather expensive way to cross the Atlantic Ocean. But the experiences of the voyage, both the pleasant ones and the unpleasant ones, more than compensated for the difference in cost. In fact, to me, they were priceless; I wouldn't have traded them for anything.

One more comment should be made. The $750 in traveler's checks I had among my miscellaneous supplies was to pay for getting *Tinkerbelle* and me back to Cleveland from England. I didn't use it, however, because the *Plain Dealer* very kindly took care of this expense.

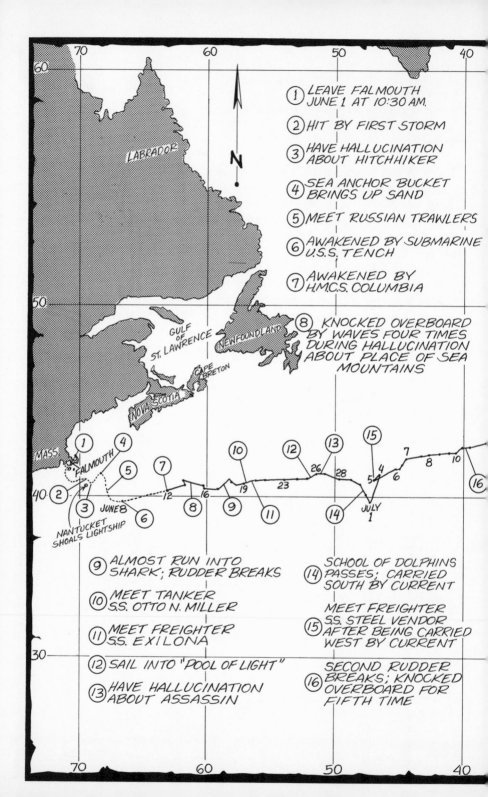

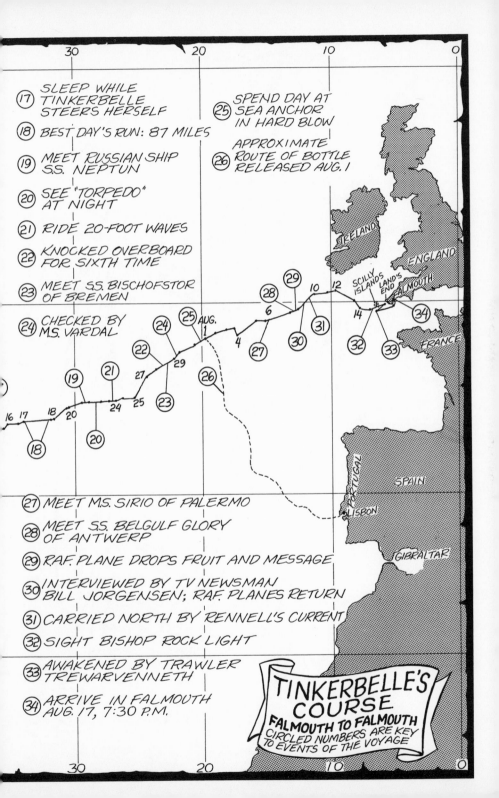

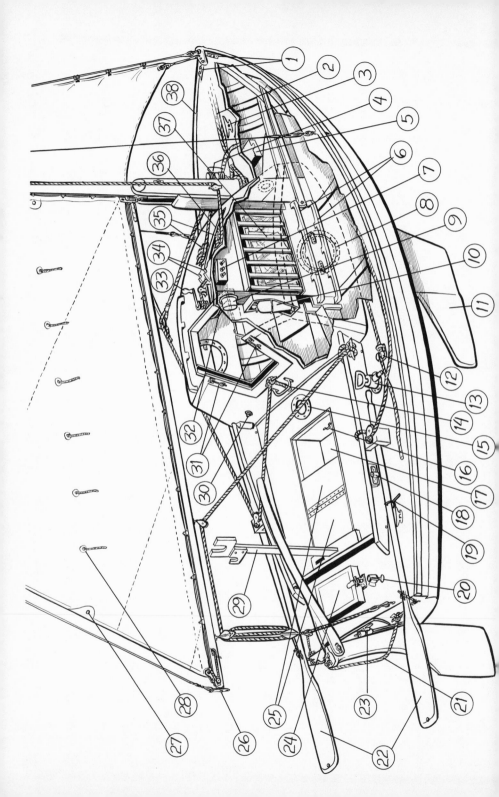

Tinkerbelle and Her Fittings

1. Chocks for mooring lines
2. Half-inch dacron line wrapped around mast, with swivel shackle at forward end for attaching sea-anchor line
3. Mooring cleat
4. Red and green combination running light
5. Case for six-volt battery powering all lights
6. Fixture to facilitate tying down supplies securely
7. Switches to control running light, stern light and masthead light
8. Porthole with ⅜-inch plastic cover to prevent breakage by waves
9. Barometer
10. Fire extinguisher
11. Lowered daggerboard-keel
12. Jam cleat for sheet used with small jib
13. Bilge pump
14. Handhold
15. Bridge-deck compass
16. Bronze strap for attaching lifeline
17. Self-bailing cockpit foot well
18. Oarlock
19. Second part of oarlock
20. Stern light
21. Safety line attaching rudder to boat
22. Oars used for rowing or to wing out twin genoas for self-steering with following wind
23. Oarlock fixture at stern
24. Lazarette hatch
25. Removable "box" designed to reduce size of cockpit foot well; flotation material in aft portion and storage space under hinged lid in forward portion
26. Swivel at end of boom to which topping lift is attached
27. Reefing cringle
28. Reef point
29. Boom and mast crutch
30. Waterproof electrical socket for attaching cord of spot-light
31. Fixtures for securing cabin hatch cover
32. Cabin dome light
33. Winch and line for raising daggerboard-keel
34. Fixture on which rod that holds daggerboard-keel in raised position rests
35. Cleats for jib and mainsheet halyards
36. Slot through which daggerboard-keel is raised or lowered
37. Rack for charts and other papers
38. Raised rub rail providing handhold for anyone in water

*

Equipment and Supplies Taken on Voyage

NAVIGATION BOOKS AND EQUIPMENT—*Radio Navigation Aids, Atlantic and Mediterranean Area; Rules of the Road; The Nautical Almanac, 1965; H.O. 214, Tables of Computed Altitude and Azimuth,* three volumes covering latitudes 30° to 59°; *Sailing Directions, South Coast of England; United States Coast Pilot No. 2,* covering Cape Cod area; *Piloting, Seamanship and Small Boat Handling,* by Charles F. Chapman; pamphlet on *Sea and Swell Observations;* book of *Tidal Current Charts* for Cape Cod area; *Primer of Navigation,* by George W. Mixter; *Navigation the Easy Way,* by Carl D. Lane and John Montgomery; light lists; universal plotting sheets; all necessary charts (protected in waterproof plastic chart cases); surplus U.S. Air Force sextant; Hallicrafters WR-3000 transistor radio receiver with earphones; 2 Danforth course protractors; 1 wind-speed meter; 1 alarm clock; 2 wristwatches; 1 stop watch; 2 dividers; 2 army-type hand-bearing compasses; 1 mounted, bridge-deck compass; 1 sounding lead and line; 1 logbook; 3 notebooks; indelible-ink ballpoint pens; pencils.

GENERAL BOOKS—*Gone With the Wind,* by Margaret Mitchell; *The Spy Who Came In from the Cold,* by John Le Carré; *The Elements of Style,* by William Strunk, Jr., and E. B. White; *Birds of the Ocean,* by W. B. Alexander; *How to Exercise Without Moving a Muscle,* by Victor Obeck; *The Stars,* by H. A. Rey; *20 Years and 20 Hits for the Harmonica; World Almanac* for 1965. (*Birds of the Ocean* was the only book I found time to read.)

TOOLS—1 saw, 3 screwdrivers, 1 adjustable-grip pliers, 1 nonadjustable pliers, 1 hand drill with assortment of bits, 1 hammer, 4 C clamps, 2 files, 1 small wood plane, 1 adjustable wrench, 1 metal measuring tape, 1 pocket emery stone, 2 pocketknives, 1 sail repair kit (containing sailor's palm, needles, twine, marlinespike, beeswax and marline), 1 cold patch kit for repairing inflatable life raft or life jacket, 1 chisel, 1 hard rubber mallet, 1 wire cutter, 1 sheath knife, and marlinespike, 1 scissors.

SPARE PARTS, MATERIALS AND EQUIPMENT—1 rudder; 1 set of gudgeons and pintles; 1 tiller; 1 stem plate; 1 chain plate; 1 mast tang; 1 stainless-steel stay (to replace either a shroud or the forestay); brass bolts and screws of all sizes; sandpaper; copper tacks; copper boat nails; liquid rubber calking material; waterproof glue; fiberglass cloth, resin and hardener; 3 sets of D batteries (8 batteries to a set) for radio; 4 sets of D batteries (2 to a set) for flashlight; 3 batteries for anchor light; 3 Hot Shot 6-volt batteries for running lights and spotlight; bulbs for flashlight, running lights and spotlight; 8 blocks (pulleys) of various sizes; 100 feet of ⅜-inch nylon line; 100 yards of light nylon cord; 2 sea-anchor buckets; 6 shackles of different sizes; assortment of pine, plywood and oak planks; various lengths of brass, copper and stainless-steel wire; pieces of sheet brass; 6 cans of gas for foghorn; 1 cylinder of gas to inflate life raft; 1 2½-pound Danforth anchor, 12 sail slides and 12 clips; 12 jib slides; calking cotton; hose for cockpit drain; wood putty; assortment of rope thimbles; 1 turnbuckle; 6 clevis pins; 1 pint of gray paint; 1 pint of spar varnish; 2 yards of sailcloth; 6 wire rope clamps; 2 rolls of chafing tape.

SAFETY EQUIPMENT—1 Mae West life jacket; 1 inflatable life raft with cylinder of gas; 1 fire extinguisher; 1 anchor light; 1 spotlight; 1 gas-operated foghorn; 6 night flares; 6 day flares; 1 deck-mounted bilge pump; 2 portable pumps; 1 signaling mirror; 1 barometer; 1 Victory Girl SOS signal transmitter; 2 dye markers; 1 life-preserver cushion; medical kit (contents listed below); 1 bucket sea anchor; 1 solar still for making freshwater from seawater; 1 white tropical helmet; 10 packets of silica gel to help keep film, sextant and radio dry; 2 pairs of sunglasses; 1 lifeline; 1 compass corrector and pelorus; 1 set of oars; 3 waterproof rubberized canvas bags for storing equipment; 1 radar reflector; 1 extra survival fishing kit; 2 rubber sleeve chafe preventers; 1 flashlight; 1 plastic emergency sextant; 5

emergency food packs (each one containing a 5-day supply of vitamin tablets, malted milk tablets, chocolate bars and biscuits); sufficient polyethylene foam flotation material to make boat unsinkable; survival kit (contents listed below).

MEDICAL KIT—(Packed in moistureproof case) 1 hemostat, 1 scalpel with spare blades, 1 tweezers, 20 disposable syringes, 12 disposable sutures, 2 tubes of bacitracin ointment, 100 3 x 3 gauze pads, 2 Ace bandages, 3 rolls of adhesive tape, 3 rolls of gauze, 24 safety pins, 8 small splints, 200 aspirin tablets, 1 package of powdered alum, 1 bottle of nose drops, 1 inhaler, 200 salt tablets, 2 pounds of Vaseline, 1 can of talcum powder, 6 small packets of toilet tissue, 1 tube of zinc ointment, 1 bottle of sun lotion, 1 bottle of Kaopectate, 1 oral thermometer, large bottle of liquid antiseptic, 1 bottle of laxative, 1 tube of anesthetic eye ointment, 1 tube of antibiotic eye ointment, large bottle of achromycin antibiotic capsules, dexedrine, nembutal, benadryl, tincture of belladonna, phenobarbital, morphine, codeine, paregoric, 4 tubes of anesthetic skin ointment, skin lotion, pills to combat motion sickness or allergy, *First Aid,* published by the American Red Cross, *The Ship's Medicine Chest and First Aid at Sea,* a U.S. Public Health Service publication.

SURVIVAL KIT—1 pound of malted milk tablets, 16 bars of tropical chocolate, 4 cans of pemmican, 30 high-energy dextrose wafers, 8 cans of vacuum-packed water, 6 night flares, 2 day flares, 1 dye marker, 1 signaling mirror, 1 fishing kit, 1 tube of suntan lotion, 2 packages of hygienic tissue, 1 bottle of insect repellant, 1 flashlight, 1 waterproof container of matches, 1 distress whistle, 1 distress flag, 1 can opener, 1 first-aid kit with instructions for use, 1 sheathed hunting and fishing knife, 1 compass.

SAILS AND GEAR—1 red nylon mains'l, 68 square feet; 1 white cotton mains'l, 68 square feet; 2 white cotton jibs, 22 square feet each; 1 white dacron genoa, 38 square feet; 1 white cotton genoa, 38 square feet; 1 green cotton storm jib, 9 square feet; 1 green cotton trysail, 25 square feet; 150-foot ½-inch nylon anchor line; all running rigging of ⅜-inch dacron line; 10 feet of ⅛-inch shock cord; 10 feet of ¼-inch shock cord; 8 sail stops made of shock cord; 2 whisker poles for winging out cotton jibs; 1 8-pound Danforth anchor; 2 plastic-foam fenders (one of which served as float for sea-anchor bucket).

GALLEY EQUIPMENT—1 canned-heat stove in gimbals, 27 large cans of canned heat, 1 frying pan, 1 saucepan, 1 knife, 1 fork, 1 spoon, 100 matchbooks in waterproof plastic container, 3 bottles of liquid salt-water soap, scouring pads and dishcloths for cleaning pans and silverware, 2 plastic nonsinkable cups, 1 seaman's knife with can opener on it, 4 folding army-type can openers.

PROVISIONS—28 gallons of water carried in 40 half-gallon, 3 one-gallon and 1 five-gallon plastic containers; 40 cans beef slices and potatoes; 30 cans turkey loaf; 24 cans peas; 23 cans peas and carrots; 23 cans corn; 6 cans chili; 6 cans Vienna sausage; 4 cans boned chicken; 5 cans beef stew; 6 cans stuffed peppers; 4 cans stuffed cabbage; 8 cans beans and wieners; 8 cans corned-beef hash; 5 cans shrimp; 5 cans tuna and noodles; 8 cans spaghetti and meat balls; 2 cans ham loaf; 3 cans chicken and noodles; 10 cans diced beets; 10 cans succotash; 10 cans sweet potatoes; 10 cans diced carrots; 30 cans assorted fruit juices; 30 cans carbonated soft drinks; 40 cans Bartlett pears; 20 cans fruit cocktail; 20 cans sliced peaches; 10 cans condensed milk; 2 cans plum pudding; 1 jar hard sauce; 8 cans oleo-margarine; 5 cans cherries; 50 small packets raisins; 140 assorted candy bars; 20 dehydrated meat bars; 10 dehydrated bacon bars; 10 cans pemmican; 10 cans egg salad; 8 cans fruitcake; 20 cans white bread; 100 cereal bars; 40 starch jelly bars; 8 dehydrated Spanish omelets; 8 servings dehydrated scrambled eggs; 200 individually packaged servings of coffee, dehydrated cream and sugar; 20 portions grape jelly; 20 portions strawberry jelly; 20 portions marmalade; 1 bottle brandy; 20 servings orange drink; 20 servings cocoa; 60 packets biscuits; 90 multivitamin capsules; 90 ascorbic acid tablets; ketchup; mustard; Tabasco sauce; curry powder; salt; pepper; turkey stuffing; bouillon cubes.

CLOTHING AND PERSONAL GEAR—1 waterproof anti-exposure suit, 1 set of oilskins, 1 pilot cap, 1 knitted watch cap, 4 cotton undershirts, 4 cotton undershorts, 2 turtle-neck sport shirts, 2 V-neck sport shirts, 2 pairs of cotton thermal underwear, 4 pairs of woolen socks,

2 pairs of cotton trousers, 1 pair of woolen trousers, 1 woolen shirt, 3 sweaters, 2 pairs of rubber-soled deck shoes, 1 pair of leather shore shoes, 2 shoregoing shirts, 1 shoregoing jacket, 2 pairs of shore-going trousers, 2 neckties, 1 visored yachting hat, 1 red nylon wind-breaker, 1 safety razor and spare blades, 2 cakes of salt-water soap, 2 washcloths, 2 face towels, 2 bath towels, 1 toothbrush, 1 tube of toothpaste.

PHOTOGRAPHY EQUIPMENT—1 Nikonos 35-mm. still camera, 1 Revere 16-mm. magazine movie camera, skylight filters for both cameras, 52 50-foot magazines of 16-mm. Kodachrome II, 12 rolls of 36-exposure 35-mm. Kodachrome II, flashgun for Nikonos, 10 dozen blue flashbulbs, Weston exposure meter, closeup lenses for Nikonos, neutral-gray test cards for determining exposure, lens shades, home-made device on a pole for thrusting the Nikonos camera into the sea and operating it remotely for taking pictures underwater.

MISCELLANEOUS—Writing paper and envelopes, $750 in traveler's checks, 10 one-dollar bills (to cover postage of letters picked up at sea), 6 ballpoint-pen refills, 3 sponges, 3 rolls of cellulose tape, 1 American flag, 1 American ensign, 1 British flag, 1 yellow "Q" flag, plastic bags of various sizes, spring clips to hold plastic bags shut, 1 ink marker, 1 chromatic harmonica, 1 hand warmer and fuel, 2 woolen blankets, passport, health certificate, boat owner-ship papers.

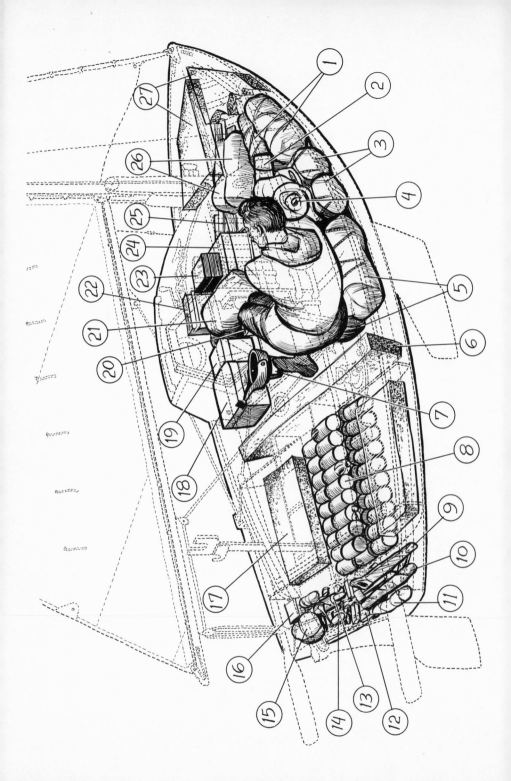

Stowage of Supplies

1. Two bags of food, one week's supply in each bag
2. Watertight, rubberized canvas bag containing navigation books, cameras and log
3. Two more bags of food
4. Blanket used as pillow while sleeping. Several positions were tested for sleeping and the one shown proved most satisfactory.
5. Bags of clothing and photographic film
6. Flotation material
7. Canned-heat stove in gimbals
8. Forty half-gallon plastic bottles of drinking water (not all shown)
9. Saw
10. Other tools
11. Survival fishing kit
12. Packages of spare parts, screws, bolts and batteries
13. Anchor light
14. Compressed-gas horn
15. Extra sails
16. Solar still for converting salt water into fresh water
17. Plank of flotation material (similar plank on starboard side)
18. Victory Girl emergency SOS transmitter
19. Survival kit
20. Five-gallon plastic container of water
21. Bag of food with another underneath
22. Radio receiver
23. Sextant
24. Medical kit in airtight case
25. Assortment of lumber for making repairs
26. Two more bags of food
27. Two more flotation planks

Glossary

ABAFT—Astern of; behind; at the rear of; toward the stern.

ABEAM—At right angles to the keel.

ADRIFT—Loose from moorings.

AFT—Toward or near the stern.

ASTERN—To the rear or behind.

BACK—To back a sail is to pull it to the windward side of the vessel. The wind is said to back when its direction shifts in a counterclockwise direction; it is the opposite of veer.

BACKWIND—When the wind hits the ordinarily leeward side of a sail.

BATTEN DOWN—To secure or to make watertight.

BEAM—The point of a vessel's greatest breadth.

BEAM ENDS—A boat is said to be on its beam ends when it is knocked over onto its side.

BEAT—To sail to windward; tack.

BEND—To bend on sails is to attach them to the vessel, before hoisting, so they are ready for use.

BILGE—The inside of a vessel near the keel where water may collect.

BLOCK—A pulley; a frame enclosing one or more sheaves or rollers over which lines are run.

BOOM—A spar at the foot of a fore-and-aft sail.

BOOM CRUTCH (OR CRADLE OR CROTCH)—A prop that lifts the boom off the deck and holds it secure when it is not in use.

BOW—Forward part of a boat.

BROACH—A vessel broaches when it swings broadside to the wind and waves when running free.

BULKHEAD—A partition or wall below decks.

BUOY—A floating object anchored to show position.

CENTERBOARD—A pivoted board-like device that can be lowered to provide lateral resistance to the water in shoal draft vessels.

CENTERBOARD TRUNK—The housing in which the centerboard is pivoted.

CLEW—Aftermost corner of a sail.

COAMING—Raised protection around a cockpit.

COCKPIT—Space within the coaming where the helmsman sits. A self-bailing cockpit has drains to allow water to run out of it.

COME ABOUT—To bring the boat from one tack to the other when sailing into the wind.

DAGGERBOARD-KEEL—Heavy, board-like surface used to provide lateral resistance to the water, raised and lowered vertically.

DEAD RECKONING—Determining a vessel's position by the course sailed and the distance covered.

DINGHY—A small rowboat that sometimes is rigged with a sail. Also called tender or dink.

DOUSE—To take in or lower a sail.

DRIFT—The leeway of a boat.

DROGUE—A canvas bucket or conical-shaped device used to provide resistance in the water and slow a vessel or keep its bow pointed into the wind and waves.

DYE MARKER—Capsule of dye used to color a patch of water to help searchers find a boat or person.

EASE—To let out the sheet so as to relieve the pressure on the sail and possibly spill some wind.

ENSIGN—A national flag flown on a boat.

FEND—To push off.

FOOT WELL—Central area of cockpit designed to accommodate helmsman's feet.

FORE—In or toward the bow of a boat.

FORE-AND-AFT—Parallel to the keel.

FORESTAY—Wire used to support mast, leading to the bow.

FREEBOARD—The distance from the top of the hull to the water.

GAM—Visiting or conversation carried on between persons from separate ships at sea.

GENOA—Large, overlapping jib. Also called a genny.

GHOST—To make headway when there is no apparent wind.

GRAB RAIL—Railing, usually on cabin top, used as handhold.

GREENWICH MEAN TIME—Time as measured at the meridian of Greenwich, England.

GUDGEON—An eye fitting into which the rudder's pintles are inserted.

GUNKHOLING—Shallow-water sailing and anchoring in out-of-the-way places.

HALYARD—A line used to hoist a sail. Also spelled halliard.

HATCH—An opening in a deck with a cover.

HEAD—The upper corner of a sail. Also, a boat's toilet.

HEAVE TO—To stop a vessel's progress by putting out a sea anchor or drogue, or hauling a headsail to windward.

HEAVING LINE—Line with a weighted end to facilitate throwing it ashore or to another vessel.

HEEL—The tilt, tip, listing or laying-over of a boat, usually due to the force of the wind.

HELM—The tiller by which the rudder is controlled.

HULL—The main body of a boat.

IN IRONS—A boat in the wind's eye which, having lost all headway, will not go off on either tack.

JIB—A triangular sail set forward of the mast.

JIBE—When running, to bring the wind on the other quarter so that the boom swings over. Also spelled gybe.

JIB SHEET—The line leading from the lower aft end of the jib to the cockpit and by which the set of the jib is controlled.

JIGGER—Another name for the mizzen or aft sail on a ketch or yawl. Such a sail was improvised on *Tinkerbelle* to help her ride better to a sea anchor.

KEEL—The backbone of a boat running fore-and-aft.

KNOT—Measure of distance: one nautical mile, 6,080 feet. Measure of speed: one nautical mile per hour.

LAPSTRAKE—Overlapping plank of a boat.

LAZARETTE—A stowage compartment in the stern.

LEE SHORE—A shore on the side of the boat away from the wind.

LEE SIDE—The side of the boat away from the wind.

LEEWARD—In the direction away from the wind.

LIFELINE—Line by which person is attached to boat.

LINE—Nautical term for rope used for riggings, anchoring, tying up, etc.

MAINSAIL OR MAINS'L—The large sail set abaft the mast.

MAINSHEET—The line that controls the mainsail.

MASTHEAD—Top of the mast.

MOOR—To secure a vessel to an object such as a dock or buoy.

PINTLE—Metal braces or hooks upon which the rudder of a boat swings.

POINT—To sail as close as possible to the wind.

PORT—Left side of a boat, facing toward the bow.

PORT TACK—Boat sailing with the wind coming over the portside.

QUARTER—The after part of a boat's side; that part of a craft which is within forty-five degrees from the stern, known as the port quarter or starboard quarter.

RADAR REFLECTOR—Metallic contrivance which reflects radar beams.

REACH—Points of sailing between running and pointing close-hauled. Close reach, sailing nearly close-hauled. Beam reach, sailing with the wind abeam. Broad reach, sailing with the wind abaft the beam.

REEF—To reduce sail area by partly lowering sail and securing the surplus material to the boom.

RUBBING STRAKE—Outer plank of hull designed to protect hull from docks.

RUB RAIL—Same as rubbing strake.

RUNNING—Sailing before the wind.

RUNNING LIGHTS—Lights carried by a vessel under way.

SEA ANCHOR—A drag device (usually a conical canvas pocket held open by a metal hoop, but a canvas bucket in *Tinkerbelle*'s case) used to keep the boat headed into the wind and waves while it is not under way, especially during heavy weather.

SECURE—To make fast; to tie or lock into position.

SELF-BAILING COCKPIT—A cockpit provided with drains to allow water washed into it to return to the sea.

SEXTANT—Instrument used to determine the altitude of the sun or stars used in navigation.

SHACKLE—A U-shaped piece of metal with a removable pin across the open end. Shackles are attached to the ends of a boat's halyards and used to link the halyards to the heads of the sails for hoisting.

SHEAVE—The wheel in a block or at the masthead.

SHOAL—Shallow.

SHROUD—Standing rigging, usually of stainless-steel wire, running from the mast to the sides of a boat to support the mast. The mast's principal lateral stays.

SLOOP—A sailing vessel with one mast and one sail (a jib) before the mast.

SPAR—General term for masts, booms, whisker poles, etc.

STANDING RIGGING—The shrouds and stays and other rigging not moved in working the boat.

STARBOARD—The right side of a vessel, looking toward the bow.

STARBOARD TACK—Sailing with the wind coming over the starboard side.

STAY—Rigging, usually wire, used to support a mast.

STEERAGEWAY—The amount of forward movement necessary to make a vessel's rudder effective.

STEM PLATE—The plate at the bow to which the jibstay (forestay) is attached.

STERN—The after part of a boat.

STIFF—A boat is said to be stiff when it is not easily heeled.

STORM SAILS—Small sails of heavy canvas for use in heavy weather.

STOW—To put away.

SQUARE SAIL—A rectangular sail attached to a spar suspended at the middle from a mast.

SWELL—The waves that continue after the wind that created them has changed in direction or vanished.

SWING THE BOAT—To rotate the vessel to check the compass on known courses.

TABERNACLE—A hinge at the base of a mast which allows the mast to be lowered easily.

TACK—The lower forward corner of a sail. Also, to sail to windward in a series of zigzags.

TILLER—A bar connected with the rudderhead and by which the rudder is moved to steer the boat.

TOPPING LIFT—A line attached at one end to the masthead and at the other to the aft end of the boom, which supports the boom while the sail is being set.

TROUGH—The valley between the peaks of successive waves.

TRYSAIL—Small storm sail set in lieu of the mainsail.

UNSHIP—To remove or detach.

VEER—Wind shift in a clockwise direction.

WAKE—The foamy path of disturbed water left behind a moving boat.

WATERLINE—The line painted on a boat's side indicating the proper trim.

WEATHER HELM—A sailboat in which the tiller must be pulled (usually only slightly) toward the wind to keep it on course.

WEATHER SIDE—Windward side of a sailboat.

WHISKER POLE—A light spar positioned between the mast and the clew of the jib to hold out the sail when running before the wind.

WINDWARD—Toward the wind.

ABOUT THE AUTHOR

Robert Manry says of himself: "I was born in June, 1918, in Landour, India, a town situated about 7,000 feet above sea level at the summit of the first range of the Himalayan Mountains, and I had most of my elementary school education and all of my high school education at Woodstock School there. With the exception of interludes totaling four or five years, I lived in India until I was 19.

"I did my first sailing on the Jumna River at Allahabad, India, where my father, Dr. James C. Manry, a Presbyterian missionary-educator, taught philosophy and English at Ewing College.

"In late December, 1936, I left India and, on my way to the United States, stopping for a semester of study at Lingnan University, Canton, China. I left China in 1937, via the port of Tientsin, the day before the Japanese attacked at the Marco Polo bridge near Peking, starting the long war that eventually involved the United States.

"I entered Antioch College in the fall of 1937 and after many vicissitudes, among them service with the 66th Infantry Division in France, Germany and Austria, earned an A.B. degree in political science. I subsequently worked as a reporter on newspapers in Washington Court House, Ohio, and Pittsburgh and Erie, Pennsylvania. In 1953 I joined the *Plain Dealer* as a copy editor and I am still with that paper, although presently on a leave of absence.

"In 1950 I married the former Virginia Place of Pittsburgh, whose father and brother were newspapermen, and we have a daughter, Robin, now fifteen, and a son, Douglas, now twelve.

"My principal sideline interest, besides sailing, is photography, especially nature photography."